HARPER FORUM BOOKS
MARTIN E. MARTY, *General Editor*

CONTEMPORARY RELIGIOUS THINKERS

*From Idealist Metaphysicians
to Existential Theologians*

HARPER FORUM BOOKS
Martin E. Marty, *General Editor*

23507

CONTEMPORARY RELIGIOUS THINKERS

From
Idealist Metaphysicians
to
Existential Theologians

Selected and Introduced by

John Macquarrie

1817

HARPER & ROW, PUBLISHERS

NEW YORK, EVANSTON, AND LONDON

FIRST EDITION

Published as a Harper Forum Book, 1968, by Harper & Row, Publishers, Incorporated, New York, Evanston, and London.

LIBRARY OF CONGRESS CATALOG CARD NUMBER: 68-11747

HARPER FORUM BOOKS

Often dismissed with a shrug or accepted with thoughtless piety in the past, religion today belongs in the forum of study and discussion. In our society, this is particularly evident in both public and private colleges and universities. Scholars are exploring the claims of theology, the religious roots of culture, and the relation between beliefs and the various areas or disciplines of life. Students have not until now had a series of books which could serve as reliable resources for class or private study in a time when inquiry into religion is undertaken with new freedom and a sense of urgency. *Harper Forum Books* are intended for these purposes. Eminent scholars have selected and introduced the readings. Respectful of the spirit of religion as they are, they do not shun controversy. With these books a new generation can confront religion through exposure to significant minds in theology and related humanistic fields.

MARTIN E. MARTY, GENERAL EDITOR
The Divinity School
The University of Chicago

PREFACE

THIS VOLUME contains readings in the religious thought of the present century, drawn from the works of about thirty philosophers and theologians. This book of readings may be used as a companion to my book, *Twentieth-Century Religious Thought* (New York: Harper & Row, 1963), but it may also be used independently, for I have provided introductions to each of the three parts into which the readings have been divided, and also brief introductory notes to each individual selection.

The first part of the book contains selections from writers who reflect the many varieties of the idealist tradition that had flourished in the nineteenth century and was still powerfully influential in the early years of the present century. The second part represents the schools of naturalism, realism, and empiricism, for long rivals to idealism and still very much alive today, especially in the English-speaking countries. The final part contains the writings of those whose thought is shaped by life and action—pragmatists, personalists, and existentialists.

Although I have included a few shorter excerpts, most of the selections are chapter-length, since it seemed to me that these would be most useful.

I wish to acknowledge with thanks the great help I have had in the preparation of this volume from Mr. Ronald Stone and Mrs. Joann Stone.

—JOHN MACQUARRIE

Union Theological Seminary
New York City

CONTENTS

xi

III. PRAGMATISM, PERSONALISM, AND EXISTENTIALISM

I

THE IDEALIST TRADITION

I

THE IDEALIST TRADITION

I

INTRODUCTION

IN ITS BROADEST SENSE, the term "idealism" is used for any philosophy which accords the primary reality to ideas or, more generally, to thought and to the experiencing subject, rather than to physical objects. The latter are supposed to exist only in relation to an experiencing subject or to some ideal reality which stands behind the phenomena of space and time. In this very broad sense of "idealism," Plato could be counted an idealist, for he supposed that reality is constituted by the eternal world of ideas or forms, and that the world of sense is only a reflection of this real world. A different kind of "idealism" is represented by Bishop Berkeley, for whom the being of physical objects is constituted by their perception by a subject (*esse est percipi*).

In this book, however, we are concerned with "idealism" in a more restricted sense. The word is used especially for a movement in modern philosophy having its roots in Germany but later spreading to other countries. Kant, Fichte, Hegel, Schopenhauer, and many other leading philosophers have belonged to the German idealist tradition, and have developed its theories and extended its influence. Yet even to mention these names shows how much diversity there is within the idealist philosophy. Apart from the fact that these philosophers accept the experiencing subject as the primary philosophical datum, one can scarcely generalize about them, and to do justice to the richness and complexity of the idealist tradition, it will be necessary to outline severally the major types of idealism. All of them were exercising a powerful influence on Western religious thought at the beginning of the twentieth century. The

3

idealist stress on mind and spirit might seem to make this style of philosophy a natural ally of religion, though in practice this was not always the case and to some Christian theologians it has seemed that even the most harmonious accommodations between idealism and Christian faith have been fundamentally mistaken and distorting.

We begin with *absolute idealism,* perhaps the most thoroughgoing development of the idealist philosophy. This absolute idealism had flourished in Germany in the early part of the nineteenth century, its best known representative being Georg Wilhelm Friedrich Hegel (1770–1831). Long after the school had declined in Germany, it had a new lease of life in the English-speaking countries, and in these lands it was probably the dominating philosophical influence in the early years of the present century. This kind of idealism is called "absolute" because it refers the world to a single all-embracing experience, to a universal subject, the Absolute (sometimes identified with God). Finite minds were usually supposed to be somehow included in the Absolute, though this led to the devaluation of individual personal existence. Indeed, the concrete tended to be swallowed up in the universal. Historical happenings, for instance, are of interest only in so far as they embody timeless universal truths. Thus the Hegelian philosopher tended to dismiss any notion of a "once-for-all" or unique character in the events of the Christian gospel. It has been said that he looked on Christianity as a "visual aid" to idealism: its myths and stories serve as pointers to the universal truths of idealist metaphysics, and especially to the truth of the unity of all things in the Absolute.

Absolute idealism is represented in this book by four selections. Edward Caird (1835–1908) stands closest to Hegel himself. He links the idealist notion of the immanence of the Absolute Spirit in all finite beings to the Christian doctrine of the incarnation, and regards the doctrine as the indispensable manifestation in a concrete form of the universal idea. Francis Herbert Bradley (1846–1924), perhaps the most brilliant of the English idealists, departed from the orthodox Hegelian tradition in holding that the Absolute is suprarational. All finite beings are shot through with contradictions that mark them as appearance, rather than reality, but the nature of this reality is beyond the grasp of conceptual thought. Our excerpt shows us the extreme depreciation of the particular and the historical in the interests of the timeless Absolute. Josiah Royce (1855–1916) was the principal representative of absolute idealism in the United States. He worked out his own version of idealism, and in this we see the influence of the social and pragmatic character of American thought. The Absolute is interpreted in social terms, and we see its manifestation in history in the emergence and development of the great community of love and loyalty. John Richardson Illingworth (1848–1915) shows the influence of absolute idealism in Christian theology. While he turned back the strong pantheistic tendency of the absolutist philosophy, he laid stress on the doctrine of divine immanence, and this enabled him to relate the Christian belief in an incarnation to the belief of all religions that the divine Spirit is present in the world.

We turn now to *personal idealism*. This was a reaction, within the idealist school itself, against the excessively exalted role that had been assigned to the Absolute. The personal idealists objected to the notion that finite persons are only "adjectives" of the Absolute and are destined to lose themselves in the all-embracing (or all-devouring) whole. They claimed that to be a person is to have a measure of privacy and independence, even a measure of ultimacy. Moreover, they claimed that it is in finite persons, rather than in a hypothetical Absolute, that we know what the reality of mind or spirit is. Early exponents of personal idealism were Andrew Seth Pringle-Pattison (1856–1931) in Scotland and George Holmes Howison (1834–1916) in California.

The emphasis on the importance of the individual person might seem to accord better with Christian theology than absolute idealism had done, and in fact the personal idealists were usually theists, and visualized the cosmos as a community of spiritual beings, presided over by a personal God. Some of them laid such stress on the independence of each individual person that they also taught that God is limited or finite, and certainly less than the Absolute. But the most interesting of all the personal idealists was John McTaggart Ellis McTaggart (1866–1925), and it is from him that we have chosen an excerpt to illustrate personal idealism. Taking the finite person as the ultimate and eternal reality, he saw no need for God. The cosmos is a system of eternal uncreated selves, living through a succession of embodied lives. Thus even personal idealism in its most thoroughgoing form turned out to be incompatible with Christian theology.

While the teaching of Hegel was undergoing a renascence in the English-speaking countries, Germany itself was exploring again the *transcendental idealism* of Immanuel Kant (1724–1804). Although Kant rejected anything like a Berkeleyan idealism, he believed that the world as we know it is shaped by the categories of the mind, so that we do not know things as they are in themselves but only as they are interpreted by the understanding. However, Kant's idealism ruled out the possibility of rational metaphysics, for the questions of God, freedom, and immortality lie beyond the reach of human thought. But although theoretical reason cannot establish the reality of God, freedom, and immortality, these are, according to Kant, postulates of the practical reason. The neo-Kantianism of the late nineteenth and early twentieth centuries accepted Kant's criticism of metaphysics, and sometimes showed markedly positivist leanings. But neo-Kantianism also followed Kant in his appeal to the practical reason and introduced the notion of objectively subsisting values, especially moral values, as a bulwark against a purely naturalistic interpretation of the world. In theology, the school of Albrecht Ritschl (1822–89) worked with similar ideas. Rejecting the metaphysical elements in traditional Christian dogma, the Ritschlians looked for the empirically ascertainable facts at the origin of Christianity. The historical Jesus, they maintained, is recognized as the Christ by a value-judgment of the practical reason, rather than by a metaphysical interpretation of his person. Both among the philosophical and theological exponents of neo-Kantianism, history and ethics are allotted a more important role than they had in the Hegelian schools.

We have included selections from three representatives of neo-Kantianism and Ritschlianism. The brief excerpt from Wilhelm

Windelband (1848–1915) comes from near the end of his history of philosophy. He has brought the story to the relativism of Nietzsche, and he sees the future of philosophy as "the science of values which are universally valid." His own philosophy consisted in a study of such values, a study sometimes called "axiology." Next there is an excerpt from Hans Vaihinger (1852–1933), who represents the skeptical and positivistic type of neo-Kantianism. It has been called "positivistic idealism" and has affinities with pragmatism. His extensive studies of Kant led him to believe that his work is properly interpreted in terms of a philosophy of "as if." Our knowledge is strictly limited to the phenomena of space and time, but our minds construct "fictions" which go beyond what we can know. These fictions (God, freedom, and immortality are examples) are infected with falsity and inconsistency, but they may nevertheless have value for the conduct of life. Finally there is an excerpt from Wilhelm Herrmann (1846–1922), one of the best-known Ritschlian theologians and teacher of both Barth and Bultmann. Herrmann looked for a positive foundation for his theology on what he took to be the solid historical facts concerning Jesus. But the inner life of Jesus, as preserved in the historical tradition, is said to make on us the same impression that it made on the first disciples, so that our innate sense of moral values leads us to acknowledge that God was in this man.

Within the idealist tradition we must take note also of *historical idealism*. This type of philosophy looks to the living panorama of culture and history for the clue to reality. It does not, like absolute idealism, try to go behind history to some timeless idea. Yet it equally rejects all naturalistic accounts of history, believing that history is the unfolding of spirit. This type of idealism was developed by Wilhelm Dilthey (1833–1911) who distinguished between the natural sciences, where we know the phenomena only from outside, and the human sciences, where we know the subject-matter through our direct participation in it. Chief among these human sciences is history. Even metaphysics is less fundamental than history, and the history of metaphysics shows us the relativism that characterizes all human thought.

From this branch of the idealist tradition we have drawn two excerpts. One is from Ernst Troeltsch (1865–1923) who owed much to Dilthey and applied his ideas to the study of Christianity as a phenomenon to be viewed within the framework of man's spiritual and cultural history. The other is from Robin George Collingwood (1889–1943), perhaps the most noted representative of this type of idealism in the English-speaking countries. He sets out clearly and concisely his basic understanding of history and its significance.

2

THE GOSPEL OF ST. JOHN AND THE IDEA OF A DIVINE HUMANITY

Edward Caird

The Evolution of Religion *contains Edward Caird's Gifford Lectures, and presents an almost purely Hegelian interpretation of religion. Reality is rational and intelligible. Reason and religion are not rivals, but different ways in which man, as a rational being, relates himself to Reality. Religion has undergone a dialectical development. In its first phase, it looked outward on nature, and assumed the forms of polytheism and pantheism. In its next phase, it turned inward on the subject, and found the transcendent God who manifests himself in the demand of the moral consciousness. The opposition between these stages is overcome in universal religion, typified by Christianity and finding its philosophical interpretation in idealism. It is with this synthesis that our excerpt deals.*

ST. PAUL at once generalized and idealized the faith of Christ, liberating it from the Judaic conditions of its origin, and at the same time lifting it into the region of theology. For him the whole life of Christ became summed up in his death; and the story of his humanity was changed into the history of a divinely commissioned Messiah, who had renounced the glories of his prenatal existence with God that he might endure all the pains and sorrows of man, and, by bearing the utmost force of evil which man can suffer or

From *The Evolution of Religion* (Glasgow: James Maclehose & Sons, 1893), Vol. II, pp. 217–34.

inflict, might emancipate man from it. For the resurrection of Christ, as St. Paul believed, had shown that the way of self-abnegation, and not the way of self-assertion, was the divinely-appointed way to glory and immortality. It had been made manifest in this transcendent example that he who empties himself of all selfish ambition, becomes filled with the power of a divine life; that he who gives up all, finds all again in God. Thus, as St. Paul maintained, through Christ's death a new principle has been introduced into humanity—a principle which, in every one who has faith in Christ, will produce the same fruits as in him. We, indeed, cannot, like Christ, renounce heaven for earth, that we may save mankind; but none the less it is possible for us, through the new spiritual force that has come into man's life, to make the "grand renunciation" of ourselves, and so to "fill up that which is behind in the afflictions of Christ"[1] to complete the salvation of men. And, when we do so, we feel within us the "earnest of the spirit," the sustaining and inspiring power of the same principle of life, which in him vanquished all the hate of man and rose victorious over death itself; and we cannot but believe that in us it will produce the same effects in life and in death.

In this way we see that St. Paul combined two things which at first might seem irreconcilable. On the one hand, he generalized the lesson of the life and death of Jesus. He extracted from it a universal principle which was not confined to Jesus Christ, but might find new organs in every human soul. Or, to put it in another way, he recognized that in Christ was revealed the essential law of man's moral life, as drawing all its strength out of surrender to the divine Spirit, which is present in all men, in so far as in them the consciousness of self is bound up with the consciousness of God. Yet, at the same time, by his identification of Jesus as an individual with this principle, he prevented it from shrinking into an abstract dogma, and gave to it the living power of an image of perception or imagination.

And what St. Paul thus initiated, was still more fully worked out in the Gospel of St. John, in which the highest view of Jesus, as not

[1] Col. 1:24.

only the Messiah but the "Logos of God," is brought into direct combination with the story of his earthly life; and, in which, on the other hand, the details of that life are consistently presented as the manifestation of the divine meaning of his personality. St. John, or the writer of the Gospel attributed to St. John, thus completed that synthesis of the universal and the individual, to which Christianity owes so much of its power over the hearts of men. And when the same writer speaks of that which "was from the beginning, which we have seen with our eyes, and our hands have handled, of the Word of life," he is uniting, with a clear consciousness of their startling contrast and antagonism, the utmost universality of the Christian idea—as a principle which embraces all the existence of man and of the universe—with the immediate personality of an individual, who is represented as living and acting under the ordinary conditions of human life. He was thus bringing together the two poles between which the spirit of man moves, as it is conscious of itself in its finitude in relation to the divine, and, therefore, conscious at the same time that the divine can be revealed in it.

What has now been said may be otherwise expressed thus: It is a law of human history that principles and tendencies which are really universal, should at first make their appearance in an individual form, as if bound up with the passing existence of a particular nation or even of a single man. The general idea needs, so to speak, to be embodied or incarnated, to be "made flesh and to dwell among men" in all the fullness of realization in a finite individuality, before it can be known and appreciated in its universal meaning. And it is only after such individual presentation has produced its effect that reflection is able to detach the idea from accidents of time and place and circumstance, and present it as a general principle. Even in the case of philosophy itself—which, as it belongs to the reflective stage of consciousness, might seem independent of the personality of its teachers—the same laws still partially holds good; for the greatest of all philosophical movements is associated with the life and death of Socrates, the first representative of the subjective principle of thought. Now, in this movement from the individual to the universal the great danger is that the idea should lose in intensity what it gains in generality; that, as it frees itself from local and temporal conditions, it should at the same time be deprived of that direct force of appeal to the souls of men which springs from its identification with an individual who is its organ and living embodiment. It is, therefore, of the highest importance that, in spite of the generalizing process which necessarily begins so soon as the individual is removed and reflection is at work upon his memory, the living impression of the person should as much as possible be retained, and kept in union with the principle he has represented. Hence

> Wisdom dealt with mortal powers,
> Where truth in closest words shall fail,
> When truth embodied in a tale,
> Shall enter in at lowly doors.[2]

Thus, while the individual influence is very limited in its operation, and the bare universal is like a disemboded soul that has lost the power of action in the finite world, the individual who is regarded as the organ of a universal principle, the universal principle which has incarnated itself for perception or imagination in an individual life, take hold upon man by both sides of his nature, and work with irresistible transforming force upon all his thought and life. Now, it may fairly be said that St. Paul's Epistles and St. John's Gospel have together discharged this office for Christendom in relation to the life of Jesus Christ: the *former* freeing the idea of the crucified Messiah from the limitations of the Jewish environment in which it is presented by the Synoptic narrative, and the *latter* reinstating the ideal image of Christ thus reached, not indeed in all the special Jewish relations of its first expression, but at least in the general conditions of an actual human life. With St. Paul, Jesus has become ideal without ceasing to be real, because, just in the same measure as he is lost as an image without, as a "Christ after the flesh," he is restored as a "quickening spirit" in the hearts of his followers. With St. John, the outward image of Christ after

[2] *In Memoriam*, xxxvi.

the flesh is revived again, though only as "Word made flesh," the individualized manifestation of God in a humanity which is perfectly conformed to that which it has to express.

Now this process of idealizing the real, and again of realizing the ideal, which we have thus just described, is not isolated, or unexampled in other spheres of human thought and life. If the spirit of Christ could not come to men till Christ after the flesh had departed, the same may be said in a measure of every human embodiment of excellence. The same psychological law renews its action in every great experience of loss or bereavement.

> 'Tis only as they spring to heaven that angels
> Reveal themselves to you: they sit all day
> Beside you, and lie down at night by you,
> Who care not for their presence—muse or sleep—
> And all at once they leave you, and you know them.[3]

In this sense it may be said that men never have full spiritual or ideal possession except of that which has ceased to be empirically present to their senses. They cannot discern the "word of life" in that which "their eyes see and their hands are" actually "handling." They need the real to be removed to some distance, ere they can fully apprehend the ideal that is behind it. This does not mean, however, that they do not really discern but only imagine it. It is not that regretful memory exaggerates the virtues of the friend, who no longer is there to refute our idealism with the limitations of mortality. It is that the conditions of life half-conceal from us that which they half-reveal, and that the immediate perception of all the details of the moment obscures the meaning of the whole. And thus it is often death which first gives the right focus, from which alone each part can be seen in its proper proportion and relation to the others.

> When he shall hear she died upon his words,
> The idea of her life shall sweetly creep
> Into his study of imagination,

[3] Browning's *Paracelsus, Part Fifth.*

> And every lovely organ of her life
> Shall come apparelled in more precious habit,
> More moving-delicate and full of life,
> Into the eye and prospect of his soul
> Than when she lived indeed.

It is only a grander illustration of the same law which we have in the great poem of the Middle Ages, the *Divina Commedia,* with its all but deification of the object of Dante's youthful love. By the long brooding gaze of the poet's imagination the purity and simplicity of maidenhood, with its single-minded instinct for what is lovely and pure—all that Dante had loved in Beatrice—were gradually transformed into a symbol, and even an embodiment of the divine light that guides man through the confusions of life; and all the faults and weakness of mortality were lost in the vision of the "eternal womanly" which is ever "drawing us upward."[4] And this example suggests another thought, viz., that the qualities which we revere in men are *growing* powers, which have their value in their promise, and can only be fully understood by one who sees in them the future to which they point. They are undeveloped germs in which a finite form hides an infinite potentiality. And though, as life goes on, such hints may acquire more definiteness, yet the veil of human individuality is generally too dark to let us discover in what ways and in what measure the individual has become and is becoming one with his ideal. The imperfections of growth and the limits of finite personality keep, so to speak, the human separated from the divine, till the idealizing touch of death removes the division between them, and enables us to see in the man, our fellow, a new organ of the universal spirit of goodness. This revelation of the divine in the human is perhaps the highest use of sorrow, as it is the one thing which has plucked from many human hearts its bitterest sting. Hence it is no irreverence, still less is it any mere poetic exaggeration, copying the irrationality of human passion, which leads Tennyson to find his final consolation for the loss of his friend in all but dissolving his individuality in the divine. Though

[4] *Das ewig Weibliche*
Zieht uns hinan.

"mixed with God and nature," he declares, "I seem to love thee more and more."

> Strange friend, past, present, and to be;
> Loved deeplier, darklier understood;
> Behold, I dream a dream of good,
> And mingle all the world with thee.[5]

Still more definitely is this felt in the case of a great original individuality who does not, so to speak, give us merely a casual glimpse of the divine through a life generally lived on the ordinary levels of mortality; but who, by the devotion of his whole existence to the realization of the one idea that possesses him, initiates a new type of human character, and creates a new ideal of human excellence. Such men as Buddha, Socrates, and Luther, whose manhood and age are the fulfillment of an idea conceived in youth, and who treat their whole life, and even it may be their death, as the clay in which the moral work of art is realized, can be seen truly only when faithfulness unto death has given as it were the last touch to their work. In such a consistent course of life what strikes us most is not this or that ray of excellence, nor even the completed course of progress, but rather the path of life which is traversed is to us as the path of a star to the astronomer, which enables him to prophesy its future course. Such men seem still to grow beyond the end which hides them from our eyes. The idea which, while they lived, was painfully seen through the personality it animated, now seems after their death to be freed from all obstacles and to go on developing, carrying their personality with it. Thus the great man in his lifetime stands before his contemporaries as an external image of excellence, which may, indeed, awaken a new spirit in those who are able even partially to appreciate it; but, when the outward presence is removed, the awakened spirit reproduces the inmost reality of the fact in an idealized vision which is truer than anything seen with the eyes of sense. For then, all the results that have sprung out of the living energy of the man, furnish us with new traits which enable us to realize more clearly

[5] *In Memoriam*, cxxix.

what he was; and this new idealized image in turn reacts in further developments of the same spiritual energy which originally produced it.

It is only the greatest of all instances of this law of development which we see in the early history of Christianity. And it is this which explains at once the intensity of the religious life which Christ called forth, and the rapid expansion of the Christian community, so long as the strength of its first impulse was maintained. In the narrative which is at the basis of the Synoptic Gospels, in the idealizing movement of St. Paul's Epistles, and finally, in the effort of St. John to bring back the highest result of this process into connection with the remembered facts of Christ's life, we see the expanding power of the idea of Christ: we see it as it flows out of his personality, and again as it reacts on the memory of the life from which it proceeds, at once deepening and widening the interpretation of it, and thus, so far as may be, raising the human in it into closer union with the divine. And if in this process the accurate lineaments of fact are in some degree lost or changed, yet in the main and with one important reservation, it is to be recognized that the change is only a sacrifice of the letter to the spirit. For the result is a more perfect combination of the real and the ideal, or, if the words are preferred, of the human and the divine, than ever has been reached in any other writings. The two terms are, indeed, stretched to the utmost point of their antagonism, and are shown in their utmost tension against each other; but the religious imagination, the intuition of faith, is still able to hold them together, and, by doing so, it gains a kind of power which is possible only in such a union of opposite poles of the consciousness of humanity.

Thus the way in which, in the thought of the disciples, the ordinary limitations of finitude and humanity—of that in the finite world and in man which separates them from God—gradually drop away from the image of Christ, has in it something which, though unexampled in degree, yet agrees in kind with the ordinary process by which the ideal reveals itself in and through the real; or, to put it more accurately, with the process by which the ideal reveals itself *as the reality* which is hid beneath the immediate appearance of things. It may even be said that Christianity is distinguished from all other religions by the fact that it supplies the *rationale* and the justification of this process. For its fundamental lesson that man must "die to live" involves as a consequence that it is just through the last sacrifice of life itself that the divine principle of life in humanity reveals itself most clearly. In such complete devotion of himself, man becomes, what it is his innate vocation to be, the organ and manifestation of God. From this principle it necessarily follows that the idealizing process which death sets on foot, and by which the individual is lifted out of the limitations of mortality, is no mere visionary or poetic exaggeration, but only a recognition of the inmost truth of things. If life and death are the process whereby the image of God is realized in man, then there is no illusion in the correlative process by which, in the thought of those that come after, the history of a man is regarded as a stage in the manifestation of God. And, if it was the founder of Christianity who first realized in its full meaning the truth which we philosophically express by saying that the consciousness of God is presupposed and implied in the consciousness of the world, and even more directly in the consciousness of self—and that therefore a self-conscious being cannot know what he really is, or realize his good except in utter self-surrender to God—then there is a supreme reason why all generations of men should call *him* divine, not, indeed, as isolated from others, but as the "first-born of many brethren." By him, as by no other individual before, the pure idea of a divine humanity was apprehended and made into the great principle of life; and, consequently, in so far as that idea can be regarded as realized in an individual—and it was a necessity of feeling and imagination that it should be regarded as so realized—in no other could it find so pure an embodiment. Nay, we may add that, so long as it was regarded as embodied in him only in the same sense in which it flowed out from him to others, so long the primacy attributed to Christ could not obscure the truth. It only furnished it with a typical expression, whereby the movement of the feelings and the imagination was kept in harmony with that of the intelligence.

Now this seems to be the ruling idea of the seventeenth chapter of St. John's Gospel, in which the principle of Christian mysticism receives its highest expression. The same divine life which manifests itself in Christ, it is there declared, is also communicated by him to all his followers. "Holy Father, keep through Thine own name those that Thou hast given me, that they may be one *as* we are. . . . Neither pray I for these alone, but for them also that shall believe through their word, that they may all be one, *as* Thou Father art in me and I in Thee, that they also may be one in us." Christ is thus proclaimed to be the unique revelation of God, but only as the first-born of many brethren, the greatest of all the servants of humanity, the most perfect organ of that divine life for which man was made, in as much as he was made in the image of God. In fact, it *was* through Jesus Christ that that capacity of men to become sons of God, which was in humanity from the first, was actualized or clearly revealed; and that, not merely in some casual voice of exalted religious feeling, or in the abstract conceptions of philosophy, but as the ruling principle of a life lived under ordinary human conditions, and, above all, in the death which was its culmination, the death of the cross to which Jesus was "lifted up that he might draw all men to him."[6] For the cross, combining as it did the loftiest and the lowest things of human existence, the deepest outward shame and the manifestation of the highest energy of spiritual life to which the soul of man can rise, was the appropriate, and, we might even say, the *necessary* symbol of a religion which, in breaking down all the walls of division between man and man, class and class, nation and nation, at the same time awoke man, in all the weakness of his finitude, to a consciousness of unity with God.

Such an interpretation of the doctrine of the divine humanity of Jesus Christ may seem to many to take away that which is the necessary support of their faith. But I believe that, when fully considered and understood, it will be found to contain all the elements of vital Christianity, all the elements in it that have really given support to the religious life of man in the past. For the power of

[6] John 12:32.

Christianity has *always* lain in its bringing Christ, at once, and in virtue of the same moral and spiritual characteristics, into unity with God and with man; and the theological doctrine of two natures in Christ which are the source of separate and even opposed attributes, has never found an echo in the voice of immediate religious experience. Read all the books of Christian devotion from the earliest to the latest, and you will find that what they dwell upon, when they are not merely repeating the words of the creeds but speaking in the language of religious experience, is that Christ is divine *just because* he is the most human of men, the man in whom the universal spirit of humanity has found its fullest expression; and that, on the other hand, he is the ideal or typical man, the Son of Man who reveals what is in humanity, *just because* he is the purest revelation of God in man. The divisions of theological logic, the dogmatic decrees of councils as to the nature of Christ, which set the human and the divine in him in opposition to each other, or only externally unite them, have never quite corresponded with the devotional language of the saints, i.e. with the language in which there is the purest utterance of the religious life. And even the history of dogma itself shows a continual reaction of that life against the distinctions of theology, and an ever-renewed effort to overcome them by new refinements and distinctions. In truth, the attempts of theology to raise Christ above the conditions of human life, and to give him a metaphysical or physical greatness of another kind, really end in lowering him and depriving him of his true position in the religious life of man. For they obscure the one point in which he really is unique, as being the first to break through the Jewish division between the divine and the human, yet without falling into the gulf of an abstract pantheism, or losing any of that moral idealism in which the purifying power of monotheism lay.

3

ABSOLUTE TRUTH AND PROBABILITY

F. H. Bradley

The Principles of Logic first appeared in 1883. It represented a new approach to logic in the English-speaking world, for instead of discussing the formal conditions for valid argument, it considered the nature of judgment and the relation of thought and reality. Absolute truth could be attained only if our judgments held good of reality as a whole. Short of that, we can only have relative truth, and one of Bradley's most distinctive doctrines was his teaching about degrees of truth. The more particular and contingent a judgment is, the lower is the degree of truth it expresses. The consequences of this doctrine for historical assertions is made clear in our excerpt, taken from one of several essays which Bradley appended to the second edition of his book. We should notice also that Bradley held absolute truth to be unattainable. He departed from the idealist view that reality is rational, holding that it is suprarational and that all our knowing is infected with contradiction.

IT MAY LEAD the reader, perhaps, to realize better the whole problem and its solution, if I end by offering an illustration not merely fanciful. Suppose (let us say) a man convinced of the truth of Christianity, and rightly or wrongly to understand Christianity as the unity of God with finite souls, a reality at once consummated

Reprinted with permission from *The Principles of Logic* (2d ed.; London: The Clarendon Press, Oxford, 1922), Vol. II, pp. 688–90.

and eternal and yet temporal and progressive. Christianity is to such a man a main aspect of the Universe, conscious of itself above time, and yet revealing itself in the historical growth of spiritual experience. And imagine the same man asked to compare with this principle the truth about some happening in time. I will not instance such events as the virgin birth and bodily ascension of Jesus of Nazareth, but I will take the historical assertion that Jesus actually at a certain time lived and taught in Galilee and actually died at Jerusalem on the cross. And by "actually" I mean so that, if *we* had been there, we should have seen these things happen.

"All such events," our supposed man might reply, "are, if you view them as occurrences, of little importance. Inquire by all means whether and how far there is good evidence for their happening. But do not imagine that Christianity is vitally concerned with the result of your inquiry. Christianity, as I conceive it, covers so much ground, fills such a space in the Universe, and makes such a difference to the world, that, without it, the world would be not so much changed as destroyed. And it counts for much that this eternal truth should have appeared on our planet (as presumably elsewhere), and should here (we hope) be developing itself more and more fully. But the rest, if you will take it as mere event and occurrence, is an affair so small—a matter grounded by the very nature of its world on so little—that between the two things there can be hardly a comparison."

23507

The principle applied here is that on which I have based myself throughout. The attempt to decide off-hand between truths, however different their orders, leads naturally to the assumption that these truths are to be placed much on the same level. And hence the one may be raised and the other degraded, in each case without warrant, and with a result inevitably mistaken and often disastrous. If truths are to be compared there must be first an inquiry into the respective nature of each. And the truths which at first may seem nearest to us and most palpable and least obscure, may turn out to be in reality the most wavering and ambiguous, and most abstract and remote, and dependent, more than all others, upon false alternatives and one-sided assumptions.

Still, even if it is here unnecessary, I am led to recall another aspect of this matter; and I will venture once more to speak through the mouth of my supposed Christian. Imagine him asked whether, thinking as he does, he cares nothing for "the historical truth" of Christianity, any more than for the detail of Christian creeds and symbols—and possibly his answer might surprise us. "I understood you to be speaking," he might reply, "about mere temporal events and happenings, just as you might speak again about mere material things such as this crucifix or that flag. These by themselves are all abstractions, mistaken for realities by what too often is called Common Sense; and these most assuredly are not the genuine facts and beliefs of religion. Religious events and symbols, though on one side things and happenings in your 'real world,' are something on the other side whose essence and life is elsewhere. Identified with what is beyond, they are no mere occurrences in time or things in space. They represent, and they are the actual incarnation of eternal reality, and for the least of them a man might feel called on to die." And, whether we can quite accept this answer or not, the main principle at least is certain. What we sometimes call our "real world," our constructed order of facts and events in space and time, is in truth an abstraction. We live really only so far as we live in the concrete, and use events and things, however confusedly, as the appearances of that larger life which transcends mere space and time. And, when we perceive this, we comprehend how something may at once offer itself as in comparison fuller and more true, and yet in reality cover and contain less of what works and what counts in the whole of things. On the other hand, failing to perceive this, we everywhere may fall into mistake, and noticeably here when we seek reflectively to measure one truth against another. But the theme on which I have now entered is too large, by far, for any brief discussion.

4

THE UNIVERSAL COMMUNITY

Josiah Royce

The theme of religion interested Josiah Royce throughout his philosophical career. In The Religious Aspect of Philosophy, *published in 1885, he tells us that it was the problem of religion that first drove him to philosophy. At that time he found a solution to his problem in the Absolute of idealist philosophy. But as his thought developed, he found the Absolute of Hegelianism too abstract and too far removed from the strivings of man. Thus he came to develop a social understanding of the Absolute, of which the earthly and temporal manifestation is the growing community of love. In his book* The Problem of Christianity *from which our excerpt is taken, Royce links his philosophy of loyalty with the religious faith which appeared in the primitive Christian community.*

PAUL indeed repeated many of his Master's words concerning love; and he everywhere is in full agreement with their spirit. And yet this agreement is accompanied by a perfectly inevitable further development of the doctrine of Christian love—a development which is due to the fact that into the world of Paul's religious life and teaching there has entered, not only a new experience, but a new sort of being—a real object whereof the Master had not made explicit mention.

God and the neighbor are beings whose general type religion

Reprinted with permission from *The Problem of Christianity* (New York: The Macmillan Co., 1913), Vol. I, pp. 91–106.

and common sense had made familiar long before Jesus taught, mysterious though God and one's neighbor were to the founder's hearers, and still remain to ourselves. Both of them are conceived by the religious consciousness of the parables as personal beings, and as individuals. God is the supreme ruler who, as Christ conceives him, is also an individual person, and who loves and wills. The neighbor is the concrete human being of daily life.

But the new, the third being, in Paul's religious world, seems to the Apostle himself novel in its type, and seems to him to possess a nature involving what he more than once calls a "mystery." To express, so far as he may, this "mystery," he uses characteristic metaphors, which have become classic.

This new being is a corporate entity—the body of Christ, or the body of which the now divinely exalted Christ is the head. Of this body the exalted Christ is also, for Paul, the spirit and also, in some new sense, the lover. This corporate entity is the Christian community itself.

Perfectly familiar is the fact that the existence and the idea of this community constitute a new beginning in the evolution of Christianity. But neglected, as I think and as I have just asserted, is the subtle and momentous transformation, the great development which this new motive brings to pass in the Pauline form of the doctrine of Christian love.

What most interests us here, and what is least generally understood, I think, by students of the problem of Christianity, is the fact that this new entity, this corporate sort of reality which Paul so emphasizes, this being which is not an individual man but a community, does not, as one might suppose, render the Apostle's doctrine of love more abstract, more remote from human life, less direct and less moving, than was the original doctrine of love in the parables. On the contrary, the new element makes the doctrine of love more concrete, and, as I must insist, really less mysterious. In speaking of this corporate entity, the Apostle uses metaphors, and knows that they are metaphors; but, despite what the Apostle calls the new "mystery," these metaphors explain much that the parables left doubtful. These metaphors do not hide, as the Master, in using the form of the parable, occasionally intended for the time to hide from those who were not yet ready for the full revelation, truths which the future was to make clearer to the disciples. No, Paul's metaphors regarding the community of the faithful in the Church bring the first readers of Paul's epistles into direct contact with the problems of their own daily religious life.

The corporate entity—the Christian community—proves to be, for Paul's religious consciousness, something more concrete than is the individual fellow-man. The question: Who is my neighbor? had been answered by the Master by means of the parable of the Good Samaritan. But that question itself had not been due merely to the hardness of heart of the lawyer who asked it. The problem of the neighbor actually involves mysteries which, as we have already seen and hereafter shall still further see, the parables deliberately leave, along with the conception of the Kingdom of Heaven itself, to be made clearer only when the new revelation, for which the parables are preparing the way, shall have been granted. Now Paul feels himself to be in possession of a very precious part of this further revelation. He has discovered, in his own experience as Apostle, a truth that he feels to be new. He believes this truth to be a revelation due to the spirit of his Lord.

In fact, the Apostle has discovered a special instance of one of the most significant of all moral and religious truths, the truth that a community, when unified by an active indwelling purpose, is an entity more concrete and, in fact, less mysterious than is any individual man, and that such a community can love and be loved as a husband and wife love; or as father or mother love.

Because the particular corporate entity whose cause Paul represents, namely, the Christian community, is in his own experience something new, whose origin he views as wholly miraculous, whose beginnings and whose daily life are bound up with the influence which he believes to be due to the spirit of his risen and ascended Lord, Paul indeed regards the Church as a "mystery." But, as a fact, his whole doctrine regarding the community has a practical concreteness, a clear common sense about it, such that he is able to restate the doctrine of Christian love so as to be fully just to all its active heroism, while interpreting much which the parables left problematic.

What can I do for my neighbor's good? The parables had answered: "Love him, help him in his obvious and bitter needs, teach him the spirit of love, and leave the rest to God." Does Paul make light of this teaching? On the contrary, his hymn in honor of love, in the first epistle to the Corinthians, is one of Christianity's principal treasures. Nowhere is the real consequence of the teaching of Jesus regarding love more completely stated. But notice this difference: For Paul the neighbor has now become a being who is primarily the fellow-member of the Christian community.

The Christian community is itself something visible; miraculously guided by the Master's spirit. It is at once for the Apostle a fact of present experience and a divine creation. And therefore every word about love for the neighbor is in the Apostle's teaching at once perfectly direct and human in its effectiveness and is nevertheless dominated by the spirit of a new and, as Paul believes, a divinely inspired love for the community.

Both the neighbor and the lover of the neighbor to whom the Apostle appeals are, to his mind, members of the body of Christ; and all the value of each man as an individual is bound up with his membership in this body, and with his love for the community.

Jesus had taught that God loves the neighbor—yes, even the least of these little ones. Paul says to the Ephesians: "Christ loved the church, and gave himself up for it, that he might sanctify it; . . . that he might present the church to himself a glorious church, not having spot: . . . but that it should be holy and without blemish." One sees: The object of the divine love, as Paul conceives it, has been at once transformed and fulfilled.

In God's love for the neighbor, the parables find the proof of the infinite worth of the individual. In Christ's love for the Church Paul finds the proof that both the community, and the individual member, are the objects of an infinite concern, which glorifies them both, and thereby unites them. The member finds his salvation only in union with the Church. He, the member, would be dead without the divine spirit and without the community. But the

Christ whose community this is, has given life to the members—
the life of the Church, and of Christ himself. "You hath he quickened, which were dead in trespasses and sins."

In sum: Christian love, as Paul conceives it, takes on the form
of Loyalty. This is Paul's simple but vast transformation of Christian love.

Loyalty itself was, in the history of humanity, already, at that
time, ancient. It had existed in all tribes and peoples that knew
what it was for the individual so to love his community as to glory
in living and dying for that community. To conceive virtue as
faithfulness to one's community, was, in so far, no new thing.
Loyalty, moreover, had long tended towards a disposition to enlarge both itself and its community. As the world had come together, it had gradually become possible for philosophers, such as
the later Stoics, to conceive of all humanity as in ideal one community.

Although this was so far a too abstract conception to conquer
the world of contending powers, the spirit of loyalty was also not
without its religious relationships, and tended, as religion tended,
to make the moral realm appear, not only a world of human communities, but a world of divinely ordained unity. Meanwhile, upon
every stage, long before the Christian virtues were conceived, loyalty had inspired nations of warriors with the sternest of their
ideals of heroism, and with their noblest visions of the destiny of
the individual. And the prophets of Israel had indeed conceived
the Israel of God's ultimate triumph as a community in and
through which all men should know God and be blessed.

But in Paul's teaching, loyalty, quickened to new life, not merely
by hope, but by the presence of a community in whose meetings
the divine spirit seemed to be daily working fresh wonders, keeps
indeed its natural relation to the militant virtues, is heroic and
strenuous, and delights to use metaphors derived from the soldier's
life. It appears also as the virtue of those who love order, and who
prefer law to anarchy, and who respect worldly authority. And it
derives its religious ideas from the prophets.

But it also becomes the fulfillment of what Jesus had taught in the parables concerning love. For the Apostle, this loyalty unites to all these stern and orderly and militant traits, and to all that the prophets had dreamed about Israel's triumph, the tenderness of a brother's love for the individual brother. Consequently, in Paul's mind, love for the individual human being, and loyalty to the divine community of all the faithful; graciousness of sentiment, and orderliness of discipline; are so directly interwoven that each interprets and glorifies the other.

If the Corinthians unlovingly contend, brother with brother, concerning their gifts, Paul tells them about the body of Christ, and about the divine unity of its spirit in all the diversity of its members and of their powers. On the other hand, if it is loyalty to the Church which is to be interpreted and revivified, Paul pictures the dignity of the spiritual community in terms of the direct beauty and sweetness and tenderness of the love of brother for brother—that love which seeketh not her own.

The perfect union of this inspired passion for the community, with this tender fondness for individuals, is at once the secret of the Apostle's power as a missionary and the heart of his new doctrine. Of loyalty to the spirit and to the body of Christ, he discourses in his most abstruse as well as in his most eloquent passages. But his letters close with the well-known winning and tender messages to and about individual members and about their intimate personal concerns.

As to the question: "What shall I do for my brother?" Paul has no occasion to answer that question *except* in terms of the brother's relations to the community. But just for that reason his counsels can be as concrete and definite as each individual case requires them to be. Because the community, as Paul conceives it—the small community of a Pauline church—keeps all its members in touch with one another; because its harmony is preserved through definite plans for setting aside the differences that arise amongst individuals; because, by reason of the social life of the whole, the physical needs, the perils, the work, the prosperity of the individual are all made obvious facts of the common experience of the church, and are all just as obviously and definitely related to the health of the whole body—Paul's gospel of love has constant and concrete practical applications to the life of those whom he addresses. The ideal of the parables has become a visible life on earth. So live together that the Church may be worthy of Christ who loves it, so help the individual brother that he may be a fitting member of the Church. Such are now the counsels of love.

All this teaching of Paul was accompanied, of course, in the Apostle's own mind, by the unquestioning assurance that this community of the Christian faith, as he knew it and in his letters addressed its various representatives, was indeed a genuinely universal community. It was already, to his mind, what the prophets had predicted when they spoke of the redeemed Israel. By the grace of God, all men belonged to this community, or would soon belong to it, whom God was pleased to save at all.

For the end of the world was very soon to come, and would manifest its membership, its divine head, and its completed mission. According to Paul's expectation, there was to be no long striving towards an ideal that in time was remote. He dealt with the interests of all mankind. But his faith brought him into direct contact with the institution that represented this world-wide interest. What loyalty on its highest levels has repeatedly been privileged to imagine as the ideal brotherhood of all who are loyal, Paul found directly presented, in his religious experience, as his own knowledge of his Master's purpose, and of its imminent fulfillment.

This vision began to come to Paul when he was called to be an apostle; and later, when he was sent to the Gentiles, the ideal grew constantly nearer and clearer. The Church was, for Paul, the very presence of his Lord.

Such, then, was the first highly developed Christian conception of the universal community. That which the deepest and highest rational interests of humanity make most desirable for all men, and that which the prophets of Israel had predicted afar off, the religious experience of Paul brought before his eyes as the daily work of the spirit in the Church. Was not Christ present whenever the faithful were assembled? Was not the spirit living in their midst? Was not the day of the Lord at hand? Would not they all soon be changed, when the last trumpet should sound?

Paul's expectations of the coming judgment were not realized. Those little apostolic churches, where the spirit daily manifested itself, gave place to the historical church of the later centuries, whose possession of the spirit has often been a matter of dogma rather than of life, and whose unity has been so often lost to human view. The letter has hidden the spirit. The Lord has delayed his coming. The New Jerusalem, adorned as a bride for her husband, remains hidden behind the heavens. The vision has become the Problem of Christianity.

5

DIVINE IMMANENCE IN NATURE

J. R. Illingworth

The Divine Immanence is one of several distinguished books written by a learned parish priest of the Church of England, John R. Illingworth. His theology was strongly colored by the influences of idealist philosophy, and this is apparent in the importance which he gave to the notion of divine immanence. His belief that God is present in all creation also led him to have a positive appreciation for natural religion and to assert a continuity between Christianity and other faiths. But he resisted the tendencies of absolute idealism toward pantheism and the depreciation of the historical, and tried to find a place for the uniqueness of the incarnation, as Christianity understands it.

THE RELIGIOUS influence of external nature is a fact of experience; nothing rare or exceptional, but an ordinary fact of normal human experience. And as the significance of this fact depends upon its magnitude—its agelong existence and world-wide extent—it is very important to bear in mind the distinction between the experience itself and its interpretations. For its interpretations being inevitably colored by the spirit of their age, have varied with every variety of culture and of creed. And as men easily tend to confuse the original impression with the philosophic or theological belief into which they instinctively translate it, they often appear to be going further than their premises allow, and so bring the whole process into dis-

From *The Divine Immanence* (London: Macmillan & Co., 1900), pp. 49–50 and 62–73.

repute. One man, for example, claims to see in nature a benevolent creator; another a dualism; another a plurality of spiritual beings; another a universally diffused spirit. But all these are interpretations of an immediate experience in the light of a general belief; and are liable to obscure, by their contradictory character, the universality of the experience in question. Still, beneath them all that experience remains; a sense, in the presence of nature, of contact with something spiritual; a sense of affinity, or kinship, as the Neo-platonists described it, with the material world, implying spirituality within or behind it. The feeling is hard to describe in more definite terms, since even the emotions that it arouses are very different in different minds; but though undefinable it is intense, and, as we have seen, unquestionably normal to humanity.

But if all this be true, and the experience in question cannot be invalidated, then it remains, a stupendous evidence that the material universe is a manifestation of spirit. This question is too often treated as if it were merely an argumentative inference—an inference from beauty, or the need of causation, or the traces of design, or the like; in oblivion of the fact that behind, and prior to, all these inferences, there is the spiritual influence, which nature does, as we have seen, undoubtedly exert. And our reason for emphasizing the distinction between this influence and its interpretations, is to bring its universality into stronger relief. However variously men interpret it, they all feel and have ever felt it alike.

Now we often hear it said that the first aspect of nature—its *prima facie* aspect—makes for materialism. But in the light of the foregoing facts, this is unquestionably not the case. The *prima facie* aspect of the world conduces to spiritual belief, and the view which makes for materialism is not the *prima facie* view, but that which we obtain by going behind the *prima facie* view, to examine its machinery. But in so doing we pass from the whole to a partial view. The *prima facie* view is the judgment of our personality as a whole, in contact with nature as a whole; that is, a judgment in which our entire being takes part. But the analytical or scientific view is a partial view, with important elements left out; it makes abstraction, for its own purpose, of certain properties of things, and omits the remainder. And though the physical sciences have been called concrete, in comparison with the still more abstract mathematics, yet they are all abstract to this extent, that they regard only the physical relations of phenomena, which possess also moral and emotional relations. Such abstraction is of course as necessary for the development of thought, as is its practical equivalent, the division of labor, for the development of life. As social progress only begins, when the different members of a society confine themselves to the performance of different functions; so intellectual progress only begins, when the various aspects of the world are distributed for analysis, each to a separate science. But neither the specialization of science, nor the division of labor, are ends in themselves. If we wish to understand human nature, in its fullness, we do not confine our attention to particular classes of the community—soldiers, statesmen, merchants, thinkers, artists, artisans; but pass on to the total society, which includes, and is enriched by all these partial lives; and supplements, and correlates, and unifies them all. In the same way, if we wish to understand material nature, in its fullness, we must pass on from its partial analysis to its total effect; from the examination of its mechanical structure, its chemical properties, its organic development, its aesthetic appearance, to the actual result of all these things in synthesis, that is, in their living combination, as presented to the personality of man. We then find that nature, in its concrete unity, has a spiritual character which cannot be discovered from its abstract parts; any more than the subject of a puzzle picture can be known before we have put its isolated portions together; or the meaning of a word before we have arranged its letters when given us to spell. In order to emphasize the fact that this spirituality of nature is not an inference but an experience, we have purposely, as above stated, set the variety of its interpretations aside; though that very variety is of course additional proof of the reality of the experience in question; since it shows that, however differing in all their theories of the world, men have always agreed that here was a fact, a persistent something, to be explained. But now that we are clear upon this point, we may return to the further question of its interpretation. What is the relation of the material universe to that Spirit of which it so persistently seems to speak? The experience with which we are dealing has, as we have seen, been historically compatible with theories of every description; but those theories are not all equally tenable on other grounds.

Polytheism and dualism, for instance, are no longer possible interpretations; for the universe is obviously one. Its unity of structure and development, though often maintained in other ages, has been placed by modern science in an entirely new light; and that unity leaves no place for the thought of contradictory beings at its helm. If the system of things be guided by spiritual power, that power must be ultimately one. And if we are to form any further conjecture of the way in which this Spirit is related to the material order, we must recur to the starting-point of all our knowledge, namely, ourselves. Human personality, however little we may comprehend it, is yet the thing that we know best, as being the only thing that we know at first hand, and from within. And further, human personality exhibits spirit and matter in combination; such intimate combination that, as we have seen above, they do not admit of being completely sundered. It is in human personality alone, therefore, that we must look for light upon our subject; the limited light indeed of a lantern carried in our own uncertain hand, but still the only light that we can possibly possess.

Now we find on reflection that what we call our spirit transcends, or is, in a sense, independent of the bodily organism on which otherwise it so entirely depends. Metaphysically speaking this is seen in our self-consciousness, or power of separating our self as subject from our self as object, a thing wholly inconceivable as the result of any material process, and relating us at once to an order of being which we are obliged to call immaterial. But as metaphysical analysis is "caviare to the general," while the metaphysically-minded will find this point amply illustrated by most modern philosophers, it will be sufficient for our purpose to appeal to the more familiar field of morals.

Morally speaking, we are responsible for our actions. That is a fact which no sane man doubts. It is the assumption on which the whole course of our political and social life is carried on; and if a man takes leave to deny it, except in theory, law soon interferes for his correction. There is no fact in the world that, in their misery, men would more gladly have denied; yet they are agreed to treat its denial as a manifest absurdity. Surely, then, it is as strong a conviction as any that can be conceived. And this conviction is amply sufficient for our purpose; for it implies that we are self-identical and free, the same personal unit today that we were when born—whereas all the matter of our bodies has changed—and capable of determining ourselves from within, whereas all matter is determined by something else, and from without. Our present object is not to argue these points, which have been argued abundantly elsewhere, but simply to refer to them, as results of past argument, in illustration of the fact that, with all our dependence upon matter, we yet transcend it; we move in a plane above it, and are, though in a limited degree, its masters and not its slaves. This, then, is one aspect of the relation between spirit and matter, as known within the circle of our own personality. And when we pass beyond that circle to mold the external world to our use, through various forms of scientific invention, and artistic creation, it becomes still more apparent that spirit has a dominant and transcendent relation to matter.

But from another point of view our spirit may be described as "immanent" in matter. It not only works through the brain and nervous system, but, as a result, pervades the entire organism, animating and inspiring it with its own "peculiar difference"; so that we recognize a man's character in the expression of his eye, the tone of his voice, the touch of his hand; his unconscious and instinctive postures, and gestures, and gait. Nor is this "immanence" confined to the bodily organism. It extends, in what may be called a secondary degree, to the inanimate objects of the external world. For a man imprints his spiritual character upon all the things with which he deals, his house, his clothes, his furniture, the various products of his hand or head. And when we speak of a man's spirit surviving in his works, the expression is no mere metaphor;

for through those works, even though dead and gone, he continues to influence his fellowmen. And when we look at the pictures of Raphael, or listen to the music of Beethoven, or read the poetry of Dante, or the philosophy of Plato, the spirit of the great Masters is affecting us as really as if we saw them face to face: it is immanent in the painted canvas and the printed page.

Spirit then, as we know it in our own personal experience, has two different relations to matter, that of transcendence, and that of immanence. But though logically distinct, these two relations are not actually separate; they are two aspects of one fact; two points of view from which the single action of our one personality may be regarded. As self-conscious, self-identical, self-determined, we possess qualities which transcend or rise above the laws of matter; but we can only realize these qualities, and so become aware of them, by acting in the material world; while conversely material objects—our bodies, and our works of art—could never possibly be regarded as expressions of spirit, if spirit were not at the same time recognized as distinct from its medium of manifestation.

If then we are to raise the question, "what is the relation of the supreme Spirit to the material universe?" this is the analogy upon which we must proceed; for we have no other. We may indeed decline the problem as wholly insoluble; but if we attempt its solution at all, it must of necessity be upon the lines of the only experience which we possess—this experience in which transcendence and immanence are combined.

This at once excludes pantheism, the belief that God is merely immanent in matter; for attractive as this creed has often seemed to worshippers of nature, it cannot really be construed into thought. Spirit which is merely immanent in matter, without also transcending it, cannot be spirit at all; it is only another aspect of matter, having neither self-identity nor freedom. Pantheism is thus really indistinguishable from materialism; it is merely materialism grown sentimental, but no more tenable for its change of name.

The logical opposite of pantheism is deism, in the sense of belief in a merely transcendent God; and this is equally inconsistent with our analogy; for as we have no experience whatever of spirit or matter as existing apart, we cannot conceive either term of the deistic universe. But deism of this kind, though it has occupied an important place in history, is scarcely a form of thought with which at the present day we need to reckon. It belongs to a metaphysical rather than a scientific atmosphere and age.

Yet another view of the question has been suggested under the name of monism; the view that "matter in motion is substantially identical with mind," that they are two aspects of one thing, which from the outside we call matter, and from the inside mind. At first sight this seems only another name for materialism; and, in fact, the word monism is expressly used by Haeckel as synonymous with scientific materialism. But its use has also been advocated in a theistic sense; the mental aspect being regarded as prior in importance, though not in existence to the material—a position very much akin to Spinozism. Now the supposed advantage of this theory is, that it abolishes all the difficulties of dualism. But it is obviously no more than an imaginative conjecture, and upon what does it rest? "We have only to suppose that the antithesis between mind and motion—subject and object—is itself phenomenal or apparent, not absolute or real."[1] That is to say that, when we are confronted in our personal experience with a dualism, whose mystery we cannot solve, we may at once attain intellectual satisfaction, by the simple expedient of assuming it to be an illusion. But this is precisely what the materialist does, and is condemned for doing; and we are no more justified in discrediting the primary facts of consciousness in the interests of spirit, than in the interests of matter. Monism, in short, whether material or spiritual, is not based upon what we know in ourselves, and what is, to that extent, solid fact; but upon distrust of what we think we know in ourselves—a sceptical foundation, which cannot possibly support a positive conclusion. It should further be noticed that, in the above quotation, mind and matter are treated as synonymous with subject and object. This in itself is a mistake, but a mistake essential to the theory. For it is only by considering mind as a mere series of subjective or mental states, that we can plausibly consider motion as its par-

[1] Romanes, *Mind, Matter, and Monism.*

allel concomitant. But the characteristic of mind, as we know it in our personal spirit, is that it is both subject and object at once; it is capable of becoming its own object, and saying I am I. It is through this power of self-consciousness, or self-diremption, that spirit transcends matter, as we have already had occasion to point out; and it is precisely this power which we are unable to conceive as having any material equivalent. Monism, in fact, started from the physical side, from analysis of the cerebral conditions of thought; it rests on physical analogies, and is colored by physical modes of thought; and the attempt to make it metaphysically tenable seems an impossible *tour de force*.

It remains then that we confine ourselves to the analogy of our personal experience, and conceive of God as at once transcending and immanent in nature; for however incomprehensible this relationship may be, we know it in our own case to be a fact, and may legitimately infer its analogue outside ourselves.

On this analogy then, the divine presence which we recognize in nature will be the presence of a Spirit, which infinitely transcends the material order, yet sustains and indwells it the while. We cannot indeed explain the method, either of the transcendence, or of the indwelling; but we come no nearer to an explanation, by attempting, with any of the above-mentioned theories, to obtain simplicity by suppressing either aspect of the only analogy that we possess. But it will be remembered that in our own case we noticed two degrees of immanence; our essential immanence in our body, which is consequently often called our person; and our contingent immanence in the works which we are free to create or not at will. The question therefore inevitably arises, under which of these analogies are we to think of God's relation to the world. Is the universe His body, or His work? Different answers have been given to this question by different thinkers; and it is obvious that no answer can be more than conjectural or hypothetical.

Under these circumstances we are entitled to urge, that the Trinitarian conception of God, which we Christians have independent reasons for believing to be true, is intellectually the most satisfactory; since it embraces both the kinds of immanence in question, and therefore harmonizes with the entire analogy of our personal experience. For according to this doctrine, the Second Person of the Trinity is the essential, adequate, eternal manifestation of the First, "the express image of His person," "in whom dwelleth the fullness of the Godhead bodily," while "by Him all things were made." Here then we have our two degrees of immanence; the complete immanence of the Father in the Son, of which our own relation to our body is an inadequate type; and, as a result of this, His immanence in creation, analogous to our presence in our works; with the obvious difference, of course, that we finite beings who die and pass away, can only be impersonally present in our works; whereas He must be conceived as ever present to sustain and animate the universe, which thus becomes a living manifestation of Himself; no mere machine, or book, or picture, but a perpetually sounding voice.

6

HUMAN PREEXISTENCE

John M. E. McTaggart

McTaggart's philosophy represents the most extreme version of the rebellion of the personal idealists against what they took to be the suffocating role assigned to the Absolute in traditional Hegelianism. In Some Dogmas of Religion, *McTaggart considers the three great problems of God, freedom, and immortality. The first two—at least, as they have usually been understood—cannot stand. But McTaggart does argue for the immortality of the soul. He claims that the universe is a community of immortal soul-substances, each of which lives through many lives and fulfills itself in the course of them. Although this philosophy is atheistic, it is not irreligious. The religious sense is the insight into the harmony of the system of selves.*

IN THIS CHAPTER I wish to point out some reasons for thinking that, if men are immortal, it is more probable that the beginning of the present life, in which each of us finds himself now, was not the beginning of his whole existence, but that he lived before it, as he will live after it. I wish, then, to consider the explanation which this theory, if true, would afford of some of the facts of our experience, and to consider what would be the practical value of such immortality as it can offer us.

The present attitude of most western thinkers to the doctrine of pre-existence is curious. Of the many who regard our life after the

Reprinted with permission from *Some Dogmas of Religion* (London: Edward Arnold, 1906), pp. 112–20 and 138–39.

death of our bodies as certain or probable, scarcely one regards our life before the birth of those bodies as a possibility which deserves discussion. And yet it was taught by Buddha and by Plato, and it is usually associated with the belief in immortality in the far east. Why should men who are so anxious today to prove that we shall live after this life is ended regard the hypothesis that we have already survived the end of a life as one which is beneath consideration?

The explanation of this, I suppose, is that in modern western thought the great support of the belief in immortality has been the Christian religion. Under these circumstances a form of the belief which was never supported by that religion was not likely to be considered of any importance. And, for some reason, Christians have almost unanimously rejected those theories which placed preexistence by the side of immortality, although there seems nothing in pre-existence incompatible with any of the dogmas which are generally accepted as fundamental to Christianity.

The most effective way of proving that the doctrine of preexistence is bound up with the doctrine of immortality would be to prove directly that the nature of man was such that it involved a life both before and after the present life. But, as I said at the beginning of the last chapter, such a demonstration, if it is possible at all, as I believe it to be, would be far beyond the scope of this book, since it would involve a determination of some of the most fundamental characteristics of reality.

I must content myself with stating in a more general manner my grounds for believing that any evidence which will prove immortality will also prove pre-existence. There are two ways in which a proof of immortality may be attempted. The first is the directly metaphysical way. We may attempt to show that the nature of man is such that he cannot cease to exist while the universe continues to exist; or that his nature is eternal, and that an eternal nature cannot have an end in time; or pursue some similar line of argument.

In this case it seems to me that, if we succeed in proving immortality, it will be by means of considerations which would also prove pre-existence. I do not see how existence in future time could be shown to be necessary in the case of any being whose existence in past time is admitted not to be necessary. If the universe got on without me a hundred years ago, what reason could be given for denying that it might get on without me a hundred years hence? Or if it is consistent with my eternal nature that its temporal manifestation should begin at some point in time, could we find any reason for supposing that the cessation of that manifestation at some point in time would be inconsistent with that nature? I do not see of what kind such a reason could be, nor do I know of any attempt that has been made to establish one.

There is another way in which attempts have been made to prove immortality. This consists in demonstrating that the universe is the work of a benevolent creator, or has a purpose harmonious with our ideals of morality, and then arguing that the absence of immortality would be inconsistent with the benevolence of such a creator, or with such a moral purpose. Arguments of this type would prove immortality more readily than they could prove pre-existence. No wrong can be done to the non-existent, and it could hardly be made a reproach to the goodness of the universe that it had waited a long time before it produced a particular person. But, once produced, any person has certain moral claims, and if it could be shown that his annihilation was inconsistent with those claims, we could argue from the goodness of the universe to the impossibility of his annihilation.

Can we, however, validly conclude from the goodness of the universe to the impossibility of a particular evil? It cannot be denied that some evil does exist. The ultimate nature of reality, then, is not incompatible with the existence of some evil. And when this is once admitted, can we hope for an *a priori* proof that any particular evil is too bad to be consistent with the nature of the universe? It seems to me that we cannot, and that we must therefore reject all arguments which attempt to prove that a thing is unreal because it would be evil.

We may call arguments of this sort ethical, since they involve the conception of the good. Modern demonstrations of immortality have almost always been of this character, and are not purely metaphysical, and this explains why it has often been held in modern times that immortality was proved, although pre-existence has almost always been disbelieved. Even the arguments of the eighteenth century, which were attacked by Kant, had an ethical element in them. Their supporters endeavored, indeed, to prove by purely metaphysical considerations that the nature of man's spirit was such that it could not be destroyed in the ordinary course of nature. But they held that each man had been created by an act of the divine will, and they admitted that a similar act could destroy him. In order to show that God never would will to destroy a man whom he had once created, they either fell back on the asserted evidence of revelation, or contended that such destruction would be inconsistent with what we knew of God's moral character, in which case their argument had passed over into the ethical class.

If, as I have maintained, ethical arguments of this sort are invalid, we are forced back on the purely metaphysical arguments, and here we seem unable to treat the past and the future differently. My conclusion is, then, that any demonstration of immortality is likely to show that each of us exists through all time—past and future—whether time is held to be finite or infinite.

We must now inquire what consequences would follow from the truth of pre-existence and immortality. Each man would have at least three lives, his present life, one before it, and one after it. It seems more probable, however, that this would not be all, and that his existence before and after his present life would in each case be divided into many lives, each bounded by birth and death. This doctrine of a plurality of future lives and of past lives may be conveniently referred to as the doctrine of plurality of lives.

There is much to be said for the view that a plurality of lives would be the most probable alternative, even on a theory of immortality which did not include pre-existence. We do not know what is the cause which produces the limitation of our present lives by birth and death, but some cause there must be, and a cause which produces so important an effect is one which plays a great part in our existence, as long as it continues to act.

If we accept immortality and reject a plurality of lives—and this is the most common opinion, though plurality of lives is accepted more frequently than pre-existence—we must hold that the causes, whatever they are, which operate on each of us so as to cause his death once, will never operate again on any of us through all future time. This is, of course, not impossible. The true nature of death may be such that there is no need, and no possibility, of its repetition. But I do not see that we have any reason to believe this to be even probable.

It is quite clear that a life which stretched on unendingly without death would in many respects be enormously different from our present lives. An attempt to imagine how our present lives would be transformed if neither we ourselves, nor our fellow men, had in future any chance of death, will make this evident. A believer in immortality who denies, or regards as improbable, the doctrine of the plurality of lives, must assert, or regard as probable, that the death which ends his present life for each of us will change profoundly and permanently the conditions of all future life. And for this there seems no justification.

If we are immortal, the value of our existence either remains permanently at about its present level, or rises or falls after death. In the first case, we should have no reason to suppose that it was so changed that death would not recur. As I have said, it is not impossible that it should be so. But when anything has a particular characteristic, the presumption is that, if that thing continues to exist, its characteristic will not suddenly vary. The presumption is certainly not strong, and it can give us no firm belief. But it is, I think, sufficient to render it rather more probable that the characteristic of periodic mortality will not be left behind at the end of our present lives.

I do not think that this would be very generally denied. The denial of the plurality of lives is generally based on the belief that our lives do not remain at the same level after death. It is not because men have died once that it is held that they cannot die again. It is because it is believed that after death they are in heaven or hell, the one much above the level of earthly life, the other much below it. It is contended that the change effected in this manner renders further deaths improbable. This is especially maintained with regard to heaven.

It might be admitted that a state of absolute perfection would render further death improbable. But even the best men are not, when they die, in such a state of intellectual and moral perfection as would fit them to enter heaven immediately, if heaven is taken as a state of absolute perfection which renders all further improvement unnecessary and impossible. This is generally recognized, and one of two alternatives is commonly adopted to meet it. The first is that some tremendous improvement—an improvement out of all proportion to any which can ever be observed in life—takes place at the moment of death, at any rate in the case of those who die under certain conditions. For this, so far as I know, there are no arguments. The other and more probable alternative is that the process of gradual improvement can go on in each of us after the death of our present bodies.

But if our existence immediately after our present life is imperfect, and a state of improvement and advance, it has not yet reached that absolute perfection which might make future deaths improbable. And it seems to me that the natural inference from this view—though it is not drawn by the majority of those who hold it—is that this life will be followed by others like it, each separated from its predecessor and successor by death and re-birth. For otherwise we should be limited to the hypothesis that a process of development, begun in a single life bounded by death, should be continued as an indefinitely long life not divided by birth and death at all. And to suppose, without any reason, such a change from the order of our present experience seems unjustifiable.

Should any persons be destined to attain a state of great and permanent degradation, there would be still less reason for supposing that this would exclude all death from their future existence. Death may possibly be incompatible with absolute perfection, but

it has no characteristic which can be suggested as incompatible with
the extreme of human degradation. In addition to this we may urge,
as in the case of heaven, that it is unreasonable to suppose an extreme change at the moment of death, and that, even if the completed degradation was likely to exclude death, there could be no
reason for supposing that the process towards it would do so from
the first.

Again, processes begun in this life are sometimes finished in it,
and sometimes left incomplete. We continually find that death
leaves a fault without a retribution, a retribution without a repent-
ance, a preparation without an achievement, while in other cases,
where the life has lasted longer, a similar process is complete between birth and death. If men survive death, we must expect that
these processes, when not worked out before death, will be worked
out in a future life. And if the content of our existence after death
has so much similarity, in essential features, with the content of
our present lives, the presumption is increased that they have not
changed so far as to have shaken off the necessity of periodical
death.

There seems, therefore, good reason for regarding plurality of
lives as the least improbable alternative, even if we accept immortality without accepting pre-existence. But if pre-existence is
also accepted, the case for a plurality of lives becomes stronger. For
then the death which alters my present life is no longer an unique
event in my existence. One life, if no more, came to an end for
me before my present life could begin. Thus any theory would be
false which should try to reject the plurality of lives on the ground
that it was probable that death could only occur once in a man's
existence. And the plurality of lives could only be regarded as
improbable, if there was reason to suppose that an event, which
happened twice in a man's existence, would never happen a third
time. Now while it might be contended—though, as I have said,
I do not think it could be rightly contended—that there were
features about death which made it probable it would only occur
once in a man's existence, it is difficult to see the slightest ground
for the suggestion that there is anything about death which should

make it improbable that it should occur three times, although it was known that it occurred twice. We can only accept immortality and pre-existence, while rejecting the plurality of lives, if we hold that the causes which break off a life by a death, after remaining dormant from the beginning of our existence, act twice within an interval of from five minutes to about a hundred years, and then never act again through all future time.

The result seems to be that, even granting that pre-existence is certain, there can be no absolute demonstration of plurality of lives, but that the plurality of lives is the more probable supposition in any case, and is still more probable on the hypothesis of pre-existence.

The prospect of a great number of lives—perhaps an infinite number, though this is not a necessary part of the theory—gives us the prospect of many dangers, many conflicts, many griefs, in an indefinitely long future. Death is not a haven of rest. It is a starting-point for fresh labors. But if the trials are great, so is the recompense. We miss much here by our own folly, much by unfavorable circumstances. Above all we miss much, because so many good things are incompatible. We cannot spend our youth both in the study and in the saddle. We cannot gain the benefit both of unbroken health and of bodily weakness, both of riches and of poverty, both of comradeship and of isolation, both of defiance and of obedience. We cannot learn the lessons alike of Galahad and of Tristram and of Caradoc. And yet they are all so good to learn. Would it not be worth much to be able to hope that what we missed in one life might come to us in another? And would it not be worth much to be able to hope that we might have a chance to succeed hereafter in the tasks which we failed in here?

It may be that the change, the struggle, and the recurrence of death, are endless, or, again, it may be that the process will eventually destroy itself, and merge in a perfection which transcends all time and change. Such an end may come, perhaps, but at any rate it cannot be near.

But though the way is long, and perhaps endless, it can be no more wearisome than a single life. For with death we leave behind us memory, and old age, and fatigue. And surely death acquires a new and deeper significance when we regard it no longer as a single and unexplained break in an unending life, but as part of the continually recurring rhythm of progress—as inevitable, as natural, and as benevolent as sleep. We have only left youth behind us, as at noon we have left the sunrise. They will both come back, and they do not grow old.

7

VALUES

Wilhelm Windelband

Windelband's History of Philosophy *was written in the conviction that to study the history of a subject is to study that subject itself. Thus the history ends with the contemporary philosophical problem, placed in the light of all the historical trends that have shaped it. For Windelband, the problem of values presented itself as the task for the philosophy of his time. Kant, he believed, had closed the door to rational metaphysics, but this did not entail the adoption of a positivist or naturalist philosophy. Kant had also pointed to the demands of practical reason and to the realm of values. There are three fundamental values —truth, goodness, beauty. Religious faith is the vision of the ultimate unity and validity of these values.*

THE REVOLT of boundless individualism culminates in the claim that all values are relative. Only the powerful will of the over-man persists as the absolute value, and sanctions every means which it brings into service. For the "higher" man there is no longer any form or standard, either logical or ethical. The arbitrary will of the over-man has superseded the "autonomy of reason"—this is the course from Kant to Nietzsche which the nineteenth century has described.

Just this determines the problem of the future. Relativism is the dismissal and death of philosophy. Philosophy can live only as the

From *A History of Philosophy,* translated by J. H. Tufts (New York: The Macmillan Co., 1901, and Harper Torchbooks, 1958), pp. 680–81.

science of values which are universally valid. It will no longer force its way into the work of the particular sciences, where psychology also now belongs. Philosophy has neither the craving to know over again from her standpoint what the special sciences have already known from theirs, nor the desire to compile and patch together generalizations from the "more general results" of the separate disciplines. Philosophy has its own field and its own problem in those values of universal validity which are the organizing principle for all the functions of culture and civilization and for all the particular values of life. But it will describe and explain these values only that it may give an account of their validity; it treats them not as facts but as *norms*. Hence it will have to develop its task as a "giving of laws"—not laws of arbitrary caprice which it dictates, but rather laws of the reason, which it discovers and comprehends. By following the path toward this goal it seems to be the aim of the present movement, divided within itself as it often is, to win back the important conquests of the great period of German philosophy. Since Lotze raised the *conception of value* to a place of prominence, and set it at the summit of logic and metaphysics as well as of ethics, many suggestions toward a "theory of values," as a new foundation science in philosophy, have arisen. It can do no harm if these move in part in the psychological and sociological realm, provided it is not forgotten that in establishing facts and making genetic explanations we have only gained the material upon which philosophy itself must perform its task of criticism.

But a no less valuable foundation for this central work is formed by the *history* of philosophy, which, as Hegel first recognized, must be regarded in this sense as an integrant part of philosophy itself. For it presents the process in which European humanity has embodied in scientific conceptions its view of the world and judgment of human life.

In this process particular experiences have furnished the occasions, and special problems of knowledge have been the instrumentalities, through which step by step reflection has advanced to greater clearness and certainty respecting the ultimate values of culture and civilization. In setting forth this process, therefore, the history of philosophy presents to our view the gradual attainment of clearness and certainty respecting those values whose universal validity forms the problem and field of philosophy itself.

8

KANT AND THE PHILOSOPHY OF "AS IF"

Hans Vaihinger

Vaihinger's book first appeared in 1911. He had already established himself as a major Kantian scholar, and his philosophy of "as if" is his interpretation of the implications of Kant's work. This is a much more pessimistic kind of neo-Kantianism than Windelband's. As Vaihinger sees things, human values have no objective validity and reality is indifferent to human thought and striving. But we project upon reality fictions of many kinds—we do this in science, law, politics, religion, and every department of life. These fictions have no truth, but they do possess a utility for life. This view comes near to pragmatism, but the pragmatist would claim that to have utility is also to have some measure of truth.

A VERY CONSISTENT, daring and frank presentation of the As-if doctrine is found in the work *Über die Fortschritte der Metaphysik.* Kant, as is well-known, planned this work for the prize offered by the University of Berlin in 1791. He never published it, and it is to this circumstance, perhaps, that we owe the frank and daring language of the essay, which has up to the present received insufficient attention. In the section on the Third Stage of Metaphysics Kant links his argument directly with the *Critique of Judgment.* Of the concept of fitness for a purpose, he says that it does not relate to

Reprinted with permission from *The Philosophy of "As If,"* translated by C. K. Ogden (New York: Barnes & Noble, 1924), pp. 302–7.

what is in the object but to what we put into it; that we consequently "only insert or interpolate this concept by a quasi-rational process"; "the concept of purpose is, at all times, made by us." Connected therewith is the concept (also "made" by us), of an end in general, the concept of the highest good; and connected with this are other "fabricated concepts"—freedom, God and immortality (or "the supersensuous *within* us, *above* us and *after* us"). Further on in the essay (in the "Solution of the Academic Problem"), he goes on to say that we "must not investigate the supersensuous from the point of view of what it is in itself, but only of how we have to conceive it and imagine its character, if we are to be in harmony with the final purpose, which is the supreme good." We are not to undertake investigations into the nature of things, "which we make for ourselves, and make only for necessary practical purposes, and which perhaps do not exist at all outside of our idea, perhaps cannot possibly exist." In this connection Kant also justifies in detail the expression "faith" for assumptions of this kind with practical object. "The proof of the correctness of this faith is no proof of the truth of the assumptions when considered theoretically; nor is it any objective indication of the reality of their objects—in regard to the supersensuous, this is impossible—but only a subjectively and practically valid, though for this purpose adequate, indication that we are to act *as if* we knew that these objects were real." What really takes place here is that, "in order to strive towards that to which we have already committed ourselves, namely the furtherance of the highest good in the world, we supplement, merely by means of rational ideas, the theory of the possibility of this highest good; we make for ourselves objects, strictly in accordance with the demands of moral law, and arbitrarily endow them with objective reality, viz. God, Freedom of the practical order, and Immortality." Further on, he says: "Practically we create these objects ourselves, according as we consider the Idea of them to be helpful to the purpose of our pure reason; and this purpose, because it is morally necessary, is able to produce the illusion that what possesses reality subjectively, namely for the use of men (because it has been exhibited to experience in actions which conform to its laws), is to be taken for knowledge of the existence of the object corresponding to this form." In reality, however, "these ideas have been arbitrarily created by us." In other words, the moral proof for the existence of God is an argument "from the rationality of *assuming* such (a being)." Man is justified in permitting an idea that he has himself constructed according to certain moral principles, to exercise an influence upon his decisions, exactly as if he had derived it from a real object. These ideas serve "to represent man's life on earth as if it were a life in heaven"; that is to say, we can and should assume the world on the analogy of physical teleology (i.e. as in the nature of a "moral teleology"). Considered theoretically this "is not, as the Leibniz-Wolff philosophy holds, a tenable but over-strained concept. It is, from a practical-dogmatic standpoint, a real concept, and one which is sanctioned by practical reason for our sense of duty." But this "practical reality" must not be misunderstood by uncritical readers of the Critical Philosophy and again applied, in a theoretical and dogmatic sense; i.e. the fiction must not be transformed into a dogma. Kant once more repeats expressly and distinctly that "we observe a certain organization of the practical reason in which (1) the subject of universal legislation, as originator of the world, (2) the object of the will of mundane beings, as conforming in their end to the subject, (3) the condition of these beings, in which alone they are capable of attaining that end [God, freedom and immortality] —are in the practical aspect self-made ideas." In other words, these concepts are and remain—self-made ideas.

Here too we see clearly the immeasurable difference between the Kantian justification of religious ideas and that of the pre- and post-Kantians. The Kantian justification of religious ideas is a purely fictive, or better perhaps, a fictionalistic one. They are for him practical, expedient fictions, whereas the pre- and post-Kantian justification of religious concepts and judgments is a rationalistic one; they are rationally grounded hypotheses. A variety only of this rationalism is the *Kantianismus vulgaris,* the popular version of Kant's doctrine, which represents Kant as justifying the principal ideas of religion on the basis of moral facts; for according to the presentation of this popular Kantianism that has become customary since Reinhold, theoretical inferences have been drawn from moral phenomena as to the existence of God, etc. i.e. we are again making hypotheses. The real and genuine Kantian criticism draws no theoretical inferences whatever, but says: You must act *as* you would *if* a God existed, etc. Therein lies Kant's critical Pragmatism.

A very important passage for the elucidation of Kant's meaning is contained in the treatise *Von einem neuerdings erhobenen vornehmen Ton in der Philosophie* (1796). There we find the expression "belief" fully explained in a note: Taken theoretically "to believe" means, "to regard a thing as likely," and is "something half-way between thinking and knowing." With regard to empirical things and empirical evidence such theoretical belief is a fact, but with regard to the supersensuous no judgment whatever is possible and, therefore, no judgment of probability: "there is therefore no such thing as theoretical belief in the supersensuous."

"But from the practical (moral-practical) point of view, not only is such a belief in the supersensuous possible. It is inevitable." For the categorical commands of the "voice of morality within me" require of us that we should co-operate in realizing the unconditioned purpose of the highest good (which, of course, is only an idea): and this highest good is, in its turn, only realizable "by means of the power of a world-ruler" (which again is only an idea). "To believe in such a ruler practically and morally, does not mean first to assume his reality as true, in order that we may realize the end imposed. For that purpose the law of reason is in itself objectively sufficient. No, it means that, in accordance with the ideal of that purpose, we are to act as we should if such a world-government really existed." "This is an imperative which enjoins not belief, but action." In other words, in the Kantian sense, in the sense of the Critical Philosophy, the expression, "I believe in God," means simply that "I act *as if* a God really existed." As a moral agent the man who thinks in the Kantian, the critical manner, acts *as if* the Good possessed an unconditioned value, such as to render it the decisive factor in the world; and the Good would be the decisive factor in the world if there were a world-government to bring about its final triumph. In spite of the fact that my theoretical reason *forbids* me to assume such a moral world-order—this concept would have no content—I yet act as if such a moral world-order might exist, since my practical reason *bids* me do good unconditionally. In following this command of practical reason I am, in strict theory, acting irrationally, for my theoretical reason tells me that such a moral world-order is merely an empty, even if a beautiful, concept. But I do actually find within me the command of practical reason to do good, and this command impresses me as though it were something sublime. I act according to this command. But in acting thus, I am, at the same time, acting as if I did make this assumption of a moral world-order which I recognize to be theoretically impossible, nay even contradictory. Not in the sense of supposing that it is the assumption which gives the command; far from it; my soul does not think of that at all. The command meets with our approval and impresses us for its own sake; it is indeed part of the content of my practical reason. In other words, to the normal moral man, the moral world-order and the author of the moral order of the world, God, are not in the least a presupposition necessary to his voluntary submission to the moral commandment. On the contrary, in obeying the moral commandment Kant's normal man not only behaves just *as if* this obedience had not only to a certain extent empirical consequences in time and in the phenomenal world, but as if this moral action of his extended into an intelligible super-sensuous world and, on the one hand, helped toward the attainment of a general eternal supreme good and, on the other, were incorporated by a divine power, as an expedient element in a system of purposes. Such is always and everywhere the nature of unconditioned, ethically-good action; for to act morally means, in contradistinction to the empirical conditions, to act *as if* the good had an unconditioned value, *as if* it had the power to extend into a super-empirical world in which a supreme ruler provided for the harmonizing of good and evil. In this sense good action is identical with a belief in God and immortality. In this sense the atheist who acts morally also believes *practically* in God and immortality, since he acts *as if* God and immortality existed. All ethical conduct, therefore, involves the fiction of God and immortality—this is the meaning of the practical rational belief in God and immortality. In this sense, too, and only in this sense, must we understand the conclusion elsewhere established by Kant regarding "a morally earnest and therefore religious endeavor towards good." The morally-good can say to himself and to his kind: "Your acts are good and, for that reason, you are, in your way, a believer, for you act as though a God existed: in short, your actions are good and therefore you believe." This Kantian *recte agis, ergo credis* is the basic axiom of practical philosophy and, as such, the counterpart to the basic axiom of Descartes' theoretical philosophy as rightly understood: *cogito, ergo sum*.

9

HOW WE SEE GOD IN JESUS

Wilhelm Herrmann

Herrmann's work is one of the clearest expressions of the Ritschlian type of theology which dominated the German schools at the turn of the century. Ritschlianism itself is the theological equivalent of neo-Kantianism. Herrmann reflects the positivist side of neo-Kantianism in rejecting the metaphysical aspects of dogma and in appealing to the empirical facts of the historical Jesus (for New Testament scholars still supposed in his time that one could penetrate to the premythical reality of Jesus of Nazareth). But we see also in Herrmann the other side of neo-Kantianism, for he believed that in the lineaments of Jesus the practical reason recognizes the embodiment of an ultimate and transcendent value, so that faith must assert the presence of God in Christ.

WE BEGIN by considering what will be admitted to be the historical reality concerning Jesus by a man of our time whose interest in Him is purely historical. It may be that here and there an earnest student of history, through no merely dull misconception, may question some of the records concerning Jesus, and declare them to be legendary, and to be the production of an actual spiritual movement which led men to imagine a historical background for that movement. Yet even then the chief point will still remain the same for him as it is for us. A historian has the right, and it may

Reprinted with the permission of Ernest Benn, Ltd., London, from *The Communion of the Christian with God,* translated by J. Sandys Stanyon (London: Williams & Norgate, 1909), pp. 84–111.

even be his duty, to declare the results of the investigation for which he is responsible. But he cannot remove the fact that in the story on which he thus passes judgment there is portrayed the consistent and clear portrait of a Personal Life that has no equal. Indeed, he may become so possessed by that portrait that it shall become impossible for him to regard it as a product of the poetical imagination. For, in truth, such a product would only present to him what he himself could produce. In that case his judgment as a historian concerning the story becomes limited by his present experience of the story's effect. Nothing else could so influence his historical judgment without doing violence to his conscience. Nothing but that definite picture given by the records when read as they stand, and so making a powerful impression upon him, could possibly limit his freedom of historical judgment. This always happens when the inquirer becomes a Christian. But even if he does not get so far, the fact remains unquestioned that the Christ of the New Testament shows a firmness of religious conviction, a clearness of moral judgment, and a purity and strength of will such as are combined in no other figure in history. If we wish, then, to make these features of His character more distinct, we have a right to begin from those parts of His story which are not, as a rule, called in question even by those who do not know Jesus Himself.

All men are willing to allow that Jesus did actually appear in the history of the world in which we live. It is admitted that many hundred years ago He claimed to be the Messiah of Israel; that through His peculiar conception of His work as Messiah He drew upon Himself the hatred of His people, thereby incurring His own overthrow, and, finally, that notwithstanding all this, He died in the confidence of victory. If we saw nothing more in Jesus than this we should admit the facts, though we should pay no further heed to them. But we become more attentive when we perceive what it meant for a man to claim to be the Messiah of Israel. Such a man necessarily conceived that his existence and his work made the world complete, and that in his person the purposes of God's creation were accomplished. The mere vital energy of such a man compels our admiration. If along with this he had shown a mind overpowered by a fevered imagination, if he had been very sensitive and had sought for honor among men, we should have counted him made of common clay, a mere visionary, like many whom we know. But the story of Jesus describes to us just the opposite case. His speech is notably temperate and His reasoning remarkably clear. He is neither conceited nor overbearing, but constantly impresses us, to our surprise, with His humility of heart. If Jesus had simply taken up the Messianic ideal of Israel, and had His purpose not ranged beyond the spiritual horizon of the Jewish people, then His character as Messiah would have displayed no feature worthy of special note. For it is quite possible to imagine that among a people whose religion formed so large a part of their life, a highly gifted man might fancy himself called upon to realize the *certain goal* for which all were ardently longing. But on close inspection the will of Jesus is seen to be by no means the mere blossom of the Jewish hope for a Messiah. In the work that He undertook, He rose above all that Israel had looked upon and hoped for as the highest good, and He was quite conscious that He was disappointing the hopes He aroused. Jesus claimed certainly, as was expected of the Messiah, that He should establish the Kingdom of God among men, and that He would thereby make the world complete. But the Kingdom of God was to Him the sovereignty of God in the inner life of personal beings and in their communion one with another. The members of the Kingdom of God, as Jesus understood it, are those men who are fully subject to God through boundless confidence in Him and unbounded love for their neighbors. In the fact that these spiritual considerations did rule His own being and that they were germinating in those few individuals who grouped themselves around Him, Jesus saw the dawn of the end of all things.

Let us review those features of the portrait of Jesus which we have thus obtained. First of all we have the outward course of His work as Messiah, which tells us little of His inner life that can claim special consideration. It has two striking features; one, the conflict into which Jesus comes with pious Judaism and its hopes of a Messiah; and the other, the remarkable assurance which He maintained over against the opposition of the world, and in the face of death.

These points need to be made more clear, and we shall make them so if we realize the peculiar nature of Jesus' life-work and His attitude towards it. It is clear without further argument that He must have regarded His work as bound to succeed, seeing that He staked His life upon it. As soon as a man makes it consciously the goal of his life to secure the realization of all that Jesus understood as the Kingdom of God, so soon also must that man advance to the further conviction that this realization will actually come to pass. No one can be forced to advance in moral development up to a grasp of the idea that the personal life of man reaches its perfection in perfect love, and in a trust in a God who is the very power of that love: but the man who does grasp that thought is sensible also that nothing can interfere with his right to attain the realization of that idea. Convinced of this right, many men have become hard as steel against those forces of destiny which shattered their outward existence. Jesus had such a consciousness, the consciousness of the soul that has come to know its own eternal life, and in such possession He was like the martyrs who have answered the summons of the moral ideal He brought into the world. That feature of His personal life stands out grandly in the recorded story. And in truth it is no small matter if we let this personal power of "the good" in the figure of Jesus work upon us and move us to reverence; for no man can be redeemed by Him who does not bow in true reverence before that personal, living goodness which exists in its original purity in Him alone.

Jesus is thus placed at the head of all those men who have joyfully suffered for the sake of the good. But to see this is by no means to reach that peculiar feature of His inner life which must work upon us as a fact if He is to redeem us. Jesus is separate from all men who seek to follow Him in self-surrender to the good, not simply as their never-equalled prototype, but also by the attitude which He assumes towards that ideal of perfect life which He reveals to men as their highest good.

In the first place, Jesus shows us the portrait of a man who is conscious of no inferiority in Himself to the ideal for which He sacrifices Himself. We do not gain this impression, of course, simply from isolated expressions which have been handed down to us as a testimony to His sinlessness. Such expressions taken by themselves have little force. But certainly the fact that Jesus thought of Himself as sinless stands out powerfully before us when we remember what He said and did at the Last Supper with His disciples. In face of a death whose horror He keenly felt, He was able to say that this death He was about to die would take away the burden of guilt from the hearts of those who should remember Him. He was able to look away from the death whose approach troubled Him to the moral need of men held captive by the consciousness of guilt, so deeply did He feel the horror of that need. And so mighty within Him was the consciousness of His own purity, that He clearly saw that the impression which His death would cause would loose the spiritual bonds of those who had found Him and could remember Him. Jesus could not have spoken as He then did if He had been conscious of guilt within Himself. In that hour when the conscience of every man who is morally alive inexorably sums up his life, this man could conceive of His own moral strength and purity as that power which alone could conquer the sinner's inmost heart and free him from the deepest need. And this He did, not after the manner of an enthusiastic visionary, but as a man to whom the deepest moral knowledge gave a most tender conscience. He was the first to declare distinctly that the command to love is not simply one of the commandments but that it is the whole moral law, because it determines the disposition which is the condition of righteousness, and which therefore alone gives moral worth to human action. He led His disciples above all to recognize that such a life of love is the highest good for man, or, in other words, that without it nothing can give the heart true joy. Through this new conception of the highest good, or the Kingdom of God, a conception which no prophet of Israel had before Him, Jesus brought moral knowledge among men to its highest possible level. He has brought it about that, as far as His influence extends, every man feels guilty whose heart is not wholly given up to love.

But now it is plain that at the same time He saw set up thus before Him the highest conceivable standard for judgment of Himself. He counted it self-evident that He must find all His own joy, His unfailing joy in the life and freedom and strength of His own love. He could count Himself inwardly pure only if He persevered in incessant effort to be pure. Nevertheless, even standing where He did at that Last Supper, He said confidently that His Personality would lift away the burden of guilt from the heart of every man who should see that Personality enter death. In view of this, any one who feels the appeal of Jesus to his own conscience, must receive the impression that Jesus actually was what He claimed to be.

Jesus has indeed been, by His suffering for the sake of what is good, an example which many have followed; in this further respect, however, He is incomparable, that He first saw what is good in all its glory, its fullness and its power, and that He nevertheless felt Himself not inferior to what He conceived and what He said. In all other cases, the very men whose goodness uplifts us give us such a conception of what is good that we see thereby how great is their own moral need. Jesus alone has had the conviction that He had no such need, and the man who learns to know Him admits that conviction to be correct. He awakens in us the deepest understanding of duty, and He remains at the same time Himself the highest standard for our conscience. This incomparable moral strength of Jesus must become clear to us if we see the simplest features of His appearance in history, and if we note in what He claimed to be the Messiah and the way in which He went to His death. When we see this, then our eyes are opened to the glory of all the rest of the record concerning Him; we see in it all the wonderful fact that it constantly gives us fresh views of other and yet other sides of the infinite life of a human soul. Such records are incomparable, and that not because of their contents alone; but their very existence is a wonderful fact, for it comes to us through the minds of men who did not experience in their own lives such untrammelled freedom in being good as He had. In spite of this, the tenderest features of such a life have been preserved in their narratives, and have become the true spiritual food for mankind. Jesus is for us a fact in His moral glory, in those inner movements of His soul which include the deepest moral knowledge, the never failing strength of His moral purpose and the bliss of knowing it; He is a fact for us which we do not accept for others' sake, but which we see for ourselves. He has thus become an integral part of all that is real to ourselves; and He fills with light all the world in which we stand. Jesus differs, then, from all men who follow Him by His conscious rising always to His own ideal and because He compels us to admit that He does rise to it.

But this is not the only difference between Him and all others.

Jesus would claim to have done more than make the best ideal clear for men, and more than live it out before them. As the Messiah of God, He claimed to set men no mere task to do, but to give to them God's perfect gift to enjoy. He was confident that He could so uplift men that they would be able actually to enjoy the highest good in a life of utter submission to God, and therefore in a life of love. The Jesus who thinks thus of Himself and who looks on men with such a confidence in His power to redeem them from the terrible misery He sees in all—that Jesus, I say, stands as a fact before us, and it is a fact that has no equal. The dying Buddha puts his confidence in the truth of his teaching; he leaves to his disciples the admonition that they may forget him, but they are to keep his teaching and the way that he has shown them. Plato says the like of Socrates. Now in the whole wide range of history there is no other figure, apart from Jesus, which so surprises us with originality of moral strength as do these two just named. But these two hid themselves modestly behind the teaching for which they lived and died, whereas Jesus knows no more sacred task than to point men to His own Person. His life and death proclaim the conviction that no man who desires true life can do without Him; every one must concern himself with Jesus, and must take to heart the fact of His personal life.

Jesus did not teach that He had brought other miraculous forces into the world, which were to be distinguished from Himself, and from the impression His Person would make on human hearts. He did not teach that souls should be set free by the mysterious operation of any such other forces. If we are told that this is the case, we must reply that such forces can in no case become to us a fact which shall master our inmost souls. Men may talk of such force, but the talking helps no one whose conscience Jesus has quickened. Of course a million voices out of the Christian church loudly proclaim this very theory a way of salvation; we are to be saved by certain mysterious forces which are organically connected with the worship and sacraments of the church. If, however, we keep our eyes fixed on Jesus, these cries will not trouble us. Even if such a thought had crept into the records concerning Jesus, and claimed to be part of His own teaching—thank God, it is not the case—but if it were, then we should certainly regret the fact, but we should not let it influence us. We should quietly declare such a doctrine to be an error of the narrator. For it would contradict that which is our sole concern, that which has become for us as an undeniable fact concerning Jesus. The fact is this, that Jesus stands before us in history claiming to be Himself alone salvation for all men. We have no right whatever to imagine in addition any mysterious powers by means of which Jesus is to bring about our redemption. He Himself "is made unto us redemption." We can only understand His assertion in that sense. Any teaching must be a matter of utter indifference to us which tells of mysterious redemptive forces which are to proceed from Christ, and which for that very reason are not Christ Himself. Such teaching can produce no proof of its truth; it remains one of those mere assertions which ramble in plenty through empty heads. That great declaration, on the other hand, which is the whole of the gospel of Jesus, may easily be tested and tried as to whether it be true.

Jesus asserts that He brings to men the highest good in the form of a Kingdom of God. Without doubt, by the Kingdom of God Jesus meant that God should rule in the inner life of men and in their intercourse with one another. God does so rule when the men on whom He works awake to unhesitating trust in Him, and hence to true-hearted love. Such men are in full submission to God. The fellowship which arises among them when their mutual love springs from a common source is the realm of God's full sovereignty. If, then, Jesus asserts that He brings such a Kingdom to men, He means simply this, that through the impression caused by His Person men are brought into submission to God. Of course, then, every one may test the truth of this assertion who has at all learned to see the Person, the human soul of Jesus. The most important thing for the man who is to submit himself to God is surely that he should be absolutely certain of the reality of God, and Jesus does establish in us, through the fact of His personal life, a certainty of God which covers every doubt. When once He has attracted us by the beauty of His Person, and made us bow before Him by its exalted character, then even amid our deepest doubts that Person of Jesus will remain present with us as a thing incomparable, the most precious fact in history, the most precious fact our life contains. If we then yield to His attraction and come to feel with deep reverence the strength and purity of His soul, disclosing to us the impurity and weakness of our own, then His mighty claim comes home to us. We learn to share His invincible confidence that He can uplift and bless perfectly those who do not turn away from Him.

Such confidence in the Person and cause of Jesus implies something else: it implies that we think and must think of a Power greater than all things, which will see to it that Jesus, who lost His life in this world, shall be none the less victorious over the same world. This thought of such a Power lays hold of us as firmly as did that view of Jesus by which we were overwhelmed. This is the beginning of the consciousness within us, that there is a living God; this is the only real beginning of an inward submission to Him. As soon as trust in Jesus awakens this thought within us, we connect the thought at once with our experience of the inner life of Jesus as a present fact in our own life. The startled sense we felt at the disclosure of actual, living goodness in His Person, and the sense of condemnation that we felt, are at once attributed by our souls to the power of God, of which we have now become conscious. The man who has felt these simple experiences cannot possibly attribute them to any other source. The God in whom he now believes for Jesus' sake, is as real and living to him as the man Jesus is in His marvellous sublimity of character. If we ask: How does our thought of God come to include for us the thought of Omnipotence? the answer is, Clearly from the Person of Jesus alone. We arrive at the thought of Omnipotence because we are obliged to pay to Jesus the homage of believing that He must certainly succeed, even if all the world besides be against Him. The Omnipotence of which we become conscious in this way must be wielded by that same purpose which produced the life-work of Jesus. Nothing else could rule it.

Thus God makes Himself known to us as the Power that is with Jesus. We are obliged, then, to confess that the existence of Jesus in this world of ours is the fact in which God so touches us as to come into communion with us. Of course, we learn at the same time how great the contrast is between Jesus and ourselves; and we feel it the more keenly, the more we become alive to that strength of His character which so overwhelms us that it makes the reality of God undeniable. But for this very reason the God we recognize is not only the God of Jesus Christ. He is our own God. This follows from the fact that the Man in whom we grasp with certainty the reality of God stands in the attitude of friendship towards men who feel themselves far removed from God. Luther says, "If we observe His loving and friendly companionship with His disciples, if we note how He rebukes without rejecting them, this will support and comfort us in every kind of trial. And this is the best and most excellent thing we have in Christ."[1] This personal attitude of Jesus assures us that His God is our God; and it thereby uplifts us into the Kingdom of God. Hence this fact, through which God touches us, not only relieves the impotence of the creature, which of itself can arrive at no certain knowledge of God, but at the same time it helps the sinner, who, when left to himself, tries to shut his eyes to the revelation of God, because God's nature is so strange to him. God enters into such sort of

[1] Luther, second enlarged edition, xv, 470; 1, 130.

communion with us that He thereby forgives us our sins. Without forgiveness we should still be uncertain of the reality of God. God will become certain to us only if His revelation of Himself confirms the moral claims we feel within us. He does this as He comes to us in Jesus, for He frees us from that moral want which the freedom and fullness of Jesus' love have compelled us to feel within ourselves. Unless we are in the grasp of the God who turns to us in Jesus, those thoughts concerning what is good which Jesus makes clear to us, only render us profoundly unhappy: for we cannot rid ourselves of these thoughts; we recognize their eternal truth; in them we first learn to understand the spiritual as distinct from the natural life. We see that we have no inner life at all until we recognize the good and let it rule in our hearts; and the clearer this becomes the more painfully are we sensible that all the force within us is in conflict with the good. The world which supports and feeds us does not seem to us to be ruled by that law which we know to be the law of life. Arrangements and movements, which seemed to open a free course to the good we desire, are upset or arrested by the stronger force of blind chance. Even human society, instead of proving to be an organism for the realization of freedom, surrounds us with so many obstacles that a communion with others in which we could find freedom and joy appears to be a far-distant and unattainable goal. At the same time the results of our own moral efforts are never of such a kind that we could trust our very life upon them; and least of all could any man do so whose conscience Jesus had quickened, for such men know well that by no strain of will can they bring forth from their own hearts that love which the law of Jesus demands. Now, if our life in the world has such an outlook, how can truth lie ultimately in the demand of the moral law that it is our duty to be good? No one can devote his life to ends which he does not fully admit to be capable of realization. So the very thoughts which we know are able to set free our inner life only throw us back again into discouragement and despondency. We are divided against ourselves: we are unable to realize that good thing which is evidently the way of true life for us.

We are saved from this self-contradiction when once we have come to understand the fact that Jesus belongs to this world of ours. If he has only won from us the trust that His cause is the cause of God, then we become sure that the good has a reality and a power in our own lives, because of the interest He showed in men, an interest which has stood the severest tests. Certainly, as soon as the law of duty is set forth and expounded to us as Jesus does it, so soon does that law receive at once our unflinching approval, whether we are sure of any fulfillment or not. But unless our existence in the world bore some sure sign that the good is not essentially foreign to human nature, we should never be certain that our knowledge of moral law could lift our very selves up to a higher life, or that we ourselves could attain to the blessed liberty of a moral life. Jesus Christ is that sure sign. His attitude towards us uplifts us and makes it possible for us to trust that the Divine Power, which must be with Him and with His work, cares for us and makes us fellow-workmen with Him in nothing less than the actual realization of His moral purposes in a Kingdom of God. Hence, by the conviction that in Christ God communes with us, we are placed inwardly in a position to overcome the opposition between our natural life and the law of duty. It thus becomes possible for us to believe that those very things in our surroundings which are hostile to the good, are by God's power being made of service for what is good. Whenever our moral striving seems to exhaust itself in vain attempts, we have still the consolation that we stand in and belong to a historical movement in which the good wields ever greater sway, for Christ's work must reach its goal, and we know through God's communion with us that we are assisting in that work. Our impression that in Christ we have to do with God gives thus such satisfaction to our moral need that that impression deepens into the very clearest of certainties. For that is the true God who creates infinite life within us by causing us to rejoice in the good.

God communes with us, therefore, by the appearance of Jesus Christ in such a way that we are perfectly certain we see Him. Any doubts whether God does actually come near to us in Jesus are removed from the Christian's mind by his experience that as soon as he understands this Man as the message of God to him, he finds a joy in bowing to what is inevitable, and in self-sacrifice for the sake of others. Our experience of the communion of God with us is, at the same time, the experience of moral deliverance. Without these things we should not have that certainty of faith which is present and active in every believer.

The rise of faith as the consciousness that God communes with us cannot be forced. It remains the subjective experience of the man who learns to believe; he cannot transfer it to another. For whether anyone should place confidence in another person is certainly his own affair; it is impossible to demonstrate the necessity for such a confidence to a man in whom it does not exist. If anyone would obtain this soul-emancipating trust in Jesus, he must turn to Jesus and place himself under Jesus' influence. We all dislike to do this, for we fear that the impression He makes upon us will tear away the veils that conceal our forlorn condition. If some men do overcome this fear and are not dismayed by the appearance of the Holy One, although they know themselves condemned before Him, that must remain a strange secret of their own inner life.

But, on the other hand, the man in whom trust towards Jesus has been aroused, does not lack objective ground for the attitude which he takes. He can justify that attitude to himself, and become free and joyful in the consciousness of standing in the truth. The Christian's consciousness that God communes with him rests on *two objective facts, the first of which is the historical fact of the Person of Jesus*. This fact is an element in our own personal reality. It must be admitted that unless we are to live half asleep, as it were, and to have an existence on the level of the brutes, we must face this fact as something in our lives, and must say what we will do with it. The Christian knows that every man who is morally alive must be able to see this fact, which L. Ranke thus describes: "more guiltless and more powerful, more exalted and more holy, has nought ever been on earth than His conduct, His life and His death; the human race knows nothing that could be brought, even afar off, into comparison with it."[2] Hence all who close their eyes to this, the most precious fact that history contains, seem to the Christian to be shut up in a fatal subjectivity, and to be shut out from reality, from that nourishment without which the inner life must starve.

The second objective ground of the Christian's consciousness that God communes with him *is that we hear within ourselves the constant demand that we do right.* And this is not merely some high ideal which perhaps might not concern us; it is something that we feel bound to obey. Here we grasp an objective fact which must be held to be valid in any historical study of life. For life as studied in history, or, in other words, actual human life, cannot be conceived of without the assumption that men know they are unconditionally bound to obey the law of duty. Now we find that the God of whose reality Jesus makes us conscious actually makes us morally free; that is, He actually brings it about that to do right ceases to be a painful problem for us, and begins instead to be the very atmosphere in which we live. Here then we find a thought which we have a right to hold to be an objective reality for every man, and we find this very thought working in us to make us certain of God. There are no other objective grounds for the truth of the Christian religion.

Anyone who has let the fact of the personal life of Jesus work upon him, and who has been led thereby to trust in Him, cannot help thinking that there is a Power over all things, and that that Power is with Jesus. In what he experiences at the hands of Jesus, he feels himself in the grip of this Power. Here his religious life begins, but this beginning is kept from being a purely subjective experience by these two objective things, viz.: by that historical fact which, when once seen, never disappears, and by his conscience. Through Jesus he has not merely a thought of God supported by proofs or authorities, but he has the Living God Himself, who is working upon him. The man who has attained that is a Christian. He is a Christian, although he is not in a position to recognize as truths all those things which other Christians have

[2] *The Popes of Rome,* 6th ed., Vol. I, p. 4.

professed. Where he notes his inability to do so, he will by no means determine, as some may expect, that he will nevertheless profess them to be truths. For example, he might be obliged to insist that it by no means follows from the new life created in him by the grace of God through Jesus Christ that he could fairly affirm all the affirmations of the so-called Apostolic Creed. At the same time, however, he might observe that other Christians, for whom he entertains the greatest respect, declare that they can heartily join in confessing that Creed as their own. Now what will a Christian do in these circumstances who has become conscious, in the way we have described, that God is working upon him? He will certainly not accuse his fellow-Christians of professing to believe what they do not believe, nor will he at once declare to be false those portions of the Creed which he cannot see to be the truth. Perhaps he may be obliged to say they are false for other reasons; but the fact that these things are strange to him will not of itself alone lead him to deny their truth. Indeed, he has just had the experience that a fact, hitherto utterly strange to him, is now true, to his certain knowledge. But, on the other hand, when he observes that other Christians join in the Apostolic Creed, he will not be induced by seeing this to resolve to do the same. In his case such a resolve would not be an act springing genuinely out of that new life which he owes to the grace of God. If he were to make such a resolve he would act, not perhaps from cowardice or vanity, but, to put it briefly, with conscious untruthfulness. At best he would be yielding to an evil habit which would tend to drive him from that standing-ground that made him sure and glad, yes, from the impregnable rock of historical reality and the Eternal One. Through a strange confusion of thought this bad habit prevails largely.

Men say that we must have firm ground beneath us, and that for that reason it is well to hold immovably to what is presented to us in the confessions of the Church, and presented to us, indeed, by the Holy Scriptures. It is certainly of the utmost importance that the Christian should be conscious of standing on objective reality, and that his view of God's working upon him should not hang in subjective mid-air. But it is clear that we can have such an objective basis for our faith only in facts which force themselves upon us as undeniable elements in the reality in which we stand. Then alone can we rejoice in the truth of our faith, for in that case our religious thinking obeys the compulsion of a sacred necessity. On the other hand, we fall precisely into the error of a false subjectivity whenever we seek to appropriate, as the contents of our faith, any conceptions which we do not see arising out of the fact that God comes into communion with us. For then we do not fit ourselves to the objective fact which is given us, but follow our own arbitrary and subjective will.

The temptation to the subjectivity of such a false attachment to creeds is pressing in on us all in Christendom with tremendous force. There is but one sure protection against it, and that is the joy we have in objective reality of the personal life of Jesus, and in His power to make us feel God working upon us. The man who is sensible of this joy knows that he is hidden in a mighty Hand; and he is able to recognize evil in the demand that he should yield to feeble and arbitrary subjectivity, an evil thing though dressed in an ecclesiastical garb. In view of the devastation this demand is causing, it is high time that the officials of the Church should be asked whether they ought to give it the weight of their approval. If they do so, they hold poor souls the tighter in their prison chains, and that is not the office of the Church, but the office of Cerberus. The Protestant people who are refusing, in increasing numbers, to join in an arbitrary confession of the faith, are simply guarding themselves against counting anything the basis of faith which does not possess the weight of undoubted fact. They are not holding by a false subjectivity, as some would-be churchly people would maintain; on the contrary, they are athirst for the objective in religion. So we mock their need if we offer them as a ground for their faith doctrines of Scripture and propositions of the Apostolic Creed in which they cannot, by any means, find an expression of what they themselves shall recognize as fact. They long for facts which shall stand firm at the moment of deepest doubt, and by which they shall feel that they are not without God in the world.

The only such facts are the inner life of Jesus and their own conscience.

Luther once said that he would argue no more with any man who did not recognize Holy Scripture as the Word of God. If we were now to take such a course, it would certainly be very convenient and very pleasing to the flesh, but it would be utterly fruitless. For even where the admission was made, in most cases it would be made no longer in the unthinking fashion of Luther's day. It would be the result, as a rule, either of arbitrary resolve, or of shallowness, or of anxiety. We ought rather to say that we will argue with every man, and will only lay down our arms when we see that men have no sense of unconditional obligation, and that in them, therefore, conscience is dumb. Where such a point has not yet been reached, we are to go on preaching to men, not of things they cannot grasp as undoubtedly real, for such things can have no power over them; but we are to preach of the inner life of the man Jesus, who rules in the world of conscience with far greater power than our weak faith is wont to imagine.

If it is true that the reality of the personal life of Jesus, when grasped as a reality, becomes evidently the touch upon us of that God for whose sake we will forsake all else, then Jesus Himself and His power over the heart are actually the vital principle of our religion. "The Christian religion consists in the personal love and adoration of Jesus Christ; not in correct morality and correct doctrines, but in homage to the King."[3] And what are we to call that joy in the personal life of Jesus with which men's hearts glow when Jesus brings them into the presence of God, and they learn there how He slays and makes alive again? I have no other name for it but this: it is the mightiest love a soul can give. That mightiest love is what we have towards Jesus when once we have tasted the experience that it is through Him that God communes with us. The religious life of the Christian is inseparable from vision of the personal life of Jesus. That vision must be the Christian's constant companion, and so it is as he finds more and more that

[3] F. W. Robertson, *Sein Lebensbild in Briefen* (his life as described in his letters), Gotha, 1888, p. 71.

in such vision he grasps that reality without which all else in the world is empty and desolate.

It is a dangerous undertaking then, and one that needs gentle handling, to say there is such a thing as a false love for Christ. And yet this must be done. The very importance of the matter demands that it shall have firm handling. If love for Jesus is anything else than reverent joy in that personal life which makes us feel the judgment and mercy of God, then that love is but the flowering of an impure heart. We are easily impressed with the spiritual beauty of Jesus, and it arouses tender emotions in the soul; but if we do not get beyond this, we show thereby that we are not letting Jesus work upon us what He would. In these tender emotions we make ourselves virtually His equals, and remain precisely what we were before; but such emotions would be stifled if we really experienced what Jesus causes to dawn upon the sinful man who does not give play to his own vain feelings, but really gives himself into Jesus' hands. True love for Jesus is a far more serious matter; its attitude is determined by the discovery that He at once destroys all the self-contentment we had before, which, of course, was the very source whence a sentimental admiration for His spiritual beauty could flow.

We have said already that the religious experience of the Christians, or the experience of God's entrance with power into our own life, is inseparable from the vision of the personal life of Jesus. It is equally true to say that we only occupy the attitude of true love towards Jesus when we are raised by Him up to God and away beyond ourselves. Jesus loses nothing by our desires in manly earnest for nothing else than to trace in our own lives the working upon us of the power of the Everlasting God; indeed, it is only then that Jesus receives the reverent love which is His due.

10

HISTORIOGRAPHY

Ernst Troeltsch

The interest in history evident in such neo-Kantians as Windelband was further developed in the thought of Dilthey and Troeltsch. In particular, they showed that history, as a human science, has a different mode of access to its subject matter and different methods from those of the natural sciences. The article of Troeltsch reproduced here gives a clear and convenient summary of his views. One may also notice the difference between Troeltsch's understanding of the historical character of Christianity and the way the Ritschlians understood it. Whereas the Ritschlians tended to isolate the events at the origin of the Christian religion, Troeltsch set Christianity in the whole context of man's spiritual history and explored its relations to culture and society.

THE PROFOUND changes which have so drastically altered the whole situation in the religious thought and practice of modern times make their appearance in various spheres, and assail the traditional Christian view of the world from the most diverse quarters and with the most manifold results. To begin with, there is the modern conception of Nature, which, as comprised in the mathematico-mechanical method, has dissolved the purely metaphysical teleology of Nature given by Aristotle, demolished the cosmology of the Bible, and provided modern philosophy with all

Reprinted with permission from the *Encyclopedia of Religion and Ethics,* edited by James Hastings (New York: Charles Scribner's Sons, 1913), Vol. VI, pp. 716–23.

its essential problems. There is, secondly, the new conception of history, which has radically altered our whole attitude to the past and the future, and with which the present is a link in the whole concatenation of things. Thirdly, there is the modern ethics of humanity, which, besides the unworldly virtues of love to God and one's neighbor, has emphasized the intrinsic excellences of artistic and scientific culture—treating them, indeed, as peculiar and indispensable ideals—and has also recognized the positive ethical imperatives involved in political, social, economical, and industrial problems. There are, finally, the new conditions of social life on its economical and industrial sides, and the sociological mode of thought issuing from them, which, in contrast to mere abstract speculation, insists upon the novelty of the whole situation in its social and economical aspects. The first three movements sprang from the Renaissance, while the fourth is a product of the Enlightenment, and, under the influence of nineteenth-century thought, has become a force that towers above all else.

Among these various tendencies, of course, there exists a manifold inter-relation and inter-action. But, if they are to be properly understood, they must be isolated and severally analyzed. In this article only the second, i.e. modern historical reflection, will be specially dealt with, and its nature and results set forth in the shortest possible compass.

The development, function, and results of modern historiography. In history, as in natural science, systematic thought is the product of a relatively high state of civilization. Primitive man is content with the recollections of his family and clan, his tribe and race. As all unknown things coalesce in his mind with religion and mythology, so, in particular, his ideas of the beginning and primitive history of things are bound up with religious cosmology, the myths of holy places, and the legends of his tribal deities. In this domain he delights in the extraordinary and the fantastic, the ingenious and the intricate. Hence the beginnings of history are found in religious traditions, legends, myths, and tales, and among almost all peoples primitive recollection is embedded in a vast romanticism. At this stage there is not the slightest trace of a desire for real knowledge or of a critical spirit. And not only does primitive man lack the sense of continuity and criticism; he likewise tends to regard himself as something apart and absolute. His origin, his mode of life, and his morality seem to him to be the only true and primordial forms, in comparison with which all that is foreign is barbarian and inferior. The ties of custom and morality avail only in his own circle, and do not concern those beyond it. He has no conception whatever of the unity of mankind or of the concatenation of events. The chronological eras with which he deals are purely fanciful—sometimes idyllically short, sometimes fabulously long. The only people of ancient times who in the fullest sense consciously passed beyond this stage of popular legendary reminiscence, of priestly tradition and royal annals, were the Greeks; and in this, as in all other provinces, it was they who laid the foundations of science. Among the Greeks, the traveller and the inquirer, untrammelled by the traditions of temples and the archives of princes, and impelled only by a thirst for knowledge, began to investigate and reflect historically. Here Herodotus, Thucydides, and Polybius, partly as a result of their contact with the non-Hellenic world, partly from the need of elucidating their own people's affairs and the operation of them, and, finally, impelled by their predilection for a philosophical generalization of knowledge, laid the foundations of history as an explanation of public movements by material or psychological causes, and, in particular, as a reasoned concatenation of events occurring in the Europaeo-Asiatic arena. Even these early writers took account of analogies and uniformities with a view to reaching general historical conceptions; and in their idea of a Hellenic civilization, and, later, of a cosmopolitan civilized State organized by the Roman Empire, they had a focus into relation with which they endeavored to bring all that occurred.

These earliest manifestations of historical reflection, however, were extinguished by Christianity and the great religious revolution of later antiquity. It is true that Christianity itself operated throughout with historical conceptions of universal application, and that for the purely anti-barbarian civilized State it substituted the central conception of humanity, and a supreme ethical and religious end for the race. These provided new and powerful incentives to historical reflection. In reality, however, they served to produce, not a scientific, but a revived mythological representation of history. The early Christian conception of mankind, alike as regards time and as regards space, was narrow in the extreme, and was involved in all manner of purely speculative pre-conceptions. The history of the human race, with respect to both its beginning and its end, was saturated with mythology; in the middle stood the miracle of the Incarnation and the rise of the Church. Interest was once more concentrated upon the inexplicable, and the desire to explain came to be regarded as the mark of a profane mind. Heathen and Biblical myths regarding the origin of things were combined: Paradise with the Golden Age, the primeval transgressions of Cain and Ham with the spiritual lapse to the Silver and Iron Ages, Nimrod's tower-building with the Trojan war; and, again, the Messianic outlook of the prophets with the hymns and eclogues of Vergil; the miracles of Elijah, of saints and martyrs, with those of Orpheus and Herakles. In the eschatological sphere, again, the Second Advent of Christ was brought into connection with the universal conflagration of the Stoics, Heaven with Elysium, Hell with Hades, and the stages of the soul's purification with the Empyraean. The history of the intervening period fell into three parts: a relatively short and wholly supernatural period, in which prophecy and miracle prepare the way for the coming of the God-man; an intermediate epoch, in which the God-man Himself appears as the bodily investment of the whole supersensual world, leaving behind Him His permanent incarnation in the Church as a Divine institution for the redemption and salvation of man; and, finally, the longer and for the most part nonmiraculous era of secular history, which, although it is largely controlled by Satan and by demons, does not wholly fail to show the intervention of a redeeming God. The mythology of redemption, assimilating the mythical traditions of the ancients, now takes the place of historical reflection. The all-embracing scheme of the four Danielic world-kingdoms was constructed by Jerome, and held its ground till the eighteenth century. Medieval thought grafted its histories of the world and of nations upon this scheme, and combined with it its love of the fabulous and its legends of the saints. The fresh narratives of fact or arid annals occasionally incorporated with them produced no essential modification.

It was in reality Humanism and the Renaissance that first reverted to the traditions of ancient historical composition and historical reflection, and thus laid the foundations of modern historiography—as in the school of Bruni, where it was influenced by the style of the ancient rhetoric; in that of Blondus, where it showed proficiency in the rendering and criticism of documents; and in that of Machiavelli and Guicciardini, where it sought to explain events by their psychological and material causes. Wherever the culture of the Renaissance took root, there also modern history was evolved, being written, for the most part, by commission of State. From this, again, sprang the historiography of the Enlightenment in the school of Voltaire, in the hands of Hume, Gibbon, Robertson, and Schlözer—a type of history which elaborated and appraised its materials with the freedom of an emancipated scholarship, extended its operations to the whole compass of human history and to the various factors of civilization, and, in its criticism of tradition as in its psychological explanations and its search for causes, far surpassed the methods of antiquity and the Renaissance. Then, in the nineteenth century, there arose philological criticism, the idea of organic evolution, the new analyses of the State and of parties, pre-historic ethnography, the historical study of economics and society, the development of a history of art, of literature, and of religion, taking a place beside the too restricted political history, and, finally, the expansion of politics on a world-wide scale in its bearing upon European events.

This vast array of facts, ideas, and judgments has greatly amplified and complicated the subject-matter of historiography, has made its procedure more delicate and more difficult, and has enormously enlarged and at the same time disintegrated the web of causality. From all this has accrued an immense mass of historical work, moving on various lines, yielding magnificent results, and, nevertheless, with every supposed solution of its problems, giving rise to a fresh group. The total result, however, is not a mere mass of unsolved problems, but is rather the full development of modern historical reflection, which, notwithstanding all misgivings as to its conclusions, consists, precisely like the modern conception of Nature, in a purely scientific attitude to facts. The history of mankind merges in the evolutionary history of the earth's surface; it takes its rise in the prehistoric life of primitive peoples; it is determined throughout by the general laws of geographical conditions, and by the various phases of social life, and forms an unspeakably complex, yet altogether coherent, whole of immeasurable duration both in the past and in the future. It is as a part of this array and system that we must survey and estimate our own existence, and find its rationale and origin. On the analogy of the events known to us we seek by conjecture and sympathetic understanding to explain and reconstruct the past. From this point, again, we advance to the criticism of extant traditions and to the correction of generally accepted historical representations. Since we discern the same process of phenomena in operation in the past as in the present, and see, there as here, the various historical cycles of human life influencing and intersecting one another, we gain at length the idea of an integral continuity, balanced in its changes, never at rest, and ever moving towards incalculable issues. The causal explanation of all that happens, the setting of the individual life in its true relations, the interpretation of events in their most intricate interaction, the placing of mankind in a rounded system of ceaseless change—these constitute the essential function and result of modern historical reflection. The latter, viewed as a whole, forms a new scientific mode of representing man and his development, and, as such, shows at all points an absolute contrast to the Biblico-theological views of later antiquity.

The purely scientific character of historiography. Modern historical reflection, precisely because of what has been said, certainly involves a multitude of fresh and difficult problems. These relate partly to the significance of such a view of history for our conceptions of ideal truth, and for our theory of the universe in general, and partly to the question regarding the scientific nature of historical study itself. The latter is the more restricted problem, and must be discussed first. It is, at the same time, the only problem that is directly concerned with historical reflection as such. Here it is necessary to emphasize one particular principle. In so far as historical thought purports to be scientific, its specifically theoretical or scientific element must be clearly marked off and defined. For, besides the purely scientific attitude to historical fact, there are numerous other attitudes which must be rigorously distinguished from it, but are seldom distinguished in a proper degree. There is, for instance, the aesthetic attitude to history, which centers in its teeming wealth of incident, and the suggestive action and romantic charm of the individual; or which is concerned with an artistically rhythmical construction of the course of events. There is mere curiosity, and that liking for the remarkable, the astonishing, and the unconformable which is ever ready to be excited and kindled to sympathy by graphic description. Then there are some whose aim it is to estimate the ethical value of human actions, and to derive from history an insight into that which reveals itself everywhere as moral force. Others, again, see in history a manual of politics and a means of educating national and political opinion—an education which, they hold, can never be acquired by merely abstract doctrines, but results only from the concrete observation of the whole historical process. Some seek in history support for the sociological and economical principles which, they believe, can be attained only by abstracting from various particular developments, and which must form the basis of our own conception and organization of society. Finally, history often serves as a school of scepticism and caution, on the ground that very divergent representations of historical facts may be given, that criticism is uncertain and tradition not uniform, and that, accordingly, history yields but little real information, and more than anything else brings home to man the limitations of his knowledge.

Now, these various attitudes to the facts of history are all quite competent in their own place and in their own way, and the idea of excluding or avoiding them altogether is not to be entertained.

Nevertheless, they all lie outside the purely cognitive and theoretical sphere, and within that of judgment and appraisement. So far as historical study is concerned with distinctively theoretical and scientific interests, these other interests, as being here of secondary importance, must be scrupulously guarded against and excluded. We may grant that, if descriptive historical works were composed upon such rigid lines, they would lack interest and charm for the majority of readers, and that the impression they make depends precisely on the effective combination of purely historical knowledge with the motives and incentives that may be drawn from it. Delineations of this type, however, are necessarily composite, and must be recognized and studied as such. They combine the interest of the first degree, i.e. that of purely historical knowledge, with interests of the second degree, i.e. those relating to the significance of such knowledge for human feeling and human action. Such works are, accordingly, not purely scientific at all, and historical knowledge is to be obtained from them only by a process of elimination.

What is it, then, that constitutes the essential element of pure historical knowledge? The answer to this question is furnished by the foregoing discussions, and it becomes increasingly clear in the history-writing of the present day. History as pure theoretical science is different from history as an element of *belles lettres,* politics, economics, and the like. In history, as in other things, purely theoretical knowledge is knowledge based upon general conceptions, and that signifies primarily knowledge derived from causal conceptions. The sole task of history in its specifically theoretical aspect is to explain every movement, process, state and nexus of things by reference to the web of its causal relations. That is, in a word, the whole function of purely scientific investigation. What is so explained may then quite well become the subject-matter of interests lying outside the sphere of theoretic science, and the resultant treatment may unite the two constituents as closely as desired. But it will always be possible and necessary to isolate either element, and this will be the more or less easy as the specifically scientific side has been the more or less conscientiously dealt with.

Only in one single point is this simple process of discrimination attended with any real difficulty. One may ask whether, in view of the peculiar nature of psychical causation, or motivation (which will be more fully discussed presently), the insight necessary to determine and appreciate it must not be drawn from personal experience and personal judgment. Such insight, it will be said, is always bound up with subjective estimates of what ought to be. Thus, e.g., only those who feel that certain ethical, political, and artistic excellences ought to exist will seek and discover them as real springs of action, while those who do not so regard them will seldom be able to recognize them as motives, and the less so as historical causes do not lie on the surface or force themselves into notice, but are, as a matter of fact, always brought to light by the sympathetic imagination. Such a view is certainly not wrong. Yet it does not subvert our fundamental principle, since the causes so discovered and realized are, in the sphere of historical study, taken account of as facts only, and not as grounds for the corrections and criticisms of the historian, whose subjective attitude to the facts must, accordingly, be once more discounted. Besides, every supposed and, on grounds of analogy, probable cause must be shown to be actually operative in the particular case. Knowledge of the power of motives is thus, as a means of discovery, doubtless bound up with personal judgments, and the knowledge of what should be often serves as a heuristic principle for the understanding of forces actually at work. But the "ought-to-be" must in turn always be separated from what really is. Historical study is concerned only with the latter, and the personal judgments which have lent keenness to the power of perception must give way before the evidence of the real facts. Historical investigation is, in practice, always subjectively conditioned by the fullness, depth, and range of the personal experience of the investigators themselves, and is thus always marked by irreducible differences in their several starting-points. But the purely scientific aim of historical reflection is not thereby surrendered.

The nature of historical causality. This brings us at length to what is really our main problem, viz. that relating to the nature of historical causation. Here we find ourselves in the sphere of the logic or epistemology of history. Of the various provinces of knowledge this was the last to be won for modern logic, and it is as yet the most imperfectly elucidated. The Aristotelian philosophy dominant in the Medieval Church found no difficulty here. It regarded the operations of Nature and the processes of history as essentially of the same kind, and it applied to both spheres a metaphysicoteleological conception of development, and knew nothing of the modern conception of a causality immanent in experience. The latter conception was first set forth by natural science, and by philosophy as modified thereby; but it was, in fact, framed originally to suit Nature only. Down to the time of Herder and Hegel, accordingly, modern philosophy either took no account of history at all, and abandoned it to historians, litterateurs, or theologians; or else brought historical occurrences under a causal conception, which was simply that of natural science philosophically generalized. Descartes surrendered history to the theologians and to revelation; Hobbes and Spinoza treated it in a naturalistic fashion. The naturalistic view prevailed also in the case of Hume and Kant, notwithstanding the great diversity in their respective views of causality. This is the case even to the present day among the successors of Hume—the adherents of the Positivism of Comte—and we need here recall only the names of Buckle and Taine. In the Kantian school, in its development toward Hegel's Panlogism, the knowledge and aetiology of Nature were, on the other hand, subjected to extreme violence by historical thought, inasmuch as the latter became simply the application of the law of dialectical movement to the cosmic process and the course of human affairs. But if this was a violation of natural science, it was no less a violation of historical thought itself, which by such procedure gained only a finer sense of order and continuity, but no clearer comprehension of its own fundamental conceptions. It was only with the return to the Kantian theory of knowledge, and the emancipation of psychology, that the task of framing a logic of historical science, in contradistinction to the logic of natural science, came to be clearly recognized. Wundt, Dilthey, Windelband, and Rickert were the pioneers of this new and powerful method of investigation.

Here the primary fact was the recognition of the difference between the causality of natural science and that of historical science. The causality of natural science implies the absolutely necessary principle that events are bound together by a changeless, all-pervading, and, in all particular cases, identical law of reciprocity. The scientist demonstrates the laws thus ascertained by artificially constructed examples or experiments, and by means of these submits natural processes to exact calculation. The method finds its highest expression in the establishment of a perfect equivalence between the amount of energy that disappears in the first form of an occurrence and that which re-appears in the second, i.e. the law of mere transformation and quantitative conservation of energy. To this end, by abstracting from all qualitative distinctions, the method of natural science reduces events to mere manifestations of energy, and attends only to the aspects of reciprocity and transformation in the quantity of energy present. Now, historical causation is something entirely different, being almost exclusively a matter of psychological motivation. In the historical sphere nearly everything passes through the medium of consciousness, and in the last resort all turns upon the constant interaction of conscious efforts, into which even the unconscious elements tend to resolve themselves. Thus the peculiar irrational quality and initiative of the individual consciousness make themselves felt in the ultimate result, alike in the individual life and in the life of groups. Here, therefore, it is not permissible to reduce events to non-qualitative forces, or to explain effects by causal equivalence. Then we must also bear in mind the infinite complexity of the motives that arise on all sides and act upon one another—a complexity which gives a special and peculiar character to every particular case, and so defies all calculation and experimental proof. Further, all occurrences, whether in the individual life or in the life of groups, are so affected by the entire psychical condition of the individual or the group that another quite incalculable element is introduced. In the historical process, moreover, there ever emerges the fact of the *new,* which is no mere transformation of existent forces, but an element of essentially fresh content, due to a convergence of historical causes. Accordingly, psychological motivation differs in all respects from natural causation.

It might thus appear that the peculiar character of historical aetiology could be interpreted and methodized by means of psychology, as is proposed by Dilthey and Wundt. But on various grounds this is impossible. For one thing, historical study does not work with psychological motivation alone, but very frequently has recourse to natural causation as well. Polar limitations, glacial periods, earthquakes, famines, destructive winters, uninhabitable regions, and the like, often play a great part in history, and certainly not always by their purely psychological effects. The destruction of Napoleon's army by the Russian winter was due only in part to the psychological effects of the cold; and even in cases where geographical and physiological conditions eventually produce psychical results, we have something very different from purely psychological motivation. Further, psychology cannot supply any kind of real precalculation of historical events and developments. If that were possible, it would imply that the facts of history were known beforehand, and then traced back to the soul, as something that had issued from it. This is the case especially with the so-called folk-psychology, which is simply a rendering of history in terms of psychological laws, but does not explain the former by the latter. Here, indeed, the facts are always anterior to the psychology, and it would be more accurate to say that the history helps to explain the psychology than to assert the converse. The peculiar nature of the causality of motives points, no doubt, to the distinctive nature of historical knowledge, but it cannot properly provide a basis for it. Nor can such basis be found in the subject-matter; it is to be derived from the method alone. The method, however, is determined, not by the subject-matter, but by the epistemological end in view; for knowledge is never a mere reproduction and experience, but always an abstract selection of particular elements of experience for a definite intellectual end. Thus, e.g., the method of natural science is determined by the interest of selecting that aspect of experience in which it manifests itself as absolutely determined by universal laws, and, accordingly, the method in question abstracts from all that is qualitative and individual. The method of historical science, on the other hand, is determined by the object of selecting from the flux of phenomena that which is qualitatively and uniquely (1) *individual*, whether on a larger or on a smaller scale, and of making this intelligible in its concrete and specific relations. It therefore abstracts from the universal laws which may possibly regulate even its subject-matter, but which fail to explain the peculiar and concrete elements of it, and it operates not with the conception of causal equivalence, but with that of individual causes, which, precisely because of their infinite complexity, produce the unique.

Now the method of history, with its logical determination by a distinct intellectual end, answers to the peculiar characteristics of the historical material, just as the method of natural science answers to those of its material. The processes of the physical world demand in greater degree the first-mentioned type of isolating interest (universal law); those of the psychical world, the second (individual causality). It is not the methods themselves, but their respective intellectual ends, that spring directly from the nature of the subject-matter; and, accordingly, the distinctive characteristics of the material correspond in either case to the ends determining the respective methods. The physical world invites us to understand it by the deduction of general laws; the psychical world by a sympathetic reconstruction of the causal connections in which the actual facts of history have taken shape. Here, then, the true nature of historical knowledge comes to light. Historical knowledge selects its materials as it may require—a national history, a state of civilization, a biography, an intellectual development, etc.—and seeks, by means of the individual causality proper to history, to make it as intelligible as if it were part of our own experience. Even the history of mankind, were it within our grasp, would be a freely selected and individually concrete subject-matter, inasmuch as its development could be understood only as a particular concatenation, and in no sense as an instance of the operation of universal laws. Such purely objective causal explanation, based upon the widest possible experience and the most methodical application of experience, constitutes the distinctive character of history as a pure theoretical science.

Precisely because of this, however, historical thought shows itself to be (2) *conceptual* thought, though the concepts which it must frame are different from those of the natural sciences. The universal application of the category of causality in the special form of individual causality subjects the entire material to a uniform conceptual mode of treatment. Moreover, the several isolated subjects of inquiry which are to be causally explained in this way are conceptual unities, for which, it is true, we have as yet no logical term, but which may be designated "historical aggregates" (*historische Totalitäten*). Such would be, e.g., a human life, a nation, a condition of affairs, the spirit of an age, a legal constitution, an economical condition, a school of art, etc. These aggregates are selected freely and one after another by the investigator, but may be re-combined, till at length the highest concept of historical totality, i.e. humanity itself, is reached. It is, indeed, true that this highest concept can be described only by the successive descriptions of its separate components and factors. The conception of mankind as a whole, just because mankind cannot be brought within a single, simultaneous, and all-embracing view, can never be more than an incomplete work of the imagination.

Now, inasmuch as these totalities are processes, and internally coherent congeries of phenomena, there emerges a third fundamental principle of historical reflection—(3) the principle of *development*. This conception must certainly be taken in its purely historico-empirical sense, and must not be confounded either with the idea of development in natural science or with that found in metaphysics. The scientific conception of development signifies the explanation of becoming by the addition of infinitesimal mechanical changes; the metaphysical conception denotes the interpretation of reality as the expression of an absolute intelligence which realizes itself therein. In contradistinction to these, the concepton of historico-empirical development denotes the progress that issues from the essential element of certain psychical efforts, the working out of the consequences that are latent in the earliest beginnings, the dynamic element in psychical forces which are not exhausted in a single manifestation, but work out towards a result—forces in which exists a tendency to a development akin to logical evolution. Thus there is development in religious, ethical, and philosophical ideas; likewise in the character of individuals and peoples, as also in forms of government and economic conditions. Wherever this tendency asserts itself, it constitutes a principle that organizes the aggregates, and moves them onward from within—a principle that absorbs and elaborates the various causes, and supplies them with a focus of attraction or repulsion.

Nevertheless, the value of the conception of historical development must not be over-estimated, as it often is at the present day. For, in the first place, it does not mean an infinite progress, but in every particular case implies only a single concrete impulse controlling a given aggregate. It manifests itself in the fact of exhaustion as well as in that of advance. All progressive developments work also towards regression, so as to make room for fresh movements. The conception in question has, therefore, nothing to do with the conception of an unlimited and continuous progress found in the philosophy of history. Then, again, besides the fact of continuity, we must also recognize the fact of historical contingency, i.e. the convergence of a series of mutually independent causes. In virtue of this contingency, processes of development are commingled, furthered, amplified, obstructed, and sometimes even completely arrested; though, of course, the syntheses thus fortuitously brought about may occasionally give rise to new and fruitful developments, for the spiritual life of man has everywhere a tendency to unify the elements of a given situation, however produced, and thus also to mould them into new stimuli to development. To the sphere of accident or contingency belong the supremely important influences of climate, atmosphere, fertility, geographical position, and natural wealth. That sphere also embraces physiological occurrences and conditions—deaths, interbreeding, mixture of races, food-supplies, and the like. To the domain of chance must likewise be reckoned, so far at least as we at present know, the distribution of individual qualities, as, e.g., talent and genius, which sometimes occur but sparely, sometimes in amazing profusion. It is true that such "accidents" are rightly so designated only when judged with reference to the conception of historical aggregates and the developmental tendencies that give rise to them. They may, to a very great extent at least, be brought under the conception of natural law. The idea of contingency is, in fact, one in regard to which the historical and scientific modes of thought are discriminated with special clearness.

In the sense specified, accordingly, the causal explanation of historical aggregates constitutes the purely theoretical function of historical investigation. It is certainly obvious that such causal explanation has a rather restricted range. It is dependent upon the existence of a tradition, upon a critical examination of that tradition, and upon the imaginative and synthetic powers of the investigator. It can never re-constitute its objects in their entirety, but must decompose them; it can depict them only consecutively, and never in their simultaneous inter-dependence. Hence it can proceed only by analyzing, and by moving from subject to subject. This explains why the work of history must ever be taken up afresh. The accession of new material, the fresh sifting of facts by criticism, new ideas and views in the linking of causes to historical aggregates—all of these call for ever new beginnings, and lead to a revision of previous delineations. The writing of history can never be exhaustive, and never complete; it will never be able to compass the All in its extension and in its intension. It will never be able fully to analyze the individual peculiarities of souls or groups of souls, or to explain that power of initiative and self-determination which we call freedom. It will never be able to find the ultimate derivation of a historical world of personalities, or even of the movements at work within that world, in anything else. There will always be limits to its realization of its intellectual end, and always residua incapable of being rationally determined. But the writing of history is not on that account futile or valueless. For it enables man to comprehend himself so far as a causal comprehension of himself is possible or necessary. It is, in fact, only on the basis of such causal self-comprehension that our own historical work can be clearly and circumspectly extended. The ages of naïve traditionalism and naïve rationalism required no such understanding of oneself. But, as they pressed against their narrow bounds, and made a beginning with historical reflection, they found it necessary to carry the latter to its ultimate issues. The cultured man of today is a person who thinks historically, and can construct his future only by means of historical self-knowledge. This holds good for every sphere of life, even for the religious sphere, in which, it is true, such self-knowledge is still opposed by the naïve traditionalism and rationalism of large masses of mankind.

The relation of historiography to the philosophy of history. Our concern with history, however, is by no means exhausted in causal interpretation and the formation of aggregates. For, on the one hand, there arises the problem regarding the relation of the historical process in the world to the fundamental forces of the universe, and, on the other, the problem regarding the significance of that process for the living and operative will of each particular age—the will which is nurtured by the events of history, and yet manifests at every instant a creative power of its own. To the former problem belong the questions concerning the foundation of the psychical world in the Universal Spirit, the connection between the physical and the psychical world, the Divine direction and sustaining of the cosmos, and the distinction between the purely natural life of the soul and the spiritual and civilized life that strives to transcend it. The second problem comprises the questions relating to the teachings of history for the active and constructive will, to the inward meaning and significance of that substance of life which takes concrete form in the process of history, the ideal values to be won from that process and to be recognized in it; and, finally, its ultimate meaning and aim. These questions all lie outside the sphere of empirical historiography, and belong in reality to the philosophy of history which explains and estimates metaphysically. Empirical and philosophical history must be clearly distinguished in principle, though in the actual delineation of events they are usually found in some degree of combination.

But the philosophy of history itself, as has just been indicated, includes very different kinds of problems. The questions of the first group noted above relate to purely metaphysical matters; and, whether they are dealt with as lying within the sphere of a complete system of metaphysics, or agnostically set aside as unanswerable, it is comparatively easy to keep them apart from history proper. The metaphysical background will be discerned only in delineations on a large and comprehensive scale, and even there it will assert itself rather in the intellectual attitude as a whole and in occasional aphorisms than in elaborately constructed theories. This is, at all events, what we find in so purely empirical a historian as Ranke. Modern historiography, as contrasted with the medieval and theological types, has certainly in principle wrenched itself free from the metaphysical element, whatever the personal views of the historian regarding the latter may be. This, however, is no more than a theoretical emancipation. In view of the practical importance of the metaphysical presuppositions, their separate consideration and discussion are matters of the highest import to philosophy, and the historian must take care to keep such vital questions open, and not to foreclose them by casual remarks and ostensible truisms.

The other group of questions in the history of philosophy is not so easily kept distinct from historical composition. It is true that purely historical delineations, like the delineations of natural science, may conceivably be given in purely empirical categories, as, e.g., Tocqueville, Fustel de Coulange, and Eduard Meyer endeavor to do. This, however, cannot possibly be the regular procedure, because the reader aspires not only to a knowledge of causes, but to a point of view from which he may pass judgment on the facts of history, and because the questions that thus arise cannot be answered by themselves alone, or apart from a mental picture of the entire field of history. Nevertheless, with a view to clearness in the questions involved, the distinction must, in principle at least, be strongly insisted upon. This is demanded also by the fact that the valuations and interpretations thus conjoined with description are sometimes contradictory to one another. We meet here with interpretations from various points of view—political, legal, artistic, moral, and religious. These may show an altogether one-sided character, or they may be combined with one another. Each of these points of view, moreover, may itself exhibit variations, and may even give rise to extreme contrasts within its own sphere. This chaos of value-judgments, the perplexing impression made by which is but intensified by the perpetually fluctuating course of history, can be transcended only by grouping the questions together and finding their answers in (1) *a complete system of values*. Such a system of values, however, is neither more nor less than Ethics—to take that term in its ancient sense of a doctrine of absolutely essential qualities and goods, as formulated anew most definitely by Schleiermacher among modern thinkers, and as employed—in effect—in the Hegelian ethics and philosophy of history. On this view history is to be interpreted and evaluated by comparison with a system of values which it is the task of ethics to construct. Every single historical aggregate must, therefore, be judged by the measure of its approximation to this system, or to particular standards forming part of it. Whether that judgment is carried out with glowing personal emotion or with graphic and impressive imagery, it is always based upon such an objective system of values, of which the writer may be unaware, but whose validity he assumes.

The great obstacle to this procedure, however, lies in the fact that ethics itself must derive its knowledge of values from the facts of history, and can furnish nothing more than a critical delimitation and adjustment of these values. We are thus confronted with a logical circle: we must interpret history by the degree in which it approximates to ethical values, and at the same time we must derive these ethical values from history. The circle is not to be evaded, and the difficulty can be solved only by the thinker's own conviction and certainty that amid the facts of history he has really recognized the tendencies that make for ethical ideals, and that he has truly discerned the dynamic movement and progressive tendency of the historic process. A complete proof of the accuracy of his view, i.e. of his system of values, is impossible, and, accordingly, ethical interpretations of history will exhibit manifold divergences in the future, just as they have done in the past. Still, such a system of values, notwithstanding its irretrievably subjective character, involves no mere abstract subjectivism; on the contrary, the critical survey of the objective phenomena is through and through a matter of *insight,* and proceeds upon a true homage to the facts. The system would be more accurately described as intuitional rather than subjective. Its demonstration can, therefore, be given only by letting the critic repeat the observation in his own experience, and by leading him to draw from the historian's view of the facts a view of his own in keeping with it. This shows how great a part imagination plays in the framing of those conceptions. But the process cannot be dispensed with except by such as claim to have received a system of the kind by revelation.

From the standpoint of such a system, the historical process appears as an approximation to the complete harmony of ethical values. But here emerges another important conception of the philosophy of history, viz. that of (2) *metaphysical or ethical development.* This, as already noted, must be carefully distinguished from the conception of historical development in the empirical sense, and is not to be demonstrated by means of the latter. The empirical conception of historical development shows only partial, or progressive and regressive, developments, but not the advance of mankind as a whole towards a final and universal end. It certainly exhibits the formation of ethical aggregates, but not their synthesis in a uniform and progressive continuity. Hegel made the mistake of reducing each of these conceptions of development to the other, and also of basing both together upon the metaphysico-logical movement of the Absolute. In reality, the conception of ethical development is merely a postulate of faith—in the Kantian sense—a postulate based upon the actual occurrence of the aggregates of ethical life, and our personal experience of them. Consequently, it must remain an open question whether this kind of development attains its end in the present life, or in a further progress of souls in a life beyond. Certainly experience does not support the former alternative. Similarly, as the system of values can be realized only approximately, and as the possibilities of an approximation are, for the individual, so varied, his share in the final system must also remain an open question.

In connection with this conception of development, mention must be made, finally, of still another important element in the philosophy of history, viz. (3) the problem of *individualization*. The system of values is no rationally demonstrable abstract system, such as would confront all the phenomena of empirical history as an absolute and everywhere identical standard. If we designate the system of values as the "Idea," then the course of history is not a sometimes more and sometimes less effective progress towards the realization of the ideal, which is everywhere the same. The truth is, rather, that all spiritual manifestations—in individuals, in groups, or in periods—are individualizations or concrete manifestations of the ideal. This accords perfectly with the earliest, merely descriptive, and non-nomothetic type of historiography; and it accords likewise with the metaphysic of spirit—which cannot be more fully dealt with here. But in that case every historical phenomenon, viewed from the standpoint of the ethical philosophy of history, bears a double character: it is, on the one hand, a concrete manifestation of the Idea, having a relative right of its own, and, on the other, a mere approximation to the absolute system of values. In spite of all obstacles and defects, there obtains everywhere an individual and concrete progress towards the ideal. Final perfection itself, indeed, might be conceived of as simply the sum of the individual realizations of the Idea. Here, however, we encounter the antithesis between universal validity and individualization—an antithesis which cannot be theoretically reconciled at all. Hence each historical phenomenon is to be estimated by reference only to that degree of approximation to the Idea which is set before it and is possible to it. In this way every epoch has a relative justification, though it must, at the same time, be judged in the light of an absolute end. This shows the necessary relativity of the philosophy of history, and yet makes it possible that the relative shall appear to be included in the movement towards the absolute. The absolute *in* the relative, yet not fully and finally in it, but always pressing towards fresh forms of self-expression, and so effecting the mutual criticism of its relative individualizations—such is the last word of the philosophy of history. This implies, however, that in the writing of history and the description of historical phenomena—in spite of all appraisements by reference to final and absolute values—there still remains the concrete individual character of the objects dealt with, and there remains also the non-rationality of personal life, with its rightful claims in face of all the ideals of universal value that hover before the human mind.

HISTORY—ITS NATURE, OBJECT, METHOD AND VALUE

R. G. Collingwood

In this posthumously published work, the British idealist philosopher,
Robin G. Collingood, drew on such Continental philosophers as Dil-
they and Croce. Collingwood himself had worked as a historian as
well as a philosopher, and had produced a notable study of Roman
Britain, so that he knew the historian's task at first hand. In the pas-
sage that follows, he strongly emphasizes the human character of
history (one might almost say, its existential character, though this
would be to introduce a terminology alien to Collingwood). The
teaching of this British philosopher has received new prominence
among students of religion because of the high estimate of his work
expressed by Bultmann.

WHAT HISTORY IS, what it is about, how it proceeds, and what it
is for, are questions which to some extent different people would
answer in different ways. But in spite of differences there is a large
measure of agreement between the answers. And this agreement
becomes closer if the answers are subjected to scrutiny with a view
to discarding those which proceed from unqualified witnesses. History, like theology or natural science, is a special form of thought.
If that is so, questions about the nature, object, method, and value

Reprinted with permission from *The Idea of History* (London: The Clarendon Press, Oxford, 1946), pp. 7–10.

of this form of thought must be answered by persons having two qualifications.

First, they must have experience of that form of thought. They must be historians. In a sense we are all historians nowadays. All educated persons have gone through a process of education which has included a certain amount of historical thinking. But this does not qualify them to give an opinion about the nature, object, method, and value of historical thinking. For in the first place, the experience of historical thinking which they have thus acquired is probably very superficial; and the opinions based on it are therefore no better grounded than a man's opinion of the French people based on a single week-end visit to Paris. In the second place, experience of anything whatever gained through the ordinary educational channels, as well as being superficial, is invariably out of date. Experience of historical thinking, so gained, is modelled on text-books, and text-books always describe not what is now being thought by real live historians, but what was thought by real live historians at some time in the past when the raw material was being created out of which the text-book has been put together. And it is not only the results of historical thought which are out of date by the time they get into the text-book. It is also the principles of historical thought: that is, the ideas as to the nature, object, method, and value of historical thinking. In the third place, and connected with this, there is a peculiar illusion incidental to all knowledge acquired in the way of education: the illusion of finality. When a student is *in statu pupillari* with respect to any subject whatever, he has to believe that things are settled because the text-books and his teachers regard them as settled. When he emerges from that state and goes on studying the subject for himself he finds that nothing is settled. The dogmatism which is an invariable mark of immaturity drops away from him. He looks at so-called facts with a new eye. He says to himself: "My teacher and text-books told me that such and such was true; but is it true? What reasons had they for thinking it true, and were these reasons adequate?" On the other hand, if he emerges from the status of pupil without continuing to pursue the subject he never rids himself of this dogmatic attitude. And this makes him a person peculiarly unfitted to answer the questions I have mentioned. No one, for example, is likely to answer them worse than an Oxford philosopher who, having read Greats in his youth, was once a student of history and thinks that this youthful experience of historical thinking entitles him to say what history is, what it is about, how it proceeds, and what it is for.

The second qualification for answering these questions is that a man should not only have experience of historical thinking but should also have reflected upon that experience. He must be not only an historian but a philosopher; and in particular his philosophical thought must have included special attention to the problems of historical thought. Now it is possible to be a quite good historian (though not an historian of the highest order) without thus reflecting upon one's own historical thinking. It is even easier to be a quite good teacher of history (though not the very best kind of teacher) without such reflection. At the same time, it is important to remember that experience comes first, and reflection on that experience second. Even the least reflective historian has the first qualification. He possesses the experience on which to reflect; and when he is asked to reflect on it his reflections have a good chance of being to the point. An historian who has never worked much at philosophy will probably answer our four questions in a more intelligent and valuable way than a philosopher who has never worked much at history.

I shall therefore propound answers to my four questions such as I think any present-day historian would accept. Here they will be rough and ready answers, but they will serve for a provisional definition of our subject-matter and they will be defended and elaborated as the argument proceeds.

The definition of history. Every historian would agree, I think, that history is a kind of research or inquiry. What kind of inquiry it is I do not yet ask. The point is that generically it belongs to what we call the sciences: that is, the forms of thought whereby we ask questions and try to answer them. Science in general, it is important to realize, does not consist in collecting what we already know and arranging it in this or that kind of pattern. It consists in fastening upon something we do not know, and trying to discover it. Playing patience with things we already know may be a useful means towards this end, but it is not the end itself. It is at best only the means. It is scientifically valuable only in so far as the new arrangement gives us the answer to a question we have already decided to ask. That is why all science begins from the knowledge of our own ignorance: not our ignorance of everything, but our ignorance of some definite thing—the origin of parliament, the cause of cancer, the chemical composition of the sun, the way to make a pump work without muscular exertion on the part of a man or a horse or some other docile animal. Science is finding things out: and in that sense history is a science.

The object of history. One science differs from another in that it finds out things of a different kind. What kind of things does history find out? I answer, *res gestae:* actions of human beings that have been done in the past. Although this answer raises all kinds of further questions many of which are controversial, still, however they may be answered, the answers do not discredit the proposition that history is the science of *res gestae,* the attempt to answer questions about human actions done in the past.

How does history proceed? History proceeds by the interpretation of evidence: where evidence is a collective name for things which singly are called documents, and a document is a thing existing here and now, of such a kind that the historian, by thinking about it, can get answers to the questions he asks about past events. Here again there are plenty of difficult questions to ask as to what the characteristics of evidence are and how it is interpreted. But there is no need for us to raise them at this stage. However they are answered, historians will agree that historical procedure, or method, consists essentially of interpreting evidence.

Lastly, *what is history for?* This is perhaps a harder question than the others; a man who answers it will have to reflect rather more widely than a man who answers the three we have answered already. He must reflect not only on historical thinking but on other things as well, because to say that something is "for" something implies a distinction between A and B, where A is good for something and B is that for which something is good. But I will suggest an answer, and express the opinion that no historian would reject it, although the further questions to which it gives rise are numerous and difficult.

My answer is that history is "for" human self-knowledge. It is generally thought to be of importance to man that he should know himself: where knowing himself means knowing not his merely personal peculiarities, the things that distinguish him from other men, but his nature as man. Knowing yourself means knowing, first, what it is to be a man; secondly, knowing what it is to be the kind of man you are; and thirdly, knowing what it is to be the man *you* are and nobody else is. Knowing yourself means knowing what you can do; and since nobody knows what he can do until he tries, the only clue to what man can do is what man has done. The value of history, then, is that it teaches us what man has done and thus what man is.

II

NATURALISM, REALISM,
AND EMPIRICISM

INTRODUCTION

WHILE WE HAVE INDICATED that the idealist philosophy, in its various forms, occupied a dominant position at the beginning of our century, its claims did not go unchallenged.

To many persons, it seemed that the idealists took insufficient note of the natural sciences. The nineteenth century had been a time of tremendous advance in these sciences. Their success seemed to indicate that in their empirical approach lies the way to reliable knowledge. The assured results of the sciences contrasted with the apparently airy and untestable speculations of metaphysics and theology.

In the nineteenth century, there had already developed a strongly naturalistic type of philosophy. This *naturalism* was of the reductionist type, believing that mental phenomena can be explicated in terms of physics. It was a kind of rival metaphysic to idealism, holding that reality is constituted by matter and energy, evolving in accordance with rigidly determinist laws. According to one of its most eloquent exponents, Ernst Haeckel (1834–1919), this naturalism precisely denied the three great assertions which, in various ways, most of the idealists had been concerned to defend —the existence of God, the immortality of the soul, and the freedom of the human will.

A related point of view was *scientific positivism,* developed by such writers as Ernst Mach (1838–1916). This might be called a methodological materialism, rather than a metaphysical materialism. Reality itself is held to be unknowable, so that it is futile to ask the question "Why?" We should restrict ourselves to the question "How?" This is the question which can be answered through the methods of the empirical sciences.

Furthermore, naturalists and positivists alike believed that there is no limit to the applicability of the scientific method. It could be extended from the fields of physics and biology to human affairs, and so in the nineteenth century we see the rise of such new sciences as anthropology, psychology, and even attempts at a scientifically based ethic. These new sciences seemed to strengthen the naturalist's case, because they made it appear possible to give an account of religion in positivistic terms. Beliefs and ceremonies could be traced by the anthropologist to primitive superstitions; or by the sociologist to the need for social stability; or by the psychologist to the demands of the individual for satisfaction and security. So one could give an account of religion without any need to suppose the existence of God or of supernatural entities, though such an account was usually taken to mean that religion is fundamentally illusory or regressive. Some writers, however, while embracing a naturalistic position, were willing to find some value in religion.

This older type of naturalism is illustrated in three of our selections. Sir James George Frazer (1854–1941) was one of the pioneers in the science of anthropology and the study of primitive religion and mythology. He spent twenty-five years writing *The Golden Bough,* which brought together the myths, legends, and cults of peoples all over the world, and showed the remarkable similarities and interrelations among them. In Frazer's interpretation of the human spirit in history, its progress has been from a primitive magic to religion, and thence from religion to science. (One might compare the rather similar view of Auguste Comte [1798–1857], the father of positivism.) Frazer's thesis is stated in our excerpt from the conclusion of his great work. Sigmund Freud (1856–1939) won fame as the founder of psychoanalysis, and perhaps more than any other person of modern times, he has revolutionized our understanding of how our minds work. Freud was from his youth an atheist in the tradition of nineteenth-century naturalism, but his researches in psychoanalysis seemed to him to confirm his atheism and to show that belief in God is infantile and neurotic. We have also included an excerpt from Carl Gustav Jung (1875–1961), who ranks alongside Freud for his great researches into the human psyche. Jung differed sharply from Freud in his estimate of religion. In Jung's view, religion is no neurosis but a strengthening and integrating factor in life. Jung's account is just as naturalistic as Freud's, in some ways at least. Jung thinks of God as an archetype of the psyche, and remains agnostic about the question of God's metaphysical reality. It seems clear, however, that Jung's naturalism is not of the old reductionist type, and that for him "nature" is not without its spiritual aspects. At the same time, his defense of religion is mainly in terms of its utility.

A further threat to the dominance of idealism was offered by the emergence in the early years of the century of the philosophical movement known as the "New Realism." The word *realism* has been variously used in the history of philosophy, but in the present context it implies that we have knowledge of a world that is quite real apart from our cognition of it. For idealism, on the other hand, the world was supposed to be somehow mind-dependent. Realism was opposed not only to idealism but also to pragmatism, because of the latter's anti-intellectual character.

The most typical manifestations of the new realism leaned toward naturalism and positivism. For the realist, mind is only one factor among others in the world, and facts count for more than values. Especially through the influence of G. E. Moore (1873–1958), the new realism took on an analytic and antimetaphysical character. From there, the line of development led on to logical positivism and to logical empiricism. Although the most influential figure in this development was Ludwig Wittgenstein (1889–1951), an Austrian who settled in England, this modern *empiricism* may be regarded as the continuation of the Anglo-Saxon empirical tradition of earlier times.

Yet there was in realism another possibility of development— the construction of a metaphysic based on the findings of modern empirical science. Especially the new developments in physics in the twentieth century rendered improbable the old-fashioned materialistic naturalism, and prepared the way for developing a type of naturalism that would find room for mental and spiritual realities, and perhaps even for God. We find this new and richer naturalism in the so-called *process* philosophies and in related philosophies of an evolutionary character.

The appearance of these realist metaphysics reminds us that there is nothing in realism inherently in conflict with a theistic or religious interpretation of the world. The philosophy of St. Thomas Aquinas (1225–74) has been for many centuries the classic philosophy of the Christian Church. This philosophy is usually called a "moderate realism" and has strong empirical traits. During the period under consideration, Thomism has undergone a remarkable revival and rehabilitation under such outstanding "neo-Thomist" philosophers as Jacques Maritain (1882–   ).

Our remaining selections in this part of the volume illustrate the developments of which we have just spoken. The excerpt from Henri Bergson (1859–1941) shows us a sympathetic interpretation of religion within the context of a philosophy that appeals to modern science for its evidences. The next excerpt from Bertrand Russell (1872–   ) shows us the more skeptical aspects of realism, and contains an explicit and telling criticism of Bergson. We move on next to Alfred North Whitehead (1861–1947). Though he collaborated with Russell in providing the logical tools on which contemporary philosophy has so much relied, he diverged from Russell's skeptical attitudes and constructed a theistic metaphysic which claims to be entirely compatible with the modern scientific view of the world, and which escapes some of the difficulties of traditional theism. Our excerpt shows how Whitehead does not shrink from drawing metaphysical inferences from the findings of the physicists, yet at the same time fights against idealist interpretations. Étienne Gilson (1884–   ) has been chosen as an exemplar of neo-Thomism. The last selection, from Richard Braithwaite (1900–   ), expounds one of the most interesting theories of religion that has so far come from a logical empiricist. While Braithwaite's interpretation is not apparently willing to accord to religion a cognitive dimension, he rejects as inadequate the emotive view of religion and tries to expound its meaning in conative terms.

2

FROM MAGIC THROUGH RELIGION TO SCIENCE

James G. Frazer

Sir James George Frazer was one of the pioneers of the science of anthropology. He spent twenty-five years in writing the twelve volumes of The Golden Bough, *completed in 1915. The work ranges over the whole field of primitive religion and folklore, and traces parallels among customs and beliefs from many parts of the world. In the excerpt quoted, he states the conclusion of his studies. Man has moved through three stages in the attempt to satisfy his needs and secure his life. The first stage was magic; the discovery of its failure led to religion; this in turn has yielded to science. One may compare with this the threefold scheme enunciated by the French positivist Auguste Comte (1798–1857), who supposed that man has progressed from religion through metaphysics to science.*

IF THEN we consider, on the one hand, the essential similarity of man's chief wants everywhere and at all times, and on the other hand, the wide difference between the means he has adopted to satisfy them in different ages, we shall perhaps be disposed to conclude that the movement of the higher thought, so far as we can trace it, has on the whole been from magic through religion to science. In magic man depends on his own strength to meet the difficulties and dangers that beset him on every side. He believes in a certain established order of nature on which he can surely count, and which he can manipulate for his own ends. When he discovers his mistake, when he recognizes sadly that both the order of nature which he had assumed and the control which he had believed himself to exercise over it were purely imaginary, he ceases to rely on his own intelligence and his own unaided efforts, and throws himself humbly on the mercy of certain great invisible beings behind the veil of nature, to whom he now ascribes all those far-reaching powers which he once arrogated to himself. Thus in the acuter minds magic is gradually superseded by religion, which explains the succession of natural phenomena as regulated by the will, the passion, or the caprice of spiritual beings like man in kind, though vastly superior to him in power.

But as time goes on this explanation in its turn proves to be unsatisfactory. For it assumes that the succession of natural events is not determined by immutable laws, but is to some extent variable and irregular, and this assumption is not borne out by closer observation. On the contrary, the more we scrutinize that succession the more we are struck by the rigid uniformity, the punctual precision with which, wherever we can follow them, the operations of nature are carried on. Every great advance in knowledge has extended the sphere of order and correspondingly restricted the sphere of apparent disorder in the world, till now we are ready to anticipate that even in regions where chance and confusion appear still to reign, a fuller knowledge would everywhere reduce the seeming chaos to cosmos. Thus the keener minds, still pressing forward to a deeper solution of the mysteries of the universe, come to reject the religious theory of nature as inadequate, and to revert in a measure to the older standpoint of magic by postulating explicitly, what in magic had only been implicitly assumed, to wit, an inflexible regularity in the order of natural events, which, if carefully observed, enables us to foresee their course with certainty and to act accordingly. In short, religion, regarded as an explanation of nature, is displaced by science.

But while science has this much in common with magic that

both rest on a faith in order as the underlying principle of all things, readers of this work will hardly need to be reminded that the order presupposed by magic differs widely from that which forms the basis of science. The difference flows naturally from the different modes in which the two orders have been reached. For whereas the order on which magic reckons is merely an extension, by false analogy, of the order in which ideas present themselves to our minds, the order laid down by science is derived from patient and exact observation of the phenomena themselves. The abundance, the solidity, and the splendour of the results already achieved by science are well fitted to inspire us with a cheerful confidence in the soundness of the method. Here at last, after groping about in the dark for countless ages, man has hit upon a clue to the labyrinth, a golden key that opens many locks in the treasury of nature. It is probably not too much to say that the hope of progress—moral and intellectual as well as material—in the future is bound up with the fortunes of science, and that every obstacle placed in the way of scientific discovery is a wrong to humanity.

Yet the history of thought should warn us against concluding that because the scientific theory of the world is the best that has yet been formulated, it is necessarily complete and final. We must remember that at bottom the generalizations of science or, in common parlance, the laws of nature are merely hypotheses devised to explain that ever-shifting phantasmagoria of thought which we dignify with the high-sounding names of the world and the universe. In the last analysis magic, religion, and science are nothing but theories of thought; and as science has supplanted its predecessors, so it may hereafter be itself superseded by some more perfect hypothesis, perhaps by some totally different way of looking at the phenomena—of registering the shadows on the screen —of which we in this generation can form no idea. The advance of knowledge is an infinite progression towards a goal that forever recedes.

3

A PHILOSOPHY OF LIFE

Sigmund Freud

The treatment of religion as a purely natural phenomenon, to be explained without any appeal to such notions as God or the supernatural, received a powerful impetus from the work of Freud. In many ways, Freud's naturalism was that of the nineteenth century, and his "model" of the human mind was in mechanical terms. But some of his criticisms, especially of infantile and neurotic religion, have validity against popular forms of religion that have been very widespread. In the following passage, he sets forth the atheistic worldview (Weltanschauung) *to which, as he believed, his psychoanalytic theories impelled him.*

I PROPOSE that we should now take a bold leap and venture upon answering a question which is constantly being asked in other quarters: does psycho-analysis lead to a particular *Weltanschauung* and, if so, to which?

Weltanschauung is, I am afraid, a specifically German concept, the translation of which into foreign languages might well raise difficulties. If I try to give you a definition of it, it is bound to seem clumsy to you. In my opinion, then, a *Weltanschauung* is an intellectual construction which solves all the problems of our existence uniformly on the basis of one overriding hypothesis, which, accordingly, leaves no question unanswered and in which

Reprinted with permission from *New Introductory Lectures on Psychoanalysis*, translated by James Strachey (New York: W. W. Norton, Inc., 1964), pp. 158–172.

everything that interests us finds its fixed place. It will easily be understood that the possession of a *Weltanschauung* of this kind is among the ideal wishes of human beings. Believing in it one can feel secure in life, one can know what to strive for, and how one can deal most expediently with one's emotions and interests.

If that is the nature of a *Weltanschauung,* the answer as regards psycho-analysis is made easy. As a specialist science, a branch of psychology—a depth-psychology or psychology of the unconscious—it is quite unfit to construct a *Weltanschauung* of its own: it must accept the scientific one. But the *Weltanschauung* of science already departs noticeably from our definition. It is true that it too assumes the *uniformity* of the explanation of the universe; but it does so only as a programme, the fulfilment of which is relegated to the future. Apart from this it is marked by negative characteristics, by its limitation to what is at the moment knowable and by its sharp rejection of certain elements that are alien to it. It asserts that there are no sources of knowledge of the universe other than the intellectual working-over of carefully scrutinized observations —in other words, what we call research—and alongside of it no knowledge derived from revelation, intuition or divination. It seems as though this view came very near to being generally recognized in the course of the last few centuries that have passed; and it has been left to *our* century to discover the presumptuous objection that a *Weltanschauung* like this is alike paltry and cheerless, that it overlooks the claims of the human intellect and the needs of the human mind.

This objection cannot be too energetically repudiated. It is quite without a basis, since the intellect and the mind are objects for scientific research in exactly the same way as any nonhuman things. Psycho-analysis has a special right to speak for the scientific *Weltanschauung* at this point, since it cannot be reproached with having neglected what is mental in the picture of the universe. Its contribution to science lies precisely in having extended research to the mental field. And, incidentally, without such a psychology science would be very incomplete. If, however, the investigation of the intellectual and emotional functions of men (and of animals) is included in science, then it will be seen that nothing is altered in the attitude of science as a whole, that no new sources of knowledge or methods of research have come into being. Intuition and divination would be such, if they existed; but they may safely be reckoned as illusions, the fulfilments of wishful impulses. It is easy to see, too, that these demands upon *Weltanschauung* are only based on emotion. Science takes notice of the fact that the human mind produces these demands and is ready to examine their sources; but it has not the slightest reason to regard them as justified. On the contrary it sees this as a warning carefully to separate from knowledge everything that is illusion and an outcome of emotional demands like these.

This does not in the least mean that these wishes are to be pushed contemptuously on one side or their value for human life under-estimated. We are ready to trace out the fulfilments of them which they have created for themselves in the products of art and in the systems of religion and philosophy; but we cannot nevertheless overlook the fact that it would be illegitimate and highly inexpedient to allow these demands to be transferred to the sphere of knowledge. For this would be to lay open the paths which lead to psychosis, whether to individual or group psychosis, and would withdraw valuable amounts of energy from endeavours which are directed towards reality in order, so far as possible, to find satisfaction in it for wishes and needs.

From the standpoint of science one cannot avoid exercising one's critical faculty here and proceeding with rejections and dismissals. It is not permissible to declare that science is one field of human mental activity and that religion and philosophy are others, at least its equal in value, and that science has no business to interfere with the other two: that they all have an equal claim to be true and that everyone is at liberty to choose from which he will draw his convictions and in which he will place his belief. A view of this kind is regarded as particularly superior, tolerant, broad-minded and free from illiberal prejudices. Unfortunately it is not tenable and shares all the pernicious features of an entirely unscientific *Weltanschauung* and is equivalent to one in practice. It is simply a fact that the truth cannot be tolerant, that it admits of no compromises or limitations, that research regards every sphere of human activity as belonging to it and that it must be relentlessly critical if any other power tries to take over any part of it.

Of the three powers which may dispute the basic position of science, religion alone is to be taken seriously as an enemy. Art is almost always harmless and beneficent; it does not seek to be anything but an illusion. Except for a few people who are spoken of as being "possessed" by art, it makes no attempt at invading the realm of reality. Philosophy is not opposed to science, it behaves like a science and works in part by the same methods; it departs from it, however, by clinging to the illusion of being able to present a picture of the universe which is without gaps and is coherent, though one which is bound to collapse with every fresh advance in our knowledge. It goes astray in its method by overestimating the epistemological value of our logical operations and by accepting other sources of knowledge such as intuition. And it often seems that the poet's derisive comment is not unjustified when he says of the philosopher:

> Mit seinen Nachtmützen und Schlafrockfetzen
> Stopft er die Lücken des Weltenbaus.[1]

But philosophy has no direct influence on the great mass of mankind; it is of interest to only a small number even of the top layer of intellectuals and is scarcely intelligible to anyone else. On the other hand, religion is an immense power which has the strongest emotions of human beings at its service. It is well known that at an earlier date it comprised everything that played an intellectual part in men's lives, that it took the place of science when there was scarcely yet such a thing as science, and that it constructed a *Weltanschauung,* consistent and self-contained to an unparalleled degree, which, although it has been profoundly shaken, persists to this day.

---

[1] Heine ["Die Heimkehr", LVIII. Literally: "With his nightcaps and the tatters of his dressing-gown he patched up the gaps in the structure of the universe."]

If we are to give an account of the grandiose nature of religion, we must bear in mind what it undertakes to do for human beings. It gives them information about the origin and coming into existence of the universe, it assures them of its protection and of ultimate happiness in the ups and downs of life and it directs their thoughts and actions by precepts which it lays down with its whole authority. Thus it fulfils three functions. With the first of them it satisfies the human thirst for knowledge; it does the same thing that science attempts to do with *its* means, and at that point enters into rivalry with it. It is to its second function that it no doubt owes the greatest part of its influence. Science can be no match for it when it soothes the fear that men feel of the dangers and vicissitudes of life, when it assures them of a happy ending and offers them comfort in unhappiness. It is true that science can teach us how to avoid certain dangers and that there are some sufferings which it can successfully combat; it would be most unjust to deny that it is a powerful helper to men; but there are many situations in which it must leave a man to his suffering and can only advise him to submit to it. In its third function, in which it issues precepts and lays down prohibitions and restrictions, religion is furthest away from science. For science is content to investigate and to establish facts, though it is true that from its applications rules and advice are derived on the conduct of life. In some circumstances these are the same as those offered by religion, but, when this is so, the reasons for them are different.

The convergence between these three aspects of religion is not entirely clear. What has an explanation of the origin of the universe to do with the inculcation of certain particular ethical precepts? The assurances of protection and happiness are more intimately linked with the ethical requirements. They are the reward for fulfilling these commands; only those who obey them may count upon these benefits, punishment awaits the disobedient. Incidentally, something similar is true of science. Those who disregard its lessons, so it tells us, expose themselves to injury.

The remarkable combination in religion of instruction, consolation and requirements can only be understood if it is subjected to a genetic analysis. This may be approached from the most striking point of the aggregate, from its instruction on the origin of the universe; for why, we may ask, should a cosmogony be a regular component of religious systems? The doctrine is, then, that the universe was created by a being resembling a man, but magnified in every respect, in power, wisdom, and the strength of his passions—an idealized super-man. Animals as creators of the universe point to the influence of totemism, upon which we shall have a few words at least to say presently. It is an interesting fact that this creator is always only a single being, even when there are believed to be many gods. It is interesting, too, that the creator is usually a man, though there is far from being a lack of indications of female deities; and some mythologies actually make the creation begin with a male god getting rid of a female deity, who is degraded into being a monster. Here the most interesting problems of detail open out; but we must hurry on. Our further path is made easy to recognize, for this god-creator is undisguisedly called "father". Psycho-analysis infers that he really is the father, with all the magnificence in which he once appeared to the small child. A religious man pictures the creation of the universe just as he pictures his own origin.

This being so, it is easy to explain how it is that consoling assurances and strict ethical demands are combined with a cosmogony. For the same person to whom the child owed his existence, the father (or more correctly, no doubt, the parental agency compounded of the father and mother), also protected and watched over him in his feeble and helpless state, exposed as he was to all the dangers lying in wait in the external world; under his father's protection he felt safe. When a human being has himself grown up, he knows, to be sure, that he is in possession of greater strength, but his insight into the perils of life has also grown greater, and he rightly concludes that fundamentally he still remains just as helpless and unprotected as he was in his childhood, that faced by the world he is still a child. Even now, therefore, he cannot do without the protection which he enjoyed as a child. But he has long since recognized, too, that his father is a being of narrowly restricted power, and not equipped with every excellence. He therefore harks back to the mnemic image of the father whom in his childhood he so greatly overvalued. He exalts the image into a deity and makes it into something contemporary and real. The effective strength of this mnemic image and the persistence of his need for protection jointly sustain his belief in God.

The third main item in the religious programme, the ethical demand, also fits into this childhood situation with ease. I may remind you of Kant's famous pronouncement in which he names, in a single breath, the starry heavens and the moral law within us. However strange this juxtaposition may sound—for what have the heavenly bodies to do with the question of whether one human creature loves another or kills him?—it nevertheless touches on a great psychological truth. The same father (or parental agency) which gave the child life and guarded him against its perils, taught him as well what he might do and what he must leave undone, instructed him that he must adapt himself to certain restrictions on his instinctual wishes, and made him understand what regard he was expected to have for his parents and brothers and sisters, if he wanted to become a tolerated and welcome member of the family circle and later on of larger associations. The child is brought up to a knowledge of his social duties by a system of loving rewards and punishments, he is taught that his security in life depends on his parents (and afterwards other people) loving him and on their being able to believe that he loves them. All these relations are afterwards introduced by men unaltered into their religion. Their parents' prohibitions and demands persist within them as a moral conscience. With the help of this same system of rewards and punishments, God rules the world of men. The amount of protection and happy satisfaction assigned to an individual depends on his fulfilment of the ethical demands; his love of God and his consciousness of being loved by God are the foundations of the security with which he is armed against the dangers of the external world and of his human environment. Finally, in prayer he has assured himself a direct influence on the divine will and with it a share in the divine omnipotence.

I feel sure that while you have been listening to me you have been bothered by a number of questions which you would be glad to hear answered. I cannot undertake to do so here and now, but I feel confident that none of these detailed enquiries would upset our thesis that the religious *Weltanschauung* is determined by the situation of our childhood. That being so, it is all the more remarkable that, in spite of its infantile nature, it nevertheless had a precursor. There is no doubt that there was a time without religion, without gods. This is known as the stage of animism. At that time, too, the world was peopled with spiritual beings resembling men—we call them demons. All the objects in the external world were their habitation, or perhaps were identical with them; but there was no superior power which had created them all and afterwards ruled them and to which one could turn for protection and help. The demons of animism were for the most part hostile in their attitude to human beings, but it appears that human beings had more self-confidence then than later on. They were certainly in a constant state of the most acute fear of these evil spirits; but they defended themselves against them by certain actions to which they ascribed the power to drive them away. Nor apart from this did they regard themselves as defenceless. If they desired something from Nature—if they wished for rain, for instance—they did not direct a prayer to the weather-god, but they performed a magical act which they expected to influence Nature directly: they themselves did something which resembled rain. In their struggle against the powers of the world around them their first weapon was *magic,* the earliest fore-runner of the technology of to-day. Their reliance on magic was, as we suppose, derived from their overvaluation of their own intellectual operations, from their belief in the omnipotence of thoughts, which, incidentally, we come upon again in our obsessional neurotic patients. We may suppose that human beings at that period were particularly proud of their acquisitions in the way of language, which must have been accompanied by a great facilitation of thinking. They attributed magical power to words. This feature was later taken over by religion. "And God said 'Let there be light!' and there was light."

Moreover the fact of their magical actions shows that animistic men did not simply rely on the power of their wishes. They expected results, rather, from the performance of an action which would induce Nature to imitate it. If they wanted rain, they themselves poured out water; if they wanted to encourage the earth to be fruitful, they demonstrated a dramatic performance of sexual intercourse to it in the fields.

You know how hard it is for anything to die away when once it has achieved psychical expression. So you will not be surprised to hear that many of the utterances of animism have persisted to this day, for the most part as what we call superstition, alongside of and behind religion. But more than this, you will scarcely be able to reject a judgement that the philosophy of today has retained some essential features of the animistic mode of thought—the overvaluation of the magic of words and the belief that the real events in the world take the course which our thinking seeks to impose on them. It would seem, it is true, to be an animism without magical actions. On the other hand, we may suppose that even in those days there were ethics of some sort, precepts upon the mutual relations of men; but nothing suggests that they had any intimate connection with animistic beliefs. They were probably the direct expression of men's relative powers and of their practical needs.

It would be well worth knowing what brought about the transition from animism to religion, but you may imagine the obscurity which to-day still veils these primaeval ages of the evolution of the human spirit. It appears to be a fact that the first form assumed by religion was the remarkable phenomenon of totemism, the worship of animals, in whose train the first ethical commandments, the taboos, made their appearance. In a volume called *Totem and Taboo* [1912–13], I once elaborated a notion which traced this transformation back to a revolution in the circumstances of the human family. The main achievement of religion as compared with animism lies in the psychical binding of the fear of demons. Nevertheless a vestige of this primaeval age, the Evil Spirit, has kept a place in the religious system.

This being the prehistory of the religious *Weltanschauung,* let us turn now to what has happened since then and to what is still going on before our eyes. The scientific spirit, strengthened by the observation of natural processes, has begun, in the course of time, to treat religion as a human affair and to submit it to a critical examination. Religion was not able to stand up to this. What first gave rise to suspicion and scepticism were its tales of miracles, for they contradicted everything that had been taught by sober observation and betrayed too clearly the influence of the activity of the human imagination. After this its doctrines explaining the origin of the universe met with rejection, for they gave evidence of an ignorance which bore the stamp of ancient times and to which, thanks to their increased familiarity with the laws of nature, people knew they were superior. The idea that the universe came into existence through acts of copulation or creation analogous to the origin of individual people had ceased to be the most obvious and self-evident hypothesis since the distinction between animate creatures with a mind and an inanimate Nature had impressed itself on human thought—a distinction which made it impossible to retain belief in the original animism. Nor must we overlook the influence of the comparative study of different religious systems and the impression of their mutual exclusiveness and intolerance.

Strengthened by these preliminary exercises, the scientific spirit gained enough courage at last to venture on an examination of the most important and emotionally valuable elements of the religious *Weltanschauung.* People may always have seen, though it was long before they dared to say so openly, that the pronouncements of religion promising men protection and happiness if they would only fulfil certain ethical requirements had also shown themselves unworthy of belief. It seems not to be the case that there is a Power in the universe which watches over the well-being of individuals with parental care and brings all their affairs to a happy ending. On the contrary, the destinies of mankind can be brought into harmony neither with the hypothesis of a Universal Benevolence nor with the partly contradictory one of a Universal Justice. Earthquakes, tidal waves, conflagrations, make no distinction between the virtuous and pious and the scoundrel or unbeliever. Even where what is in question is not inanimate Nature but where an individual's fate depends on his relations to other people, it is by no means the rule that virtue is rewarded and that evil finds its punishment. Often enough the violent, cunning or ruthless man seizes the envied good things of the world and the pious man goes away empty. Obscure, unfeeling and unloving powers determine men's fate; the system of rewards and punishments which religion ascribes to the government of the universe seems not to exist. Here once again is a reason for dropping a portion of the animistic theory which had been rescued from animism by religion.

The last contribution to the criticism of the religious *Weltanschauung* was effected by psycho-analysis, by showing how religion originated from the helplessness of children and by tracing its contents to the survival into maturity of the wishes and needs of childhood. This did not precisely mean a contradiction of religion, but it was nevertheless a necessary rounding-off of our knowledge about it, and in one respect at least it was a contradiction, for religion itself lays claim to a divine origin. And, to be sure, it is not wrong in this, provided that our interpretation of God is accepted.

In summary, therefore, the judgement of science on the religious *Weltanschauung* is this. While the different religions wrangle with one another as to which of them is in possession of the truth, our view is that the question of the truth of religious beliefs may be left altogether on one side. Religion is an attempt to master the sensory world in which we are situated by means of the wishful world which we have developed within us as a result of biological and psychological necessities. But religion cannot achieve this. Its doctrines bear the imprint of the times in which they arose, the ignorant times of the childhood of humanity. Its consolations deserve no trust. Experience teaches us that the world is no nursery. The ethical demands on which religion seeks to lay stress need, rather, to be given another basis; for they are indispensable to human society and it is dangerous to link obedience to them with religious faith. If we attempt to assign the place of religion in the evolution of mankind, it appears not as a permanent acquisition but as a counterpart to the neurosis which individual civilized men have to go through in their passage from childhood to maturity.

You are of course free to criticize this description of mine; I will even go half way to meet you on this. What I told you about the gradual crumbling away of the religious *Weltanschauung* was certainly incomplete in its abbreviated form. The order of the different processes was not given quite correctly; the co-operation of various forces in the awakening of the scientific spirit was not followed out. I also left out of account the alterations which took place in the religious *Weltanschauung* itself during the period of its undisputed sway and afterwards under the influence of growing criticism. Finally, I restricted my remarks, strictly speaking, to one single form taken by religion, that of the Western peoples. I constructed an anatomical model, so to speak, for the purpose of a hurried demonstration which was to be as impressive as possible. Let us leave on one side the question of whether my knowledge would in any case have been sufficient to do the thing better and more completely. I am aware that you can find everything I said to you said better elsewhere. Nothing in it is new. But let me express a conviction that the most careful working-over of the material of the problems of religion would not shake our conclusions.

The struggle of the scientific spirit against the religious *Weltanschauung* is, as you know, not at an end: it is still going on to-day under our eyes. Though as a rule psycho-analysis makes little use of the weapon of controversy, I will not hold back from looking into this dispute. In doing so I may perhaps throw some further light on our attitude to *Weltanschauungen*. You will see how easily some of the arguments brought forward by the supporters of religion can be answered, though it is true that others may evade refutation.

The first objection we meet with is to the effect that it is an impertinence on the part of science to make religion a subject for its investigations, for religion is something sublime, superior to any operation of the human intellect, something which may not be approached with hair-splitting criticisms. In other words, science is not qualified to judge religion: it is quite serviceable and estimable otherwise, so long as it keeps to its own sphere. But religion is not its sphere, and it has no business there. If we do not let ourselves be put off by this brusque repulse and enquire further what is the basis of this claim to a position exceptional among all human concerns, the reply we receive (if we are thought worthy of any reply) is that religion cannot be measured by human measurements, for it is of divine origin and was given us as a revelation by a Spirit which the human spirit cannot comprehend. One would have thought that there was nothing easier than the refutation of this argument: it is a clear case of *petitio principii,* of begging the question—I know of no good German equivalent expression. The actual question raised is whether there *is* a divine spirit and a revelation by it; and the matter is certainly not decided by saying that this question cannot be asked, since the deity may not be put in question. The position here is what it occasionally is during the work of analysis. If a usually sensible patient rejects some particular suggestion on specially foolish grounds, this logical weakness is evidence of the existence of a specially strong motive for the denial—a motive which can only be of an affective nature, an emotional tie.

We may also be given another answer, in which a motive of this kind is openly admitted: religion may not be critically examined because it is the highest, most precious, and most sublime thing that the human spirit has produced, because it gives expression to the deepest feelings and alone makes the world tolerable and life worthy of men. We need not reply by disputing this estimate of religion but by drawing attention to another matter. What we do is to emphasize the fact that what is in question is not in the least an invasion of the field of religion by the scientific spirit, but on the contrary an invasion by religion of the sphere of scientific thought. Whatever may be the value and importance of religion, it has no right in any way to restrict thought—no right, therefore, to exclude itself from having thought applied to it.

Scientific thinking does not differ in its nature from the normal activity of thought, which all of us, believers and unbelievers, employ in looking after our affairs in ordinary life. It has only developed certain features: it takes an interest in things even if they have no immediate, tangible use; it is concerned carefully to avoid individual factors and affective influences; it examines more strictly the trustworthiness of the sense-perceptions on which it bases its conclusions; it provides itself with new perceptions which cannot be obtained by everyday means and it isolates the determinants of these new experiences in experiments which are deliberately varied. Its endeavour is to arrive at correspondence with reality—that is to say, with what exists outside us and independently of us and, as experience has taught us, is decisive for the fulfilment or disappointment of our wishes. This correspondence with the real external world we call "truth." It remains the aim of scientific work even if we leave the practical value of that work out of account. When, therefore, religion asserts that it can take the place of science, that, because it is beneficent and elevating, it must also be true, that is in fact an invasion which must be repulsed in the most general interest. It is asking a great deal of a person who has learnt to conduct his ordinary affairs in accordance with the rules of experience and with a regard to reality, to suggest that he shall hand over the care of what are precisely his most intimate interests to an agency which claims as its privilege freedom from the precepts of rational thinking. And as regards the protection which religion promises its believers, I think none of us would be so much as prepared to enter a motor-car if its driver announced that he drove, unperturbed by traffic regulations, in accordance with the impulses of his soaring imagination.

The prohibition against thought issued by religion to assist in its self-preservation is also far from being free from danger either for the individual or for human society. Analytic experience has taught us that a prohibition like this, even if it is originally limited to a particular field, tends to widen out and thereafter to become the cause of severe inhibitions in the subject's conduct of life. This result may be observed, too, in the female sex, following from their being forbidden to have anything to do with their sexuality even in thought. Biography is able to point to the damage done by the religious inhibition of thought in the life stories of nearly all eminent individuals in the past. On the other hand intellect—or let us call it by the name that is familiar to us, reason—is among the powers which we may most expect to exercise a unifying influence on men—on men who are held together with such difficulty and whom it is therefore scarcely possible to rule. It may be imagined how impossible human society would be, merely if everyone had his own multiplication table and his own private units of length and weight. Our best hope for the future is that intellect—the scientific spirit, reason—may in process of time establish a dictatorship in the mental life of man. The nature of reason is a guarantee that afterwards it will not fail to give man's emotional impulses and what is determined by them the position they deserve. But the common compulsion exercised by such a dominance of reason will prove to be the strongest uniting bond among men and lead the way to further unions. Whatever, like religion's prohibition against thought, opposes such a development, is a danger for the future of mankind.

It may then be asked why religion does not put an end to this dispute which is so hopeless for it by frankly declaring: "It is a fact that I cannot give you what is commonly called 'truth'; if you want that, you must keep to science. But what I have to offer you is something incomparably more beautiful, more consoling and more uplifting than anything you could get from science. And because of that, I say to you that it is true in another, higher sense." It is easy to find the answer to this. Religion cannot make this admission because it would involve its forfeiting all its influence on the mass of mankind. The ordinary man only knows one kind of truth, in the ordinary sense of the word. He cannot imagine what a higher or a highest truth may be. Truth seems to him no more capable of comparative degrees than death; and he cannot join in the leap from the beautiful to the true. Perhaps you will think as I do that he is right in this.

4

PSYCHOTHERAPY AND RELIGION

Carl Gustav Jung

*While Freud considered religion to be neurotic, Jung held that it can
frequently be an integrating and health-giving factor in the life of the
psyche. In the following excerpt, he criticizes the Freudian view, and
advances his own positive estimate of religion. It should be noted that
although Jung is just as naturalistic in his approach to religion as
Freud, Jung has broken away from the reductive and mechanistic
naturalism of the nineteenth century. His conception of nature (like
that of Whitehead) allows for spirit and personal being as distinct
forms of being, irreducible to merely physical constituents and incomprehensible on purely mechanical models.*

IT IS WELL known that Freudian psychoanalysis is limited to the
task of making conscious the shadow-side and the evil within us.
It simply brings into action the civil war that was latent, and lets
it go at that. The patient must deal with it as best he can. Freud
has unfortunately overlooked the fact that man has never yet been
able singlehanded to hold his own against the powers of darkness
—that is, of the unconscious. Man has always stood in need of
the spiritual help which each individual's own religion held out
to him. The opening up of the unconscious always means the
outbreak of intense spiritual suffering; it is as when a flourishing
civilization is abandoned to invading hordes of barbarians, or

Reprinted with permission from *Modern Man in Search of a Soul*, translated by W. S. Dell and Cary F. Baynes (New York: Harcourt, Brace &
World, Inc., 1933), pp. 277–82.

when fertile fields are exposed by the bursting of a dam to a raging torrent. The World War was such an irruption which showed, as nothing else could, how thin are the walls which separate a well-ordered world from lurking chaos. But it is the same with every single human being and his reasonably ordered world. His reason has done violence to natural forces which seek their revenge and only await the moment when the partition falls to overwhelm the conscious life with destruction. Man has been aware of this danger since the earliest times, even in the most primitive stages of culture. It was to arm himself against this threat and to heal the damage done, that he developed religious and magical practices. This is why the medicine-man is also the priest; he is the saviour of the body as well as of the soul, and religions are systems of healing for psychic illness. This is especially true of the two greatest religions of man, Christianity and Buddhism. Man is never helped in his suffering by what he thinks for himself, but only by revelations of a wisdom greater than his own. It is this which lifts him out of his distress.

Today this eruption of destructive forces has already taken place, and man suffers from it in spirit. That is why patients force the psychotherapist into the rôle of a priest, and expect and demand of him that he shall free them from their distress. That is why we psychotherapists must occupy ourselves with problems which, strictly speaking, belong to the theologian. But we cannot leave these questions for theology to answer; the urgent, psychic needs of suffering people confront us with them day after day. Since, as a rule, every concept and viewpoint handed down from the past fails us, we must first tread with the patient the path of his illness—the path of his mistake that sharpens his conflicts and increases his loneliness till it grows unbearable—hoping that from the psychic depths which cast up the powers of destruction the rescuing forces will come also.

When first I took this direction I did not know where it would lead. I did not know what lay hid in the depths of the psyche—that region which I have since called the "collective unconscious," and whose contents I designate as "archetypes." Since time immemorial, eruptions of the unconscious have taken place, and ever and again they have repeated themselves. Consciousness did not exist from the beginning, and in every child it has to be built up anew in the first years of life. Consciousness is very weak in this formative period, and history shows us that the same is true of mankind—the unconscious easily seizes power. These struggles have left their marks. To put it in scientific terms: instinctive defence-mechanisms have been developed which automatically intervene when the danger is greatest, and their coming into action is represented in fantasy by helpful images which are ineradicably fixed in the human psyche. These mechanisms come into play whenever the need is great. Science can only establish the existence of these psychic factors and attempt a rational explanation by offering an hypothesis as to their sources. This, however, only thrusts the problem a stage back and in no way answers the riddle. We thus come to those ultimate questions: Whence does consciousness come? What is the psyche? And at this point all science ends.

It is as though, at the culmination of the illness, the destructive powers were converted into healing forces. This is brought about by the fact that the archetypes come to independent life and serve as spiritual guides for the personality, thus supplanting the inadequate ego with its futile willing and striving. As the religious-minded person would say: guidance has come from God. With most of my patients I have to avoid this formulation, for it reminds them too much of what they have to reject. I must express myself in more modest terms, and say that the psyche has awakened to spontaneous life. And indeed this formula more closely fits the observable facts. The transformation takes place at that moment when in dreams or fantasies themes appear whose source in consciousness cannot be shown. To the patient it is nothing less than a revelation when, from the hidden depths of the psyche, something arises to confront him—something strange that is not the "I" and is therefore beyond the reach of personal caprice. He has gained access to the sources of psychic life, and this marks the beginning of the cure.

This process, if it is to be made clear, should undoubtedly be discussed with the help of suitable examples. But it is almost impossible to find one or more convincing illustrations, for it is usually a most subtle and complicated matter. That which is so effective is often simply the deep impression made on the patient by the independent way in which his dreams treat of his difficulties. Or it may be that his fantasy points to something for which his conscious mind was quite unprepared. Most often it is contents of an archetypal nature, connected in a certain way, that exert a strong influence of their own whether or not they are understood by the conscious mind. This spontaneous activity of the psyche often becomes so intense that visionary pictures are seen or inner voices heard. These are manifestations of the spirit directly experienced today as they have been from time immemorial.

Such experiences reward the sufferer for the pains of the labyrinthine way. From this point forward a light shines through his confusion; he can reconcile himself with the warfare within and so come to bridge the morbid split in his nature upon a higher level.

The fundamental problems of modern psychotherapy are so important and far-reaching that their discussion in an essay precludes any presentation of details, however desirable this might be for clarity's sake. My main purpose was to set forth the attitude of the psychotherapist in his work. A proper understanding of this is after all more rewarding than to cull a few precepts and pointers as to methods of treatment, for these are in any case not effective unless they are applied with the right understanding. The attitude of the psychotherapist is infinitely more important than the theories and methods of psychotherapy, and that is why I have been concerned to make this attitude known. I believe that I have given a trustworthy account. As for the questions in what way and how far the clergyman can join the psychotherapist in his efforts and endeavors, I can only impart information which will allow others to decide. I also believe that the picture I have drawn of the spiritual outlook of modern man corresponds to the actual state of affairs—though, of course, I make no claim to infallibility. In any case, what I have had to say about the cure of the neuroses, and the problems involved, is the unvarnished truth. We doctors would naturally welcome the sympathetic understanding of the clergy in our endeavors to heal psychic suffering, but we are also fully aware of the fundamental difficulties which stand in the way of a full cooperation. My own position is on the extreme left wing of the congress of Protestant opinion, yet I would be the first to warn people against generalizing from their own experience in an injudicious way. As a Swiss, I am an inveterate democrat, yet I recognize that nature is aristocratic and, what is even more, eso- teric. *Quod licet Jovi, non licet bovi* is an unpleasant but an eternal truth. Who are forgiven their many sins? Those who have loved much. But as to those who love little, their few sins are held against them. I am firmly convinced that a vast number of people belong to the fold of the Catholic Church and nowhere else, be- cause they are most suitably housed there. I am as much persuaded of this as of the fact, which I have myself observed, that a primi- tive religion is better suited to primitive people than Christianity, which is so incomprehensible to them and so foreign to their blood that they can only ape it in a disgusting way. I believe, too, that there must be protestants against the Catholic Church, and also protestants against Protestantism—for the manifestations of the spirit are truly wondrous, and as varied as Creation itself.

The living spirit grows and even outgrows its earlier forms of expression; it freely chooses the men in whom it lives and who proclaim it. This living spirit is eternally renewed and pursues its goal in manifold and inconceivable ways throughout the history of mankind. Measured against it, the names and forms which men have given it mean little enough; they are only the changing leaves and blossoms on the stem of the eternal tree.

5

DYNAMIC RELIGION

Henri Louis Bergson

The philosophy of Henri Bergson, though naturalistic in its approach and appealing to science for its evidences, stands in sharp opposition to the mechanistic and deterministic naturalism of the nineteenth century. The processes of life and consciousness have a dynamic flow and spontaneity that is broken up and destroyed when we try to conceptualize them in mechanical terms. The mechanistic view is compared by Bergson to the cinematograph, which substitutes for the moving reality a series of static pictures. Thus mechanism and its conceptuality prevent us from perceiving the truly dynamic, creative impetus (élan vital) that constitutes the inner reality of the universe. Religion too can become static and mechanical, but a dynamic and creative religion affords a mystical participation in the cosmic process.

LET US CAST a glance backward at Life, this life which we had previously followed in its development up to the point where religion was destined to emerge from it. A great current of creative energy is precipitated into matter, to wrest from it what it can. At most points, remember, it came to a stop; these stops are equivalent, in our eyes, to the phenomena of so many living species, that is to say, of organisms in which our perception, being essentially analytical and synthetic, distinguishes a multitude of elements combining to fulfill a multitude of functions; yet the work

Reprinted with permission from *The Two Sources of Morality and Religion,* translated by R. Ashley Audra and Cloudsley Brereton (New York: Holt, Rinehart and Winston, Inc., 1935), pp. 178–84.

of organization was but the step itself, a simple act, like the making of a footprint, which instantly causes a myriad grains of sand to cohere and form a pattern. Along one of these lines, the one along which it succeeded in going furthest, we might have thought that this vital energy, carrying the best of itself with it, would go straight on; but it swerved inward, and the whole circle reformed: certain creatures emerged whose activity ran indefinitely in the same circle, whose organs were ready-made instruments and left no room for the ceaselessly renewed invention of tools, whose consciousness lapsed into the somnambulism of instinct instead of bracing itself and revitalizing itself into reflective thought. Such is the condition of the individual in those insect societies where organization is highly perfected, but the effect of it is sheer automatism.

The creative effort progressed successfully only along that line of evolution which ended in man. In its passage through matter, consciousness assumed in that case, as it were from a mould, the shape of tool-making intelligence. And invention, which carries reflection with it, was at liberty to develop.

But intelligence was not without its dangers. Up to that point, all living creatures had drunk greedily of the cup of life. They lapped up with relish the honey which nature had smeared on the rim; they were prepared to gulp down the rest blindly. Not so intelligence, which peered into the bottom of the cup. For the intelligent being was not living in the present alone; there can be no reflection without foreknowledge, no foreknowledge without apprehension, no apprehension without a momentary slackening of the attachment to life. Above all, there is no humanity without society, and society demands of the individual an abnegation which the insect, in its automatism, carries to the point of an utter obliviousness of self. Reflection cannot be relied upon to keep up this selflessness. Intelligence, except it be that of a subtle utilitarian philosopher, would more likely counsel egoism. Thus, from two directions it called for a counterpoise. Or rather it was already provided with one, for nature, we repeat, does not make her creatures piecemeal; what is multiple in its manifestation may well be simple in its genesis. A new species coming on to the scene brings with it, in the indivisibility of the act creating it, all the elements that impart life to it. The very check of the creative impetus which has expressed itself in the creation of our species has provided, along with intelligence, within human intelligence, the myth-making function that contrives the pattern of religions. That then is the office, that is the significance of the religion we have called static or natural. Religion is that element which, in beings endowed with reason, is called upon to make good any deficiency of attachment to life.

It is true that the possibility of another solution at once occurs to the mind. Static religion, such as we find it when it stands alone, attaches man to life, and consequently the individual to society, by telling him tales on a par with those with which we lull children to sleep. Of course they are not like other stories. Being produced by the myth-making function in response to an actual need and not for mere pleasure, they counterfeit reality as actually perceived, to the point of making us act accordingly: other creations of the imagination have this same tendency, but they do not demand our compliance; they can remain just ideas; whereas the former are ideo-motory. They are none the less myths, which critical minds, as we have seen, often accept in fact, but which they should, by rights, reject. The active, moving principle, whose mere stopping at an extreme point expresses itself in mankind, doubtless requires of all created species that they cling to life. But, as we have previously shown, if this principle produces all species in their entirety, as a tree thrusts out on every side branches which end in buds, it is the depositing, in matter, of a freely creative energy, it is man, or some other being of like significance—we do not say of like form—which is the explanation of the entire process of evolution. The whole might have been vastly superior to what it is, and this is probably what happens in worlds where the current rushes through matter less refractory than ours: just as the current might never have found a free outlet—even to this inadequate extent—in which case the quality and quantity of creative energy represented by the human species would never have been released at all on our planet. But whichever way we look at it, life is a thing at least as desirable, even more desirable, to man than to the other species, since the latter receive it as the effect, produced in passing, by the creative energy, whereas in man life is that successful effort itself, however precarious and incomplete this success may be. This being so, why should man not recover the confidence he lacks, or which has perhaps been undermined by reflection, by turning back for fresh impetus, in the direction whence that impetus came? Not through intelligence, at least not through intelligence alone, could he do so: intelligence would be more likely to proceed in the opposite direction; it was provided for a definite object, and when it attempts speculation on a higher plane, it enables us, at the most, to conceive possibilities, it does not attain any reality. But we know that all around intelligence there lingers still a fringe of intuition, vague and evanescent. Can we not fasten upon it, intensify it, and above all, consummate it in action, for it has become pure contemplation only through a weakening in its principle, and, if we may put it so, by an abstraction practiced on its own substance?

A soul strong enough, noble enough to make this effort would not stop to ask whether the principle with which it is now in touch is the transcendent cause of all things or merely its earthly delegate. It would be content to feel itself pervaded, though retaining its own personality, by a being immeasurably mightier than itself, just as an iron is pervaded by the fire which makes it glow. Its attachment to life would henceforth be its inseparability from this principle, joy in joy, love of that which is all love. In addition it would give itself to society, but to a society comprising all humanity, loved in the love of the principle underlying it. The confidence which static religion brought to man would thus be transfigured: no more thought for the morrow, no more anxious heart-searching; materially the object would no longer be worth while, and morally would take on too high a significance. Now detachment from each particular thing would become attachment to life in general. But should we, in such a case, still speak of religion? Or were we right to have used the word before for all the preceding argument? Are not the two things so different as to exclude each other, and to make it impossible to call them by the same name?

Yet there are many reasons for using the word religion in both cases. In the first place mysticism—for that is what we have in mind—may, it is true, lift the soul to another plane: it none the less insures for the soul, to a pre-eminent degree, the security and the serenity which it is the function of static religion to provide. But we must above all bear in mind that pure mysticism is a rare essence, that it is generally found in a diluted form, that even then it still gives to the substance with which it mingles its color and fragrance, and that it must be taken together with the substance, to be regarded as practically inseparable from it, if it is to be observed in its active state—since it was in this state that it finally imposed its sway upon the world. Looking at it from this angle, we should perceive a series of transitions, and, as it were, differences of degree, whereas really there is a radical difference of nature. Let us go back briefly over each of these points.

In defining mysticism by its relation to the vital impetus, we have implicitly admitted that true mysticism is rare. We shall deal presently with its significance and its value. Let us confine ourselves for the moment to noting that it lies, according to the above, at a point which the spiritual current, in its passage through matter, probably desired to reach but could not. For it makes light of obstacles with which nature has had to come to terms, and, on the other hand, we can only understand the evolution of life, setting aside any by-paths it has been compelled to follow, if we view it as seeking for something beyond its reach, something to which the great mystic attains. If all men, if any large number of men, could have soared as high as this privileged man, nature would not have stopped at the human species, for such a one is in fact more than a man. The same can be said of other forms of genius: they are one and all rare. It is not by chance, then, it is by reason of its very essence that true mysticism is exceptional.

But when it does call, there is in the innermost being of most men the whisper of an echo. Mysticism reveals, or rather would reveal to us, if we actually willed it, a marvellous prospect: we do not, and in most cases we could not, will it; we should collapse under the strain. Yet the spell has worked; and just as when an artist of genius has produced a work which is beyond us, the spirit of which we cannot grasp, but which makes us feel how commonplace were the things we used to admire, in the same way static religion, though it may still be there, is no longer what it was, above all it no longer dares to assert itself, when truly great mysticism comes on the scene. To static religion, mainly at any rate, humanity will still turn for the support of which it is in need; it will leave the myth-making function, remoulding it as best it can, to go on with its work; in a word, man's confidence in life will remain much the same as it was ordained by nature. But he will sincerely feign to have sought and indeed to some extent to have found that contact with the very principle of nature which expresses itself in quite a different attachment to life, in a transfigured confidence. Incapable of rising to these heights, he will go through the motions, assume the appropriate attitudes and in his speech reserve the foremost place for certain formulae which he can never see filled with their whole meaning, the whole operation being reminiscent of some ceremony where certain chairs, reserved for high dignitaries, are standing empty. Thus may arise a mixed religion, implying a new direction given to the old, the more or less marked aspiration of the ancient god, emanating from the myth-making function, to be merged into the God Who effectively reveals Himself, Who illuminates and warms privileged souls with His presence. Thus do we find interposed, as we were suggesting, transitions and differences, ostensibly of degree, between two things which are as a matter of fact radically different in nature and which, at first sight, we can hardly believe deserve the same name. The contrast is striking in many cases, as for instance when nations at war each declare that they have God on their side, the deity in question thus becoming the national god of paganism, whereas the God they imagine they are evoking is a God common to all mankind, the mere vision of Whom, could all men but attain it, would mean the immediate abolition of war. And yet we should not, on the strength of this contrast, disparage religions born of mysticism, which have generalized the use of its formulae and yet have been unable to pervade all humanity with the full measure of its spirit. It sometimes happens that wellnigh empty formulae, the veriest magical incantations, contrive to summon up here and there the spirit capable of imparting substance to them. An indifferent schoolmaster, mechanically teaching a science created by men of genius, may awaken in one of his pupils the vocation he himself has never possessed, and change him unconsciously into an emulator of those great men, who are invisible and present in the message he is handing on.

Yet there is a difference between the two cases, and if we take it into account, we shall notice, in the matter of religion, a gradual disappearance of the opposition between the static and the dynamic, on which we have just insisted in order to bring out the characteristics of the two religions. The great majority of men may very well know practically nothing about mathematics and yet admire the genius of a Descartes or a Newton. But those who have, from afar off, bowed their heads to the mystic word, because they heard a faint echo of it within themselves, will not remain indifferent to its message. If they already have their different faiths, from which they will not or cannot break away, they will persuade themselves that they are effecting a transformation of them, as indeed they are: the same elements will subsist, but they will be magnetized and by this very magnetizing process be diverted into another direction. A religious historian will have no difficulty in discovering in the material form of a vaguely mystic belief, which has spread far and wide among mankind, so many mythical and even magic elements. He will prove thereby that there exists a static religion, natural to man, and that human nature is unchanging. But, if he stops at that, he will have overlooked something, and perhaps the essential. At any rate he will, unwittingly perhaps, have bridged the gulf between the static and the dynamic, and justified the use of the same word in such widely different instances. He will indeed be still dealing with a religion, but with a new one.

6

MYSTICISM AND LOGIC

Bertrand Russell

*Earl Russell has for long been a champion of realism and of the ap-
plication of the methods of the natural sciences to the problems of
philosophy. The following excerpt gives a good account of his position, and is of special interest because of its criticism of the author
of the preceding selection, Henri Bergson. Basically, Russell's question is: Are there two ways of knowing, that of the empirical sciences
and that of mysticism, or is there only one? His essay is devoted to
showing that it is to empirical science that we must look for reliable
knowledge.*

FOUR QUESTIONS arise in considering the truth or falsehood of
mysticism, namely:

    I. Are there two ways of knowing, which may be called re-
spectively reason and intuition? And if so, is either to be preferred
to the other?

    II. Is all plurality and division illusory?

    III. Is time unreal?

    IV. What kind of reality belongs to good and evil?

    On all four of these questions, while fully developed mysticism
seems to me mistaken, I yet believe that, by sufficient restraint,
there is an element of wisdom to be learned from the mystical way
of feeling, which does not seem to be attainable in any other man-

Reprinted with permission from *Mysticism and Logic, and Other Essays*
(London: Longmans, Green & Co., 1918), pp. 11–32.

ner. If this is the truth, mysticism is to be commended as an attitude towards life, not as a creed about the world. The metaphysical creed, I shall maintain, is a mistaken outcome of the emotion, although this emotion, as coloring and informing all other thoughts and feelings, is the inspirer of whatever is best in Man. Even the cautious and patient investigation of truth by science, which seems the very antithesis of the mystic's swift certainty, may be fostered and nourished by that very spirit of reverence in which mysticism lives and moves.

I. REASON AND INTUITION

Of the reality or unreality of the mystic's world I know nothing. I have no wish to deny it, nor even to declare that the insight which reveals it is not a genuine insight. What I do wish to maintain—and it is here that the scientific attitude becomes imperative —is that insight, untested and unsupported, is an insufficient guarantee of truth, in spite of the fact that much of the most important truth is first suggested by its means. It is common to speak of an opposition between instinct and reason; in the eighteenth century, the opposition was drawn in favor of reason, but under the influence of Rousseau and the romantic movement instinct was given the preference, first by those who rebelled against artificial forms of government and thought, and then, as the purely rationalistic defence of traditional theology became increasingly difficult, by all who felt in science a menace to creeds which they associated with a spiritual outlook on life and the world. Bergson, under the name of "intuition," has raised instinct to the position of sole arbiter of metaphysical truth. But in fact the opposition of instinct and reason is mainly illusory. Instinct, intuition, or insight is what first leads to the beliefs which subsequent reason confirms or confutes; but the confirmation, where it is possible, consists, in the last analysis, of agreement with other beliefs no less instinctive. Reason is a harmonizing, controlling force rather than a creative one. Even in the most purely logical realm, it is insight that first arrives at what is new.

Where instinct and reason do sometimes conflict is in regard to single beliefs, held instinctively, and held with such determination that no degree of inconsistency with other beliefs leads to their abandonment. Instinct, like all human faculties, is liable to error. Those in whom reason is weak are often unwilling to admit this as regards themselves, though all admit it in regard to others. Where instinct is least liable to error is in practical matters as to which right judgment is a help to survival: friendship and hostility in others, for instance, are often felt with extraordinary discrimination through very careful disguises. But even in such matters a wrong impression may be given by reserve or flattery; and in matters less directly practical, such as philosophy deals with, very strong instinctive beliefs are sometimes wholly mistaken, as we may come to know through their perceived inconsistency with other equally strong beliefs. It is such considerations that necessitate the harmonizing mediation of reason, which tests our beliefs by their mutual compatibility, and examines, in doubtful cases, the possible sources of error on the one side and on the other. In this there is no opposition to instinct as a whole, but only to blind reliance upon some one interesting aspect of instinct to the exclusion of other more commonplace but not less trustworthy aspects. It is such one-sidedness, not instinct itself, that reason aims at correcting.

These more or less trite maxims may be illustrated by application to Bergson's advocacy of "intuition" as against "intellect." There are, he says, "two profoundly different ways of knowing a thing. The first implies that we move round the object: the second that we enter into it. The first depends on the point of view at which we are placed and on the symbols by which we express ourselves. The second neither depends on a point of view nor relies on any symbol. The first kind of knowledge may be said to stop at the *relative;* the second, in those cases where it is possible, to attain the *absolute.*"[1] The second of these, which is intuition, is, he says, "the kind of *intellectual sympathy* by which one places oneself within an object in order to coincide with what is unique in it

[1] *Introduction to Metaphysics,* p. 1.

and therefore inexpressible" (p. 6). In illustration, he mentions self-knowledge: "there is one reality, at least, which we all seize from within, by intuition and not by simple analysis. It is our own personality in its flowing through time—our self which endures" (p. 8). The rest of Bergson's philosophy consists in reporting, through the imperfect medium of words, the knowledge gained by intuition, and the consequent complete condemnation of all the pretended knowledge derived from science and common sense.

This procedure, since it takes sides in a conflict of instinctive beliefs, stands in need of justification by proving the greater trust-worthiness of the beliefs on one side than of those on the other. Bergson attempts this justification in two ways, first by explaining that intellect is a purely practical faculty to secure biological suc-cess, secondly by mentioning remarkable feats of instinct in animals and by pointing out characteristics of the world which, though intuition can apprehend them, are baffling to intellect as he inter-prets it.

Of Bergson's theory that intellect is a purely practical faculty, developed in the struggle for survival, and not a source of true beliefs, we may say, first, that it is only through intellect that we know of the struggle for survival and of the biological ancestry of man: if the intellect is misleading, the whole of this merely inferred history is presumably untrue. If, on the other hand, we agree with him in thinking that evolution took place as Darwin believed, then it is not only intellect, but all our faculties, that have been devel-oped under the stress of practical utility. Intuition is seen at its best where it is directly useful, for example in regard to other peo-ple's characters and dispositions. Bergson apparently holds that capacity for this kind of knowledge is less explicable by the strug-gle for existence than, for example, capacity for pure mathematics. Yet the savage deceived by false friendship is likely to pay for his mistake with his life; whereas even in the most civilized societies men are not put to death for mathematical incompetence. All the most striking of his instances of intuition in animals have a very direct survival value. The fact is, of course, that both intuition and intellect have been developed because they are useful, and that, speaking broadly, they are useful when they give truth and become harmful when they give falsehood. Intellect, in civilized man, like artistic capacity, has occasionally been developed beyond the point where it is useful to the individual; intuition, on the other hand, seems on the whole to diminish as civilization increases. It is greater, as a rule, in children than in adults, in the uneducated than in the educated. Probably in dogs it exceeds anything to be found in human beings. But those who see in these facts a recommendation of intuition ought to return to running wild in the woods, dyeing themselves with woad and living on hips and haws.

Let us next examine whether intuition possesses any such infallibility as Bergson claims for it. The best instance of it, according to him, is our acquaintance with ourselves; yet self-knowledge is proverbially rare and difficult. Most men, for example, have in their nature meannesses, vanities, and envies of which they are quite unconscious, though even their best friends can perceive them without any difficulty. It is true that intuition has a convincingness which is lacking to intellect: while it is present, it is almost impossible to doubt its truth. But if it should appear, on examination, to be at least as fallible as intellect, its greater subjective certainty becomes a demerit, making it only the more irresistibly deceptive. Apart from self-knowledge, one of the most notable examples of intuition is the knowledge people believe themselves to possess of those with whom they are in love: the wall between different personalities seems to become transparent, and people think they see into another soul as into their own. Yet deception in such cases is constantly practised with success; and even where there is no intentional deception, experience gradually proves, as a rule, that the supposed insight was illusory, and that the slower more groping methods of the intellect are in the long run more reliable.

Bergson maintains that intellect can only deal with things in so far as they resemble what has been experienced in the past, while intuition has the power of apprehending the uniqueness and novelty that always belong to each fresh moment. That there is something unique and new at every moment is certainly true; it is also true that this cannot be fully expressed by means of intellectual concepts. Only direct acquaintance can give knowledge of what is unique and new. But direct acquaintance of this kind is given fully in sensation, and does not require, so far as I can see, any special faculty of intuition for its apprehension. It is neither intellect nor intuition, but sensation, that supplies new data; but when the data are new in any remarkable manner, intellect is much more capable of dealing with them than intuition would be. The hen with a brood of ducklings no doubt has intuition which seems to place her inside them, and not merely to know them analytically; but when the ducklings take to the water, the whole apparent intuition is seen to be illusory, and the hen is left helpless on the shore. Intuition, in fact, is an aspect and development of instinct, and, like all instinct, is admirable in those customary surroundings which have moulded the habits of the animal in question, but totally incompetent as soon as the surroundings are changed in a way which demands some non-habitual mode of action.

The theoretical understanding of the world, which is the aim of philosophy, is not a matter of great practical importance to animals, or to savages, or even to most civilized men. It is hardly to be supposed, therefore, that the rapid, rough and ready methods of instinct or intuition will find in this field a favorable ground for their application. It is the older kinds of activity, which bring out our kinship with remote generations of animal and semi-human ancestors, that show intuition at its best. In such matters as self-preservation and love, intuition will act sometimes (though not always) with a swiftness and precision which are astonishing to the critical intellect. But philosophy is not one of the pursuits which illustrate our affinity with the past: it is a highly refined, highly civilized pursuit, demanding, for its success, a certain liberation from the life of instinct, and even, at times, a certain aloofness from all mundane hopes and fears. It is not in philosophy, therefore, that we can hope to see intuition at its best. On the contrary, since the true objects of philosophy, and the habit of thought demanded for their apprehension, are strange, unusual, and remote, it is here, more almost than anywhere else, that intellect proves superior to intuition, and that quick unanalyzed convictions are least deserving of uncritical acceptance.

In advocating the scientific restraint and balance, as against the self-assertion of a confident reliance upon intuition, we are only urging, in the sphere of knowledge, that largeness of contemplation, that impersonal disinterestedness, and that freedom from practical preoccupations which have been inculcated by all the great religions of the world. Thus our conclusion, however it may conflict with the explicit beliefs of many mystics, is, in essence, not contrary to the spirit which inspires those beliefs, but rather the outcome of this very spirit as applied in the realm of thought.

II. UNITY AND PLURALITY

One of the most convincing aspects of the mystic illumination is the apparent revelation of the oneness of all things, giving rise to pantheism in religion and to monism in philosophy. An elaborate logic, beginning with Parmenides, and culminating in Hegel and his followers, has been gradually developed, to prove that the universe is one indivisible Whole, and that what seem to be its parts, if considered as substantal and self-existing, are mere illusion. The conception of a Reality quite other than the world of appearance, a reality one, indivisible, and unchanging, was introduced into Western philosophy by Parmenides, not, nominally at least, for mystical or religious reasons, but on the basis of a logical argument as to the impossibility of not-being, and most subsequent metaphysical systems are the outcome of this fundamental idea.

The logic used in defense of mysticism seems to be faulty as logic, and open to technical criticisms, which I have explained elsewhere. I shall not here repeat these criticisms, since they are lengthy and difficult, but shall instead attempt an analysis of the state of mind from which mystical logic has arisen.

Belief in a reality quite different from what appears to the senses arises with irresistible force in certain moods, which are the source of most mysticism, and of most metaphysics. While such a mood is dominant, the need of logic is not felt, and accordingly the more thorough-going mystics do not employ logic, but appeal directly to the immediate deliverance of their insight. But such fully developed mysticism is rare in the West. When the intensity of emotional conviction subsides, a man who is in the habit of reasoning will search for logical grounds in favor of the belief which he finds in himself. But since the belief already exists, he will be very hospitable to any ground that suggests itself. The paradoxes apparently proved by his logic are really the paradoxes of mysticism, and are the goal which he feels his logic must reach if it is to be in accordance with insight. The resulting logic has rendered most philosophers incapable of giving any account of the world of science and daily life. If they had been anxious to give such an account, they would probably have discovered the errors of their logic; but most of them were less anxious to understand the world of science and daily life than to convict it of unreality in the interests of a super-sensible "real" world.

It is in this way that logic has been pursued by those of the great philosophers who were mystics. But since they usually took for granted the supposed insight of the mystic emotion, their logical doctrines were presented with a certain dryness, and were believed by their disciples to be quite independent of the sudden illumination from which they sprang. Nevertheless their origin clung to them, and they remained—to borrow a useful word from Mr. Santayana—"malicious" in regard to the world of science and common sense. It is only so that we can account for the complacency with which philosophers have accepted the inconsistency of their doctrines with all the common and scientific facts which seem best established and most worthy of belief.

The logic of mysticism shows, as is natural, the defects which are inherent in anything malicious. The impulse to logic, not felt while the mystic mood is dominant, reasserts itself as the mood fades, but with a desire to retain the vanishing insight, or at least to prove that it *was* insight, and that what seems to contradict it is illusion. The logic which thus arises is not quite disinterested or candid, and is inspired by a certain hatred of the daily world to which it is to be applied. Such an attitude naturally does not tend to the best results. Everyone knows that to read an author simply in order to refute him is not the way to understand him; and to read the book of Nature with a conviction that it is all illusion is just as unlikely to lead to understanding. If our logic is to find the common world intelligible, it must not be hostile, but must be inspired by a genuine acceptance such as is not usually to be found among metaphysicians.

III. TIME

The unreality of time is a cardinal doctrine of many metaphysical systems, often nominally based, as already by Parmenides, upon logical arguments, but originally derived, at any rate in the founders of new systems, from the certainty which is born in the moment of mystic insight. As a Persian Sufi poet says:

> Past and future are what veil God from our sight.
> Burn up both of them with fire! How long
> Wilt thou be partitioned by these segments as a reed?[2]

The belief that what is ultimately real must be immutable is a very common one: it gave rise to the metaphysical notion of substance, and finds, even now, a wholly illegitimate satisfaction in such scientific doctrines as the conservation of energy and mass.

It is difficult to disentangle the truth and the error in this view. The arguments for the contention that time is unreal and that the world of sense is illusory must, I think, be regarded as fallacious. Nevertheless there is some sense—easier to feel than to state—in which time is an unimportant and superficial characteristic of reality. Past and future must be acknowledged to be as real as the present, and a certain emancipation from slavery to time is essential to philosophic thought. The importance of time is rather practical than theoretical, rather in relation to our desires than in relation to truth. A truer image of the world, I think, is obtained by picturing things as entering into the stream of time from an eternal world outside, than from a view which regards time as the

[2] Whinfield's translation of the *Masnavi* (Trübner, 1887), p. 34.

devouring tyrant of all that is. Both in thought and in feeling, even though time be real, to realize the unimportance of time is the gate of wisdom.

That this is the case may be seen at once by asking ourselves why our feelings towards the past are so different from our feelings towards the future. The reason for this difference is wholly practical: our wishes can affect the future but not the past, the future is to some extent subject to our power, while the past is unalterably fixed. But every future will some day be past: if we see the past truly now, it must, when it was still future, have been just what we now see it to be, and what is now future must be just what we shall see it to be when it has become past. The felt difference of quality between past and future, therefore, is not an intrinsic difference, but only a difference in relation to us: to impartial contemplation, it ceases to exist. And impartiality of contemplation is, in the intellectual sphere, that very same virtue of disinterestedness which, in the sphere of action, appears as justice and unselfishness. Whoever wishes to see the world truly, to rise in thought above the tyranny of practical desires, must learn to overcome the difference of attitude towards past and future, and to survey the whole stream of time in one comprehensive vision.

The kind of way in which, as it seems to me, time ought not to enter into our theoretic philosophical thought, may be illustrated by the philosophy which has become associated with the idea of evolution, and which is exemplified by Nietzsche, pragmatism, and Bergson. This philosophy, on the basis of the development which has led from the lowest forms of life up to man, sees in *progress* the fundamental law of the universe, and thus admits the difference between *earlier* and *later* into the very citadel of its contemplative outlook. With its past and future history of the world, conjectural as it is, I do not wish to quarrel. But I think that, in the intoxication of a quick success, much that is required for a true understanding of the universe has been forgotten. Something of Hellenism, something, too, of Oriental resignation, must be combined with its hurrying Western self-assertion before it can emerge from the ardour of youth into the mature wisdom of manhood. In spite of its appeals to science, the true scientific philosophy, I think, is something more arduous and more aloof, appealing to less mundane hopes, and requiring a severer discipline for its successful practice.

Darwin's *Origin of Species* persuaded the world that the difference between different species of animals and plants is not the fixed immutable difference that it appears to be. The doctrine of natural kinds, which has rendered classification easy and definite, which was enshrined in the Aristotelian tradition, and protected by its supposed necessity for orthodox dogma, was suddenly swept away for ever out of the biological world. The difference between man and the lower animals, which to our human conceit appears enormous, was shown to be a gradual achievement, involving intermediate beings who could not with certainty be placed either within or without the human family. The sun and the planets had already been shown by Laplace to be very probably derived from a primitive more or less undifferentiated nebula. Thus the old fixed landmarks became wavering and indistinct, and all sharp outlines were blurred. Things and species lost their boundaries, and none could say where they began or where they ended.

But if human conceit was staggered for a moment by its kinship with the ape, it soon found a way to reassert itself, and that way is the "philosophy" of evolution. A process which led from the amoeba to Man appeared to the philosophers to be obviously a progress—though whether the amoeba would agree with this opinion is not known. Hence the cycle of changes which science had shown to be the probable history of the past was welcomed as revealing a law of development towards good in the universe— an evolution or unfolding of an idea slowly embodying itself in the actual. But such a view, though it might satisfy Spencer and those whom we may call Hegelian evolutionists, could not be accepted as adequate by the more whole-hearted votaries of change. An ideal to which the world continuously approaches is, to these minds, too dead and static to be inspiring. Not only the aspiration, but the ideal too, must change and develop with the course of evolution: there must be no fixed goal, but a continual fashioning of fresh needs by the impulse which is life and which alone gives unity to the process.

Life, in this philosophy, is a continuous stream, in which all divisions are artificial and unreal. Separate things, beginnings and endings, are mere convenient fictions: there is only smooth un-broken transition. The beliefs of today may count as true today, if they carry us along the stream; but tomorrow they will be false, and must be replaced by new beliefs to meet the new situation. All our thinking consists of convenient fictions, imaginary congealings of the stream: reality flows on in spite of all our fictions, and though it can be lived, it cannot be conceived in thought. Somehow, without explicit statement, the assurance is slipped in that the future, though we cannot foresee it, will be better than the past or the present: the reader is like the child which expects a sweet because it has been told to open its mouth and shut its eyes. Logic, mathematics, physics disappear in this philosophy, because they are too "static"; what is real is no impulse and movement towards a goal which, like the rainbow, recedes as we advance, and makes every place different when it reaches it from what it appeared to be at a distance.

I do not propose to enter upon a technical examination of this philosophy. I wish only to maintain that the motives and interests which inspire it are so exclusively practical, and the problems with which it deals are so special, that it can hardly be regarded as touching any of the questions that, to my mind, constitute genuine philosophy.

The predominant interest of evolutionism is in the question of human destiny, or at least of the destiny of Life. It is more inter-ested in morality and happiness than in knowledge for its own sake. It must be admitted that the same may be said of many other philosophies, and that a desire for the kind of knowledge which philosophy can give is very rare. But if philosophy is to attain truth, it is necessary first and foremost that philosophers should acquire the disinterested intellectual curiosity which characterizes the genuine man of science. Knowledge concerning the future— which is the kind of knowledge that must be sought if we are to know about human destiny—is possible within certain narrow limits. It is impossible to say how much the limits may be enlarged with the progress of science. But what is evident is that any proposition about the future belongs by its subject-matter to some particular science, and is to be ascertained, if at all, by the methods of that science. Philosophy is not a short cut to the same kind of results as those of the other sciences: if it is to be a genuine study, it must have a province of its own, and aim at results which the other sciences can neither prove nor disprove.

Evolutionism, in basing itself upon the notion of *progress,* which is to change from the worse to the better, allows the notion of time, as it seems to me, to become its tyrant rather than its servant, and thereby loses that impartiality of contemplation which is the source of all that is best in philosophic thought and feeling. Metaphysicians, as we saw, have frequently denied altogether the reality of time. I do not wish to do this; I wish only to preserve the mental outlook which inspired the denial, the attitude which, in thought, regards the past as having the same reality as the present and the same importance as the future. "In so far," says Spinoza,[3] "as the mind conceives a thing according to the dictate of reason, it will be equally affected whether the idea is that of a future, past, or present thing." It is this "conceiving according to the dictate of reason" that I find lacking in the philosophy which is based on evolution.

IV. GOOD AND EVIL

Mysticism maintains that all evil is illusory, and sometimes maintains the same view as regards good, but more often holds that all Reality is good. Both views are to be found in Heraclitus: "Good and ill are one," he says, but again, "To God all things are fair and good and right, but men hold some things wrong and some right." A similar twofold position is to be found in Spinoza, but he uses the word "perfection" when he means to speak of the good that is not merely human. "By reality and perfection I mean

[3] *Ethics,* Bk. IV, Prop. LXII.

the same thing," he says;[4] but elsewhere we find the definition: "By *good* I shall mean that which we certainly know to be useful to us."[5] Thus perfection belongs to Reality in its own nature, but goodness is relative to ourselves and our needs, and disappears in an impartial survey. Some such distinction, I think, is necessary in order to understand the ethical outlook of mysticism: there is a lower mundane kind of good and evil, which divides the world of appearance into what seem to be conflicting parts; but there is also a higher, mystical kind of good, which belongs to Reality and is not opposed by any correlative kind of evil.

It is difficult to give a logically tenable account of this position without recognizing that good and evil are subjective, that what is good is merely that towards which we have one kind of feeling, and what is evil is merely that towards which we have another kind of feeling. In our active life, where we have to exercise choice, and to prefer this to that of two possible acts, it is necessary to have a distinction of good and evil, or at least of better and worse. But this distinction, like everything pertaining to action, belongs to what mysticism regards as the world of illusion, if only because it is essentially concerned with time. In our contemplative life, where action is not called for, it is possible to be impartial, and to overcome the ethical dualism which action requires. So long as we remain *merely* impartial, we may be content to say that both the good and the evil of action are illusions. But if, as we must do if we have the mystic vision, we find the whole world worthy of love and worship, if we see

> The earth, and every common sight. . . .
> Apparell'd in celestial light,

we shall say that there is a higher good than that of action, and that this higher good belongs to the whole world as it is in reality. In this way the twofold attitude and the apparent vacillation of mysticism are explained and justified.

The possibility of this universal love and joy in all that exists

4 *Ethics,* Pt. II, Df. VI.
5 Ib., Pt. IV, Df. I.

is of supreme importance for the conduct and happiness of life, and gives inestimable value to the mystic emotion, apart from any creeds which may be built upon it. But if we are not to be led into false beliefs, it is necessary to realize exactly *what* the mystic emotion reveals. It reveals a possibility of human nature—a possibility of a nobler, happier, freer life than any that can be otherwise achieved. But it does not reveal anything about the non-human, or about the nature of the universe in general. Good and bad, and even the higher good that mysticism finds everywhere, are the reflections of our own emotions on other things, not part of the substance of things as they are in themselves. And therefore an impartial contemplation, freed from all preoccupation with Self, will not judge things good or bad, although it is very easily combined with that feeling of universal love which leads the mystic to say that the whole world is good.

The philosophy of evolution, through the notion of progress, is bound up with the ethical dualism of the worse and the better, and is thus shut out, not only from the kind of survey which discards good and evil altogether from its view, but also from the mystical belief in the goodness of everything. In this way the distinction of good and evil, like time, becomes a tyrant in this philosophy, and introduces into thought the restless selectiveness of action. Good and evil, like time, are, it would seem, not general or fundamental in the world of thought, but late and highly specialized members of the intellectual hierarchy.

Although, as we saw, mysticism can be interpreted so as to agree with the view that good and evil are not intellectually fundamental, it must be admitted that here we are no longer in verbal agreement with most of the great philosophers and religious teachers of the past. I believe, however, that the elimination of ethical considerations from philosophy is both scientifically necessary and —though this may seem a paradox—an ethical advance. Both these contentions must be briefly defended.

The hope of satisfaction to our more human desires—the hope of demonstrating that the world has this or that desirable ethical characteristic—is not one which, so far as I can see, a scientific philosophy can do anything whatever to satisfy. The difference between a good world and a bad one is a difference in the particular characteristics of the particular things that exist in these worlds: it is not a sufficiently abstract difference to come within the province of philosophy. Love and hate, for example, are ethical opposites, but to philosophy they are closely analogous attitudes towards objects. The general form and structure of those attitudes towards objects which constitute mental phenomena is a problem for philosophy, but the difference between love and hate is not a difference of form or structure, and therefore belongs rather to the special science of psychology than to philosophy. Thus the ethical interests which have often inspired philosophers must remain in the background: some kind of ethical interest may inspire the whole study, but none must obtrude in the detail or be expected in the special results which are sought.

If this view seems at first sight disappointing, we may remind ourselves that a similar change has been found necessary in all the other sciences. The physicist or chemist is not now required to prove the ethical importance of his ions or atoms; the biologist is not expected to prove the utility of the plants or animals which he dissects. In pre-scientific ages this was not the case. Astronomy, for example, was studied because men believed in astrology: it was thought that the movements of the planets had the most direct and important bearing upon the lives of human beings. Presumably, when this belief decayed and the disinterested study of astronomy began, many who had found astrology absorbingly interesting decided that astronomy had too little human interest to be worthy of study. Physics, as it appears in Plato's Timaeus for example, is full of ethical notions: it is an essential part of its purpose to show that the earth is worthy of admiration. The modern physicist, on the contrary, though he has no wish to deny that the earth is admirable, is not concerned, as physicist, with its ethical attributes: he is merely concerned to find out facts, not to consider whether they are good or bad. In psychology, the scientific attitude is even more recent and more difficult than in the physical sciences: it is natural to consider that human nature is either good or bad, and to suppose that the difference between good and bad, so all-important in practice, must be important in theory also. It is only during the last century that an ethically neutral psychology has grown up; and here too, ethical neutrality has been essential to scientific success.

In philosophy, hitherto, ethical neutrality has been seldom sought and hardly ever achieved. Men have remembered their wishes, and have judged philosophies in relation to their wishes. Driven from the particular sciences, the belief that the notions of good and evil must afford a key to the understanding of the world has sought a refuge in philosophy. But even from this last refuge, if philosophy is not to remain a set of pleasing dreams, this belief must be driven forth. It is a commonplace that happiness is not best achieved by those who seek it directly; and it would seem that the same is true of the good. In thought, at any rate, those who forget good and evil and seek only to know the facts are more likely to achieve good than those who view the world through the distorting medium of their own desires.

We are thus brought back to our seeming paradox, that a philosophy which does not seek to impose upon the world its own conceptions of good and evil is not only more likely to achieve truth, but is also the outcome of a higher ethical standpoint than one which, like evolutionism and most traditional systems, is perpetually appraising the universe and seeking to find in it an embodiment of present ideals. In religion, and in every deeply serious view of the world and of human destiny, there is an element of submission, a realization of the limits of human power, which is somewhat lacking in the modern world, with its quick material successes and its insolent belief in the boundless possibilities of progress. "He that loveth his life shall lose it"; and there is danger lest, through a too confident love of life, life itself should lose much of what gives it its highest worth. The submission which religion inculcates in action is essentially the same in spirit as that which science teaches in thought; and the ethical neutrality by which its victories have been achieved is the outcome of that submission.

The good which it concerns us to remember is the good which it lies in our power to create—the good in our own lives and in our attitude towards the world. Insistence on belief in an external realization of the good is a form of self-assertion, which, while it cannot secure the external good which it desires, can seriously impair the inward good which lies within our power, and destroy that reverence towards fact which constitutes both what is valuable in humility and what is fruitful in the scientific temper.

Human beings cannot, of course, wholly transcend human nature; something subjective, if only the interest that determines the direction of our attention, must remain in all our thought. But scientific philosophy comes nearer to objectivity than any other human pursuit, and gives us, therefore, the closest constant and the most intimate relation with the outer world that it is possible to achieve. To the primitive mind, everything is either friendly or hostile; but experience has shown that friendliness and hostility are not the conceptions by which the world is to be understood. Scientific philosophy thus represents, though as yet only in a nascent condition, a higher form of thought than any pre-scientific belief or imagination, and, like every approach to self-transcendence, it brings with it a rich reward in increase of scope and breadth and comprehension. Evolutionism, in spite of its appeals to particular scientific facts, fails to be a truly scientific philosophy because of its slavery to time, its ethical preoccupations, and its predominant interest in our mundane concerns and destiny. A truly scientific philosophy will be more humble, more piecemeal, more arduous, offering less glitter of outward mirage to flatter fallacious hopes, but more indifferent to fate, and more capable of accepting the world without the tyrannous imposition of our human and temporary demands.

7

THE PHILOSOPHICAL ASPECTS OF THE PRINCIPLE OF RELATIVITY

Alfred North Whitehead

Whereas Bertrand Russell, as we have seen in the last selection, has stayed with a more reductive type of naturalism, his former collaborator, A. N. Whitehead, became one of the major exponents of a new and richer kind of naturalism, working with a concept of nature that has room for the reality of both material and spiritual phenomena, and that avoids the sharp separation or "bifurcation" of these. Whitehead's naturalism appeals in large measure to the new physics of Einstein, Planck, and others, whereas Bergson's naturalism had based itself on biology. The essay printed here was written in 1922 and is specially interesting because it shows how Whitehead rejected idealist interpretations of nature equally with materialistic ones, and tried to go beyond both of these positions to an inclusive concept of nature.

THE MOST obvious contribution of the scientific doctrine of Relativity to the problems of philosophy is to strengthen the type of argument on which Berkeley relied. Accordingly, those systems of philosophy which rely on this type of argument thereby receive additional support. I will endeavor to explain my meaning, but I am painfully conscious that it would have been better to have had

Reprinted with permission from *Proceedings of the Aristotelian Society* (London: The Aristotelian Society, 1922), Copyright 1922 by The Aristotelian Society.

the grounds of this evening's discussion laid out by an adequately trained philosopher.

I presume that the fundamental position of idealism is that all reality can be construed as an expression of mentality. For example, I suppose that Mr. Alexander is a realist because for him mind is one among other items occurring in that evolution of complexes which is the very being of space-time. On the other hand, Mr. Wildon Carr is an idealist because he finds ultimate reality in the self-expression of monadic mentality. The test, therefore, of idealism is the refusal to conceive reality apart from explicit reference to some or all of the characteristic processes of mentality; it may be either thought, or experience, or knowledge, or the expression of valuation in the form of a historical process, the valuation being both the efficient and the final cause of the process. Now Berkeley's argument in favor of this central position of idealism is that when you examine the objects of sense-perception they are essentially personal to the observer. He enforces by a variety of illustrations the doctrine that there is nothing left when you have torn the observer out of the observation. The planet, which is no bigger than a sixpence, is the observer's planet, and he walks off with his own property.

It stands to reason that modern relativity strengthens this argument, since previously there were two elements in our experience which the argument did not touch. I mean space and time. Berkeley's argument rests on the basis that appearances in space and through time are personal to the observer. But space and time were left as common facts. But now it has been shown that space and time cannot be excluded from the scope of Berkeley's argument. Accordingly, you can no longer meet the argument by showing that there are exceptions to it. Hence, so far as idealism is concerned with the facts of nature—and it must be concerned with them—its characteristic type of argument has been strengthened by the recent scientific bombshell. The realist is now left hugging the multiplication table as the sole common fact untouched by each immediate expression of mind. But the multiplication table is no good to a realist. It shuts him up with Plato's ideas, out of

space and out of time, which is just where he does not want to be
—poor man, like Wordsworth and the rest of us, he wants to hear
the throstle sing.

We seem to be left, then, with the idealist position that nature
is nothing else than a common expression for diverse processes of
mentality. I do not believe that this is the sole choice; I have been
trying to sketch in a few sentences the line of thought according to
which relativity strengthens the argument for idealism. But, before
proceeding, the immediate moral that I want to draw is that
Berkeley must be stopped at the very beginning. The presupposition of the whole line of argument must be challenged. Later on
there is no resting place.

Let us now begin again and scan carefully the main point of
Berkeley's argument.

He attacks the presumption that we observe subjects as qualified
by attributes, subject and attribute being independent of ourselves.
He easily—ridiculously easily—establishes this point so far as it
goes, and it is the scope of this argument which is widened by the
modern doctrine of relativity in physical science, so as to include
time and space. The exact conclusion which we ought to draw,
and must draw, is that the form of thought of a two-termed relation of predicate to subject imposed by the Aristotelian logic is
not adequate to express the immediate deliverance of observation.
A wider relativity is necessary in the sense that the fact of nature
observed—the crimson cloud, to take another of Berkeley's examples—cannot be expressed in terms of the two factors "crimson" and "cloud." In other words, the proposition "the cloud is
crimson" is in reality a highly elliptical form of expression and is
meaningless unless the suppressed factors are supplied. In practice
these suppressed factors always are supplied; in truth they are so
obvious to us that it is difficult for us to believe that language has
shirked its job of exposing the fact.

Furthermore, everyone would agree that in some sense the suppressed factor includes the observer. Berkeley's argument is that
it stands in the essential nature of the case that different observers
perceive different things. Accordingly, in the realm of things ob-

served there can be nothing common to diverse observers. Accordingly, there is no common realm of things observed, whose interrelations can be expressed apart from reference to observers. Accordingly, the only common ground for observers is the common stock of abstract ideas which they individually apply to their diverse experiences. Furthermore, these diverse experiences now lose all claim to any objectivity other than that of being phases in the process of the self-development of the observer.

Now I see no escape from this argument provided that the concept of an "observer" is not ambiguous. Unfortunately, it is very ambiguous. Berkeley—tacitly presupposing the Aristotelian logical forms—has thereby presupposed that in the fact observed there can only be the two-termed relation of predicate to subject, for example, "crimson to cloud." Accordingly, for him the additional factor introduced must be something underlying and in a sense creating the realm of the observed. This additional factor is, accordingly (for Berkeley), the mentality of the observer which is expressing itself in these observations. In other words, for Berkeley the observer is mind, and therefore Berkeley is an idealist. But when a realist admits that—as above—the suppressed factor includes the observer, he is (or should be) using the term "observer" in a quite different sense. He is thinking of the observer's body. I do not think that for the exposition of the realist position the term "observer" is at all well-chosen. I put it in, to start with, because, after all, Berkeley started the whole train of thought, so that the idealists are entitled to the initial phraseology which suits their line of development of the argument. But whereas Berkeley puts in an additional factor, namely, mind, which underlies the whole realm observed, the additional factor added by the realists consists of other items within the realm observed. Among these other items is the body of the observer, and this is why a realist carelessly, and in a loose unsatisfactory sense of the term, may assent to the statement that the additional factor includes the observer.

But note that now the realist has admitted that the simple proposition, "the cloud is crimson," is a meaningless statement about nature unless other items of nature are implicitly included in the proposition. In other words, a fact of nature cannot be expressed in the simple two-termed relation of predication which is the standard form of the Aristotelian logic. In allowing that it is essential to add other items of nature to crimson and the cloud in order to express the immediately apparent fact, he has admitted that the essential facts of apparent nature involve irreducible relations of more than two terms. Owing to the influence of training and custom, as embodied in the phraseology of philosophical literature, it is habitual to us to presuppose that all relations—even if they are not that of predication—are two-termed, and to acquiesce in arguments which tacitly make this presupposition. Accordingly, it is the more necessary for me to emphasize this point, since I consider that, apart from this admission of irreducible many-termed relations, there is no escape from the full force of Berkeley's argument.

If you ask how many other items of nature enter into the relation of crimson to cloud, I think that we must answer that every other item of nature enters into it. At first sight, this would appear to make knowledge impossible for poor finite human beings. But we can classify grades of relata in this multiple relation which I term that of crimson to cloud. The lowest grade sweeps all nature into itself. It is the grade of relata whereby all nature expresses its patience for this relationship of crimson to cloud. There is no such thing as crimson lone and by itself apart from nature as involving space-time, and the same is true of cloud. The crimson cloud is essentially connected with every other item of nature by the spatio-temporality of nature, and the proposition, "the cloud is crimson," has no meaning apart from this spatio-temporality. In this way all nature is swept into the net of the relationship.

You may put it this way, nature as a system is presupposed in the crimsonness of the cloud. But a system means systematic relations between the items of a system. Accordingly, you cannot know that nature is a system unless you know what these systematic relations are. Now we cannot know these systematic relations by any observational method involving enumeration of all the items of nature. It follows that our partial knowledge must disclose a uniform type of relationship which reigns throughout the system. For if we do not know that, we know nothing: and there is simply nothing to talk about. For example, we should have no reason to believe that there is an interior to the earth, or any lapse of time applying to it. We ask whether this interior is occupied with condensed matter or is empty, and whether this matter be hot or cold, solid or gaseous, because we know that the uniform systematic spatio-temporal relations must supply entities which have the status of forming the interior of the earth.

I call this principle, by which a systematic nature is known to us, the uniform significance of events. This uniform significance is disclosed to us as expressing the patience of nature for every item of our experience—for example, the crimsonness of the cloud.

Another grade of items in the relationship "crimson to cloud" entirely lacks the uniformity which attaches to the first grade. Accordingly, in contrast to "uniformity," I will speak of its "contingency." The principle of the contingence of appearance means that a set of items of nature are presupposed in the relationship crimson to cloud, whose status in the relationship requires detailed examination in each particular instance; though the laws of nature enable us to make a shrewd guess at the types of status which are possible. But there is one item in this contingent grade which is so pre-eminent that it almost deserves a whole grade to itself. I mean the observer's body. It is an empirical fact, which in no way seems to enter into the character of knowledge as such, that our knowledge of nature consists of knowledge of those relationships for which our bodies are important members of the contingent grade of items. The cloud is crimson, as perceived by a person B, because B is aware of a certain multiple relationship involving processes within his body and other items of nature. We may put it in this way, that B is aware of nature from the standpoint of his body. Thus the relativity to an observer is dominated by the physical state of the observer's body. It is therefore relative to his body.

Apart from the empirical fact that it so happens, I cannot convince myself that the character of awareness of nature necessarily involves this reference to the observer's body. In the first place, it is quite easy to imagine an infinite observer, such as God, whom in this connection I call infinite as being impartially aware of all relationships of items within nature. Each one of us is a finite observer because we are only aware of that selection among the relationships which are dominated by our body. But I cannot see that idealism would gain even if this reference to the body were absent. We can imagine that the perceptions of the sociable arch-angel, as he chatted with Adam and Eve in the garden, were not from the standpoint of his body, because he had no body, but that his selection of relationships observed was made on some other principle. What is essential as an argument for realism (under this heading of relativity) is that the relationships observed should form a closed system whose characters refer to each other. There is a process of nature which is obstinately indifferent to mind. This is why I feel difficulty in assigning to mind, or knowledge, or consciousness any essential role in the flux of fact—essential, I mean, beyond the roles played by other abstractions from that flux, such as chairs and tables.

I cannot persuade myself that relativity in any way weakens this obstinate indifference of nature. It simply shows that there are more various relationships within nature than we had anticipated—no new discovery, for every advance of science adds to the complexity of nature. If Einstein had established the affirmative answer to Pope's question, "Shall gravitation cease as you go by," he would have done something to advance the claims of idealism. But all he has done is to make it more difficult for us to compare our watches with those of the inhabitants of Mars, entirely owing to circumstances over which we have no control; and also he has produced a law of gravitation more complicated than that of Newton—but, again, this law depends on circumstances over which we have no control. I don't see how it is any easier to bend space now than it was to alter the strains and stresses in the ether. Accordingly, I cannot appreciate what accession there has been to the arguments on behalf of idealism. We still find mental processes faced with an obstinately independent nature, so that the correlations of mental processes with natural processes appear as unessential for the course of natural events. I am not denying that there are such correlations, or that when they occur the natural and the mental are not the same fact with different aspects of it emphasized. But what I am denying is that some correlation with mentality can be proved to be essential for the very being of natural fact. I will summarize the foregoing discussion by saying that the modern doctrine of relativity is calculated to hearten idealists by emphasizing certain of their lines of argument, but that it does not essentially touch the validity of the controversial arguments as between the two sides.

I should, however, not like it to be concluded that I am maintaining that relativity has no philosophical importance. The general character of its importance arises from the emphasis which it throws upon relatedness. It helps philosophy resolutely to turn its back upon the false lights of the Aristotelian logic. Ultimate fact is not a mere aggregate of independent entities which are the subjects for qualities. We can never get away from an essential relatedness involving a multiplicity of relata. Every factor A, discerned as an entity within fact, expresses in its very being its capacity for the relationships into which it enters, and requires that all other factors of fact should express their capacities as relata in relationships involving it. This is the doctrine that any factor A is significant of the relationships into which it enters, and that conversely all factors within fact must express the patience of fact for A.

The more special aspect of the importance of relativity in philosophy is its treatment of space and time, particularly time. Space and time can never be mere side shows in philosophy. Their treatment must color the whole subsequent development of the subject. The relational treatment of space is a well-established principle, and I doubt whether relativity has made much difference here, so far as philosophers are concerned. But it has made an immense difference to the treatment of time. The unique serial character of time has gone by the board; also a thoroughgoing relational treatment of time is now necessitated and made possible. I am told that there are phrases in Aristotle which look that way. Am I right in recollecting that he defines time as an ordering or disposition of events in respect to each other?

Furthermore, the fusion of time with space and the dropping of the unique seriality involves the necessity of looking on ultimate fact as essentially a process. Accordingly, wherever the idea of "process" has been lost, we are dealing with a very advanced type of abstraction. This is why, in treating this subject, I have always insisted that our lowest, most concrete type of abstractions, whereby we express the diversification of fact, must be regarded as "events," meaning, thereby, a partial factor of fact which retains process.

Now I conceive that nothing of this is really new in philosophical thought. It is as old as the hills. But I still think that a scientific doctrine which enforces consistent emphasis on these ideas has the utmost importance for philosophy, even although it does not settle the established controversies between realism and idealism.

8

THE TWOFOLD CERTITUDE

Étienne Gilson

Toward the end of the nineteenth century there began a great revival of interest in the philosophy of St. Thomas Aquinas, itself reaching back to the earlier philosophy of Aristotle. The neo-Thomism that resulted from this revival of interest has been a major philosophical force in the present century. It has special significance for religious thought, because the realist and empiricist characteristics of Thomism are well suited to the scientific age, while on the other hand this philosophy has been traditionally allied with Catholic theology. Étienne Gilson, one of the most distinguished representatives of neo-Thomism, expounds some of its basic positions in the following extract, and shows how it tries to reconcile the claims of reason and revelation.

FAR FROM seeing in Christian revelation the downfall of philosophy. Thomas Aquinas saw philosophy, in Eusebius of Cesarea's own words, as a kind of *praeparatio evangelica* by which divine providence prepared the minds of men to receive the truth of the Gospel. In a perhaps still more striking image—conceived as early as the end of the second century after Christ—Saint Justin held the astonishing view that God had given philosophy to the Greeks even as He had given his Law to the Jewish people. Let us pause for a moment to assimilate the import of this statement. According to Justin, it was God's intention that philosophy should play for

Reprinted with permission from *The Spirit of Thomism* (New York: P. J. Kenedy & Sons, 1964), pp. 11–32.

the Gentiles a role similar to that which his own revealed Law had played for the Jews. In other words, both the Greek philosophy and the Jewish Law were included in the general economy of the divine providence.

Now this exactly defines the constant attitude of Thomas Aquinas toward philosophy, particularly that of its best exponents, namely, Plato, Aristotle, and Plotinus among the ancients, and in modern times Avicenna and Averroes. While as late as the seventeenth century, Father Malebranche, a priest of the Oratory, was still to feel scandalized at the sight of Christian theologians allowing themselves to be seduced by the pagan philosophy of Aristotle, which he called "the philosophy of the snake," Thomas Aquinas often marveled, on the contrary, at its deeply religious inspiration. Judging from the metaphysics of Plato and Aristotle, Thomas Aquinas saw philosophy as bent upon the contemplation of God as the goal of human life: *omnes qui recte senserunt posuerunt finem humanae vitae Dei contemplationem.*[1]

Let us try to understand this correctly. Of course, Thomas does not mean to say that Aristotle anticipated the revelation of the Gospel. The Philosopher could not guess that God himself would later on invite men to share, through grace, in his own beatitude. Aristotle had but a foggy notion of immortality and he knew nothing of the possibility of what we call future life. He never spoke of any happiness other than that accessible to man in this mortal life, yet he considered temporal happiness to be the supreme reward of a steady pursuit of philosophical speculation. That is the reason Aristotle assigned the intellectual contemplation of the highest intelligible objects as the supreme end of this mortal life. Now among such objects, God reigns supreme.

True enough, it is a far cry from the most perfect philosophical knowledge of the deity to the sight of God face to face promised to man by the Christian revelation. In fact, the distance is infinite, yet it is remarkable that Aristotle—going in the right direction as far as human reason unaided by revelation could possibly go— saw the whole of philosophical speculation as ordained to the kind

[1] Thomas Aquinas, *In I Sent.,* Prol., q. 1, a. 1.

of felicity man finds only in knowing God as he can be known through our scientific knowledge of nature: *et ad hanc (felicitatem) ordinatur tota cognitio philosophica.*[2] Nor was this a chance statement. At a later date, in more carefully weighed terms (because, after all, some parts of philosophy are less immediately related to God than others) Thomas will say that natural theology is the supreme part of philosophy, because philosophical inquiry is *almost* totally ordained to the knowledge of God: *cum fere totius philosophiae consideratio ad Dei cognitionem ordinetur.*[3]

Was this an illusion of perspective on the part of Thomas Aquinas? Or was Aristotle really convinced that the supreme end of man consists in the philosophical contemplation of the divinity? One thing at least is certain, and it is that to Aristotle the ultimate goal of human life was the conquest of happiness to be found in the steady practice of philosophical speculation. Such was to him the ideal life: not the search for truth, but its contemplation after it has been attained.

But even the mere searching for truth was to Aristotle a promise of happiness due to the favor of the gods: "He who exercises and cultivates his reason, seems to be most excellently disposed and, by the same token, to be a favorite with the gods. For if the gods care for man, as they are said to do, it is reasonable to think that they chiefly care for that in man which, being more akin to them, is also the best, namely the intellect. It is likewise reasonable to think that the men who thus cherish and cultivate that which, in themselves, is dearest to the gods, are living both right and nobly. Now, surely these qualities are those of the philosopher. So the philosopher is the man the gods prefer, and since the man the gods love best must also be the happiest, the philosopher must be the happiest of men."[4]

Far from finding fault with this notion of human blessedness, Thomas Aquinas never ceased to wonder at the truth of such a

[2] *Loc. cit.*, solutio.

[3] *De veritate catholicae fidei contra gentiles* (to be quoted as *Contra gentiles*), I, 4, 3.

[4] *In decem libros Aristotelis ad Nicomachum*, X, 9, ed. R. M. Spiazzi, O.P., 2133–36.

purely philosophical profession of faith. Here was a pagan philosopher who, following the light of natural reason alone, had discovered that there is something divine in intellectual knowledge and that its philosophical exercise is the surest way to blessedness. And why? Because the intellect itself is highest in human affairs (*optimum in rebus humanis*), nay, because the intellect is that in man which is most cognate to the gods, *cognatissimum*—a word which means, according to Thomas, that which in man is most similar to God: *id est simillimum Deo*. So Thomas concludes with Aristotle that to love the intellect is to love that which God prefers over all other things: *quid maxime amatur a Deo inter res humanas*.

At this point, I myself feel I have to stop. I cannot do more. It is up to you to do the rest. Or rather let us say: up to us, for in this I am one of you, a pupil listening to Thomas Aquinas and striving to understand what the master says. And my own question now is: If we were asked to name the supreme wonder of the world, how many of us would answer, "Intellectual knowledge"? Do we realize what a prodigy the existence of knowing beings actually is? Of all knowable things, knowledge itself is by far the most amazing there is.

Sensation is the first wonder of the world. Think of the solemn moment in the history of the universe when under circumstances unknown to us the first eye opened to light. Then think of the far more solemn moment when for the first time an intelligent being conceived an abstract concept as standing for a plurality of individuals, and expressed it by a gesture or by some sort of grunt that was a word. At that very moment, all the future intellectual conquests of man in science and in philosophy were becoming possible. If there is nothing in nature more noble than the intellectual activity of man, it is small wonder that the steady pursuit of scientific and philosophical knowledge should lead the mind to the knowledge of God as its own origin and end.

Yes indeed—and the history of philosophy shows it—philosophical inquiry is almost totally ordained to the cognition of God as its end, but more remarkable still is the fact that Christ once said in the Gospel: "This is eternal life, that they may know thee, the only true God" (John 17:3). There is something amazing in this first coincidence of what philosophy says and what revelation teaches; but there will be other ones.

To recapture that feeling of unity between two distinct sources of knowledge is a first step toward a proper understanding of the spirit of Thomism. In order to confirm ourselves in that feeling, let us try to discover the origin of their unity.

Thomas not only loves and admires the intellect, he trusts it implicitly. There is in him no trace of the sophisticated relativism or quasi-skepticism of so many philosophers and scientists of today. Strangely enough, the reason for this difference was a religious one. Thomas Aquinas entertained the deep-seated conviction that to cultivate science and philosophy was to be about God's own business. He felt certain that all that is true for man owes its invincible certitude to the fact that it first is true for God. I know of no stronger expression of that conviction than the passage of the *Contra gentiles* (I, 7, 2) in which Thomas says that the knowledge of the first principles evident to the mind has been implanted in us by God, who is the author of our nature. This is the reason they cannot possibly not be true, since the very same principles from which human knowledge is derived, are likewise contained in the wisdom of God. An astounding statement indeed! *Haec ergo principia etiam divina sapientia continet.*

Some of our contemporaries love to speak of the utter relativity of human knowledge. They think that what is true to us could appear untrue in the light of a differently constituted intellect. Far from sharing such views, Thomas Aquinas expressly teaches that what is true to us cannot fail to be true even to God.

It could not be otherwise, since the principles of human knowledge are part and parcel of divine wisdom. A curious passage of Thomas' commentary on the Book of Job confirms this interpretation of the doctrine. Thomas is there reaching the point where Job, goaded into exasperation by the reproaches of his talkative friends, suddenly exclaims: "Shut up! Shut up! Let me say something! I want to speak to the Almighty; I want to argue my case with God" (Job 13:3). Whereupon Thomas Aquinas starts wondering: Is not this rather unseemly? A disputation between a man and God does not look right because of the inequality between the parties. But Thomas goes on to say, "It should be remembered that truth does not vary according to persons; when what a man says, is true, he is invincible; whomsoever he may be disputing with."[5]

To be sure, Job was aware of his own righteousness; he felt comforted by the gifts of wisdom and of science, but to him the main point was that he knew that what he had to say was true, God or no God. Don't browbeat me, Job tells God, and I shall not be afraid of disputing with thee: *non timebo tecum disputare.* Only speak to me and I shall answer, or else I surely shall speak and thou wilt answer me: *aut certe loquar et tu respondebis mihi.* To be true disciples of Thomas Aquinas, we would first have to put so much trust in the natural light of reason that nothing could make us doubt it, not even God.

Let us now look at the other side of the picture, for Thomas everywhere assents to the truth of Scripture, and this sort of assent has nothing to do with the evidence of reason; on the contrary, faith assents to the word of God in spite of the fact that reason does not clearly see it to be true. Thomas Aquinas was fully aware of the difference. At the very beginning of his career, in his commentary on the *Sentences* of Peter Lombard, as he was establishing the scientific nature of theology, he addressed to himself the well known objection: how can the theologian be wholly certain of his conclusions, since they hang on premises of which at least one is not known to be true in the light of reason, but is held on the strength of faith?

To the assertion that the theologian is not fully certain of his conclusions, Thomas answers that this is not true: *dicimus quod falsum est.* And passing straightway to the limit, Thomas adds this remark, almost unbelievable after what he has said about the evidence of the first principles: the believer assents to the truth of faith even more, and more firmly, than to the first principles of reason: *magis enim fidelis est et firmius assentit his quae sunt fidei*

[5] *In Job,* 13, lect. 2; ed. Fretté, vol. XVIII, p. 90.

quam etiam primis principiis rationis.[6] In other words, the true believer is more certain of the dogma of the Trinity, for instance, than of the principle that one and the same thing cannot be at the same time itself and something else. So the believer assents more confidently to a proposition he does not *know* to be true, than to the propositions of which the truth is evident to him in the natural light of reason. This does not imply any doubt in his mind about the absolute validity of the first principles; what is at stake here is not the truth of those propositions but, quite precisely, the firmness of our assent to them.

Now, in the case of the first principles, we assent to the evidence of the natural light of a human, created, and finite mind, whereas faith is an assent of the intellect and heart to the truthfulness of the word of God. We are here reaching key positions of which every Christian is bound to know something, but which are seldom grasped in the fullness of their implications. They all are related to faith, a very simple thing indeed, since every Christian can make an act of faith, but an exceedingly complex notion and, at any rate, an often misunderstood one.

A first point is that religious faith never assents to anything except for one single reason, to wit, because God has revealed it. There are always reasons to believe, but such reasons are never sufficient to cause the assent of the believer to the proposition he believes; otherwise he would not believe its truth, he would know it.

A second point, which is the foundation of the whole theology of faith, is that the proper object of revelation of itself and in itself is always something man needs to know in order to achieve salvation in beatitude. There is such a distance from God to man that if we were left to our own resources, we could never bridge the ontological gap. Revelation precisely instructs us of what we need to know in order to attain an end far exceeding our natural means. This is so essential a notion that it could almost serve as a definition of the object of faith, namely "that through which man attains beatitude."[7] The notion is simple; the trouble is that, along with

[6] *In I Sent.,* Prol., q. 1, a. 3, quaestiuncula 3, solutio.
[7] *Summa theologiae,* II–II, 1, 1, resp.

what belongs to the object of faith properly and by itself, many other things are included in it indirectly and incidentally; most of the difficulties that beset the doctrine, at least in the mind of its readers, originate in that fact.

In discussing or interpreting these matters, we refer to *philosophy* and *theology,* but Thomas himself seldom uses the word "theology." True enough, we find it in the very title of the *Summa theologiae,* and for a good reason. Written for the use of students in faculties of theology, the work could bear no other title, but it was an ambiguous one because the word "theology" had long been used by the philosophers, especially by Aristotle, to point to the crowning part of metaphysics and therefore of philosophy.

Now the kind of theology Thomas intends to teach has nothing in common with the philosophical knowledge of God, except its object. The two theologies are about God, hence their name, but their respective ways of knowing that same object are widely different. In order to mark the distinction, we ourselves now call "natural theology" the theology of the philosophers, and "revealed theology" the doctrine taught by the men we call theologians; Thomas himself does not use those expressions, and the better to avoid ambiguity, he calls theology *sacra doctrina.* Comparing it with the theologies of the philosophers, such as Plato, Aristotle, Proclus and others, Thomas says that there is between them and "sacred doctrine" a wider difference than is to be found between a species and another species within one and the same genus; they differ as one genus from another genus. *Differt secundum genus,* Thomas says of sacred doctrine as developed in his *Summa.*[8]

And indeed it is wholly distinct from the metaphysical knowledge of God, for the theology of the philosophers is the cognition of God such as man can obtain it; it is their own cognition of God, born of the human mind and limited to what we can know of God from our knowledge of his creatures. The theology of the philosophers belongs to the order of the things that are of this world and are, in the proper acceptation of the word, profane. Unlike that

[8] *Summa theologiae,* I, 1, 1, ad 2m.

nonsacred theology, *sacra doctrina* proceeds from God; it imparts to us something of God's own self-knowledge so that through faith there is in us a finite and participated creation of the literally divine knowledge God has of himself. Because it proceeds from God, the sacred doctrine is in us something essentially divine. Faith is God already with us. Of course, the philosophical cognition of God is in itself an excellent thing, only it is a purely natural knowledge. The kind of information man naturally acquires about God leaves us completely out of the inner life of the divinity.

Such is the meaning of the word "supernatural." It points to the divine order which as such distinguishes the *secundum genus* from the natural order. There is no passing from the natural to the supernatural, but the supernatural can come down to inform the natural and to perfect it. Revelation does precisely that with respect to man's natural cognition of God. It divinizes it.

Being a participation in the knowledge God has of himself, faith already is, by mode of cognition, a substantial possession of God. Hence the classical doctrine of Scripture, followed by Thomas as well as by all Catholic theologians, that faith is *the substance of things to be hoped for* (Heb. 11:1). As Thomas understands them, these words signify "the relation of the act of faith to its end," which is God. Faith is said to be the substance of the things to be hoped for because it is the beginning of those very things, already possessed by the assent of the act of faith in which all are virtually included.

Its essential relation to beatitude, then, is what radically distinguishes sacred doctrine from a mere philosophical knowledge of God. It is not simply information about God, it is an invitation from God to man; unless we accept that divine invitation, no beatitude is possible. Now the act of the virtue of faith is our acceptance of it; in the words of Scripture, *sine fide impossibile est placere Deo* (Heb. 11:6): without faith it is impossible to please God. To which the Epistle presently adds that he who wants to approach God (not merely to know about him) must believe that He exists and that He rewards those who seek Him: *Credere oportet accedentium ad Deum quia est, et quod inquirentibus se remunerator est.* Thomas Aquinas has made that doctrine his own. Philosophy avails nothing to salvation; faith is its very beginning.

Such is the concrete situation with which Thomas is concerned. Most of our own controversies are inspired by a different spirit. Instead of dealing with the actual condition of man with respect to salvation, we focus our attention on the definition of abstract terms such as philosophy and theology, faith and reason. It is legitimate, even necessary, to do so. Thomas himself is careful to introduce such distinctions to clear up the meaning of terms around which certain discussions revolve, but the notions at stake interest him only to the extent that they help him to understand the complex structure of reality.

In the present case, one fact dominates the whole discussion: that it is the free decision of God, in creating the universe, to elevate man to perfect beatitude. Such a beatitude can only be found in the vision of God face to face, and since that vision exceeds the natural power of the human mind, God must reveal what man needs to know in order to be saved.

But that is not the whole question. Granting that at least some of the cognitions required for man's salvation are accessible to the natural light of reason, how many men in fact will be able to acquire them? This amounts to asking: how many men are there who enjoy the natural gifts of intellect, the moral qualities of will, and the leisure and social privileges without which a life successfully dedicated to metaphysical inquiry is practically impossible? This is one of those questions on which differences of opinion can be expected, but Thomas himself was far from entertaining an optimistic view of the situation.

According to him, metaphysicians are rare; there are few of them (*pauci*), indeed very few (*paucissimi*). Whatever their number, since God wanted the saving knowledge to be at the disposal of all men, he freely decided to reveal to them, not the whole of philosophy to be sure, nor even the whole of metaphysical truth, but at least those conclusions of natural theology which exceed the grasp, not indeed of the human mind, but of many human minds.

Such is the situation we are in. While the professors are pains-takingly explaining that we cannot simultaneously know the truth of a proposition and believe it, God simply reveals the whole saving truth to all men so that even those who are not able to discover it by means of reason will nevertheless be able to hold it by faith. So we have to make our own choice—either to analyze the component elements of the situation or to envisage the situation itself and what it pleased God to do about it.

From this second point of view, which is that of theologian Thomas Aquinas, it is a fact that a certain amount of philo-sophically knowable truth has been revealed to man. God did not reveal it as philosophy; in Scripture there are no metaphysical demonstrations of the existence of God, of his oneness, of his providence, or even of the immortality of the soul. In short, Scrip-ture contains no metaphysics at all, but it does contain—or imply —positive information on points of metaphysical interest. Given the complexity of the data, a practically infinite variety of indi-vidual situations are likely to arise. Their detail escapes prevision, but the theologian must at least account for their very possibility.

Thomas Aquinas does more than foresee this; his own theology is calculated to include the totality of saving truth in all its forms and whatever its origin. What of it can be believed only, such as the mysteries of the Trinity and the Incarnation, will be taught as such; as to the parts of it that can be philosophically known, they will be received, first as revealed, since theological knowledge is at stake, then as philosophically justifiable in the light of reason. What is going to happen? The theologian does not know, nor does he need to know. Some of his readers will believe, others will try to know all that which they think they can know, still others will neither know nor believe. A phenomenological de-scription of these concrete situations or at least of some of their general patterns, is a task which Thomas Aquinas left undone, because he was doing something else, but he has left directives to be observed in investigating such problems.

Thus far, our discussion has been concerned with the meaning of two terms only, reason and faith, or philosophical knowledge and revelation. Such are the traditional data of the problem, but one term is missing, and its absence is largely responsible for the failure of those who discuss it to find a satisfactory answer to the question.

As was said, revelation is an invitation. What God reveals to be believed is what man needs to know in order to obtain eternal life. Since eternal life is the sovereign good and since by faith in revelation man holds a promise of it, the truth of faith is itself part of that good. As such this truth is an object of love as much as of cognition. He who is aware of holding in the object of his faith the very substance of the things to be hoped for—and finally the First Truth, God himself—is bound to love this object with his will at the same time that he knows it by his understanding. That is also why the understanding assents to truths it fails to see clearly and is unable to demonstrate. Such truths are beyond the grasp of cognition, not of love.

It is truly said that Thomism essentially is an intellectualism, but it is many other things, if only because in it the will is the prime mover of all the other powers of the soul. This is particularly true in acts of the virtue of faith. Because intellectual evidence is lacking, "the intellect assents to matters of faith at the command of the will,"[9] and the will itself is directed to the object of faith as its own good, which is the vision of God. The act of faith remains inexplicable if one omits to say that at the same time that God is infusing in the intellect the knowledge of the First Truth, he likewise infuses in the will, as a moving force, the grace of loving it. A participation in the love by which God eternally loves himself, the love in us of the object of revelation: this is charity. Because it quickens faith and prompts it to elicit its acts, the theologians say that the form of faith is—charity.

From this conclusion as from a vantage point, the whole doctrine is seen in its full intelligibility. And not only the personal doctrine of Thomas Aquinas, but the whole Augustino-Anselmian tradition as well. Why should faith seek understanding, if not because the understanding of faith is a halfway house on the road

[9] *"Ex imperio voluntatis intellectus credibilibus assentit"* (*Summa theologiae,* II–II, 4, 2, ad 1m).

from plain faith to the beatific vision? Thomas Aquinas is not speaking of philosophy as it can be found in the mind of an unbeliever. Himself a theologian, living in the thirteenth century after Christ, Thomas speaks of the philosophizing reason of baptized men.

Now, of such men Thomas Aquinas says that their faith, so far as it is in its power, sufficiently inclines them to assent not only to all that is of faith essentially and absolutely, but also to all that precedes faith, accompanies it or follows it. This statement covers a very wide field and we are far from the kind of classroom Thomism in which philosophical reason jealously protects its integrity against all religious influences. On the contrary, "when the will of a man is willing to believe, he loves the truth he believes, he turns it over in his mind (*super ea excogitat*) and if he can find reasons for it, he makes them his. And in this too reason does not exclude the merit of faith, but, rather, one should see in it the sign of a greater merit."[10]

Such is the climate in which Thomas Aquinas has always philosophized. There are other ways to philosophize, if only for the simple reason that there have been, still are, and always will be philosophies unrelated to Christian revelation. The man for whom Thomas Aquinas reserved his greatest philosophical admiration, Aristotle, had developed a philosophy entirely free from all religious influences, and of course Thomas was well aware of this fact, but it had nothing to do with his own personal problem. For he at least was a Christian, and the question for him was, could he himself philosophize as though he had never heard of the Christian revelation? Of course he could not. If a Christian undertakes to speak of God, how can he presume to neglect revelation, which is not a merely human knowledge of God, but a certain participation in the knowledge that God has of himself and an assimilation of the divine knowledge inasmuch as by infused faith we adhere to the First Truth itself for its own sake?

Whenever I attempt to define the spirit of Thomas Aquinas' doctrine, I find myself confronted with a sort of antinomy, and so

[10] *Summa theologiae,* II–II, 2, 10, resp).

I start wondering what kind of man he was. In order to teach such a doctrine, he had to entertain an unqualified confidence in the aptitude of human reason to know scientific and philosophical truth; at the same time, he had to entertain an equally absolute confidence in the truth of the divine revelation as received by faith. Last, not the least, he must have been a man who could do both at one and the same time.

Unless we too begin to share in that twofold certitude, we cannot hope to participate in the true spirit of Thomism. Personal dispositions are at stake here, and they defy analysis, but ideas are also involved. Only a certain notion of the world, of man's place in the world, and of man's destiny, can provide a justification for such an attitude.

9

EMPIRICISM AND RELIGIOUS BELIEF

Richard B. Braithwaite

Logical empiricism has become the dominant philosophy nowadays in Great Britain and the United States. It has fused the empiricist tradition, going back to Locke, Berkeley, and Hume, with the contemporary interest in language and logic. For the philosophy of religion, this has meant a study of the language of religion—what it means, and whether it has any empirical basis. The earlier positivists were inclined to dismiss religious language as merely emotive, but there are many objections to such an oversimplified account of the matter. In the following excerpt, Richard Braithwaite argues that religious assertions are to be understood as conative rather than emotive.

THE MEANING of any statement will be taken as being given by the way it is used. The kernel for an empiricist of the problem of the nature of religious belief is to explain, in empirical terms, how a religious statement is used by a man who asserts it in order to express his religious conviction.

Since I shall argue that the primary element in this use is that the religious assertion is used as a moral assertion, I must first consider how moral assertions are used. According to the view developed by various moral philosophers since the impossibility of regarding moral statements as verifiable propositions was recognized, a moral assertion is used to express an *attitude* of the man

Reprinted with permission from *An Empiricist's View of the Nature of Religious Belief* (New York: Cambridge University Press, 1955), pp. 11–18.

making the assertion. It is not used to assert the proposition that he has the attitude—a verifiable psychological proposition; it is used to show forth or evince his attitude. The attitude is concerned with the action which he asserts to be right or to be his duty, or the state of affairs which he asserts to be good; it is a highly complex state, and contains elements to which various degrees of importance have been attached by moral philosophers who have tried to work out an "ethics without propositions." One element in the attitude is a feeling of approval towards the action; this element was taken as the fundamental one in the first attempts, and views of ethics without propositions are frequently lumped together as "emotive" theories of ethics. But discussion of the subject during the last twenty years has made it clear, I think, that no emotion or feeling of approval is fundamental to the use of moral assertions; it may be the case that the moral asserter has some specific feeling directed on to the course of action said to be right, but this is not the most important element in his "pro-attitude" towards the course of action: what is primary is his intention to perform the action when the occasion for it arises.

The form of ethics without propositions which I shall adopt is therefore a conative rather than an emotive theory: it makes the primary use of a moral assertion that of expressing the intention of the asserter to act in a particular sort of way specified in the assertion. A utilitarian, for example, in asserting that he ought to act so as to maximize happiness, is thereby declaring his intention to act, to the best of his ability, in accordance with the policy of utilitarianism: he is not asserting any proposition, or necessarily evincing any feeling of approval; he is subscribing to a policy of action. There will doubtless be empirical propositions which he may give as reasons for his adherence to the policy (e.g. that happiness is what all, or what most people, desire), and his having the intention will include his understanding what is meant by pursuing the policy, another empirically verifiable proposition. But there will be no specifically moral proposition which he will be asserting when he declares his intention to pursue the policy. This account is fully in accord with the spirit of empiricism, for whether or not a man has the intention of pursuing a particular behavior policy can be empirically tested, both by observing what he does and by hearing what he replies when he is questioned about his intentions.

Not all expressions of intentions will be moral assertions: for the notion of morality to be applicable it is necessary either that the policy of action intended by the asserter should be a general policy (e.g. the policy of utilitarianism) or that it should be subsumable under a general policy which the asserter intends to follow and which he would give as the reason for his more specific intention. There are difficulties and vaguenesses in the notion of a general policy of action, but these need not concern us here. All that we require is that, when a man asserts that he ought to do so-and-so, he is using the assertion to declare that he resolves, to the best of his ability, to do so-and-so. And he will not necessarily be insincere in his assertion if he suspects, at the time of making it, that he will not have the strength of character to carry out his resolution.

The advantage this account of moral assertions has over all others, emotive non-propositional ones as well as cognitive propositional ones, is that it alone enables a satisfactory answer to be given to the question: What is the reason for my doing what I think I ought to do? The answer it gives is that, since my thinking that I ought to do the action is my intention to do it if possible, the reason why I do the action is simply that I intend to do it, if possible. On every other ethical view there will be a mysterious gap to be filled somehow between the moral judgment and the intention to act in accordance with it: there is no such gap if the primary use of a moral assertion is to declare such an intention.

Let us now consider what light this way of regarding moral assertions throws upon assertions of religious conviction. The idealist philosopher McTaggart described religion as "an emotion resting on a conviction of a harmony between ourselves and the universe at large,"[1] and many educated people at the present time would agree with him. If religion is essentially concerned with

[1] J. M. E. McTaggart, *Some Dogmas of Religion* (1906), p. 3.

emotion, it is natural to explain the use of religious assertions on the lines of the original emotive theory of ethics and to regard them as primarily evincing religious feelings or emotions. The assertion, for example, that God is our Heavenly Father will be taken to express the asserter's feeling secure in the same way as he would feel secure in his father's presence. But explanations of religion in terms of feeling, and of religious assertions as expressions of such feelings, are usually propounded by people who stand outside any religious system; they rarely satisfy those who speak from inside. Few religious men would be prepared to admit that their religion was a matter merely of feeling: feelings—of joy, of consolation, of being at one with the universe—may enter into their religion, but to evince such feelings is certainly not the primary use of their religious assertions.

This objection, however, does not seem to me to apply to treating religious assertions in the conative way in which recent moral philosophers have treated moral statements—as being primarily declarations of adherence to a policy of action, declarations of commitment to a way of life. That the way of life led by the believer is highly relevant to the sincerity of his religious conviction has been insisted upon by all the moral religions, above all, perhaps, by Christianity. "By their fruits ye shall know them." The view which I put forward for your consideration is that the intention of a Christian to follow a Christian way of life is not only the criterion for the sincerity of his belief in the assertions of Christianity; it is the criterion for the meaningfulness of his assertions. Just as the meaning of a moral assertion is given by its use in expressing the asserter's intention to act, so far as in him lies, in accordance with the moral principle involved, so the meaning of a religious assertion is given by its use in expressing the asserter's intention to follow a specified policy of behavior. To say that it is belief in the dogmas of religion which is the cause of the believer's intending to behave as he does is to put the cart before the horse: it is the intention to behave which constitutes what is known as religious conviction.

But this assimilation of religious to moral assertions lays itself open to an immediate objection. When a moral assertion is taken as declaring the intention of following a policy, the form of the assertion itself makes it clear what the policy is with which the assertion is concerned. For a man to assert that a certain policy ought to be pursued, which on this view is for him to declare his intention of pursuing the policy, presupposes his understanding what it would be like for him to pursue the policy in question. I cannot resolve not to tell a lie without knowing what a lie is. But if a religious assertion is the declaration of an intention to carry out a certain policy, what policy does it specify? The religious statement itself will not explicitly refer to a policy, as does a moral statement; how then can the asserter of the statement know what is the policy concerned, and how can he intend to carry out a policy if he does not know what the policy is? I cannot intend to do something I know not what.

The reply to this criticism is that, if a religious assertion is regarded as representative of a large number of assertions of the same religious system, the body of assertions of which the particular one is a representative specimen is taken by the asserter as implicitly specifying a particular way of life. It is no more necessary for an empiricist philosopher to explain the use of a religious statement taken in isolation from other religious statements than it is for him to give a meaning to a scientific hypothesis in isolation from other scientific hypotheses. We understand scientific hypotheses, and the terms that occur in them, by virtue of the relation of the whole system of hypotheses to empirically observable facts; and it is the whole system of hypotheses, not one hypothesis in isolation, that is tested for its truth-value against experience. So there are good precedents, in the empiricist way of thinking, for considering a system of religious assertions as a whole, and for examining the way in which the whole system is used.

If we do this the fact that a system of religious assertions has a moral function can hardly be denied. For to deny it would require any passage from the assertion of a religious system to a policy of action to be mediated by a moral assertion. I cannot pass from asserting a fact, of whatever sort, to intending to perform an action, without having the hypothetical intention to intend to do the action if I assert the fact. This holds however widely fact is understood—whether as an empirical fact or as a non-empirical fact about goodness or reality. Just as the intention-to-act view of moral assertions is the only view that requires no reason for my doing what I assert to be my duty, so the similar view of religious assertions is the only one which connects them to ways of life without requiring an additional premise. Unless a Christian's assertion that God is love (*agape*)—which I take to epitomize the assertions of the Christian religion—be taken to declare his intention to follow an agapeistic way of life, he could be asked what is the connection between the assertion and the intention, between Christian belief and Christian practice. And this question can always be asked if religious assertions are separated from conduct. Unless religious principles are moral principles, it makes no sense to speak of putting them into practice.

III

PRAGMATISM, PERSONALISM,
AND EXISTENTIALISM

III

I

INTRODUCTION

BOTH THE IDEALISTS considered in the first part of this volume and the naturalists and positivists considered in the second part could be accused of abstraction. Admittedly, no uniform charge could be leveled against such a varied selection of philosophers as came to our notice. Yet in so far as idealism takes the thinking subject as its starting point, it deals in an abstraction, though this is in some degree overcome in the forms of personal and historical idealism. Likewise, naturalism and empiricism begin from the abstraction of the object, and an extremely distorting type of abstraction is characteristic both of reductive naturalism and of logical positivism. On the other hand, the naturalism of Whitehead has a much more concrete character, and seeks explicitly to avoid the "bifurcation" that vitiates the reductive type.

We turn now to a series of philosophies which try to bridge the gap between subject and object and to overcome the abstractness which so easily arises when either the subject or the object is taken in isolation as philosophy's starting point. The initial datum is man already involved in his world, and man in the whole range of his relationships, not merely as a knowing subject. We are concerned now with philosophies of life, action, existence.

We begin with *pragmatism*. This philosophy, which has been enormously influential in the United States, subordinates thought to action and protests against all abstract intellectualism. In the words of Charles Sanders Peirce (1839–1914), "the whole function of thought is to produce habits of action." Hence the meaning and perhaps even the truth of beliefs is to be judged from their practical consequences. Religious belief, for instance, is to be judged by its consequences in individual and social life.

We include an excerpt from perhaps the most famous of all pragmatists, William James (1842–1910). It shows both his antipathy to speculative idealism on the one hand and to agnosticism on the other, for the very fact that we have to decide about our lives means that we cannot help taking up a stance on the issue of faith or unfaith. James' type of pragmatism comes very near in some respects to the existentialism of a later generation. We should note too that James was too wise to think that pragmatism allows us simply to bypass questions about "the way things are." His point is that however we try to answer these questions, we must test our answers in lived experience. We have included also an excerpt from Walter Rauschenbusch (1861–1918), one of the most distinguished representatives of the "Social Gospel." His activist and ethical interpretation of Christianity is very typical of American Protestantism, but whereas much of the latter is theologically very thin, Rauschenbusch tried to match his activist concerns with a viable theology, and found the basis for this in the Ritschlian preoccupation with the Kingdom of God as the central *motif* of theology.

Pragmatism shifts attention from man as subject to man as agent. Yet man's being is not exhausted by what he does, any more than by what he thinks. What is perhaps most distinctive about the personal being of man is his capacity for love and friendship, in other words, his capacity for entering into relations with other persons. Just as we are dealing with an abstraction if we think of man apart from what he is doing in the world, so too we are dealing with an abstraction if we do not recognize that to be a person, one must stand in relation to other persons. Furthermore, this "I-Thou" relation is fundamentally different from my relation to the things which I use in the world. The personal dimension of human life cannot be measured in terms of utility or practical results. I have used the word *personalism* in the broadest sense to stand for those recent and contemporary philosophical attempts to explore the richness and complexity of personal and interpersonal being, without sacrificing its concreteness or attempting to reduce it to that which is less than personal. Undoubtedly Martin Buber (1878–1965) has been the outstanding philosopher of personal being in this century, and we include an excerpt from his best-known work.

Yet Buber's poetic style is perhaps more typical of the sage than of the strict philosophical practitioner. If the philosophy of personal being was to be put on a firmer methodological basis, it has to find some more stringent way of dealing with its theme. This methodological basis was supplied by the phenomenology of Edmund Husserl (1859–1938). Phenomenology is, at bottom, simply description, letting the phenomena be seen for what they really are. Yet description is notoriously difficult, for so often our unspoken prejudices and expectations cause us to see what is not there or to fail to see what is there. The phenomenologist carefully strives to find ways of describing human experience that will show us the essence of the matter without distortion. Rudolf Otto's classic description of the experience of the holy is a splendid example of the phenomenology of religious experience. Otto lived from 1869–1937.

The above-mentioned trends are gathered up in contemporary *existentialism*. It seeks to span the gap between subject and object, and begins from the concrete awareness of existing in the world. The existent is, from the beginning, a being-in-the-world, engaged in all kinds of practical concerns, and also a being-with-others, situated in a web of interpersonal relations. The existentialist philosopher begins from this datum in all its concreteness, and seeks to analyse it and to trace its structure. For this task, the leading existentialist philosophers, such as Martin Heidegger (1889–   ), have employed the phenomenological method. But the very fact that existence is to be studied in its concreteness implies that existentialism cannot be simply an anthropology (doctrine of man) but must expand into an ontology. The major features of existentialism, including its differences from pragmatism and vitalism, are set forth very clearly and persuasively by Nikolai Berdyaev (1874–1948) at the beginning of one of his books. The passage is printed below, and we should notice also that Berdyaev shows very effectively that even if Kant discredited traditional rational metaphysics, this leaves unaffected the possibility of an existential metaphysic or ontology.

We conclude with selections from three theologians, illustrating how the philosophies of existence are being applied to concrete theological problems. Emil Brunner (1889–1966) was specially influenced by the notion of personal encounter, as this is described by Buber and others, and this is apparent in our excerpt, which deals with the nature of revelation. Rudolf Bultmann (1884–   ) has perhaps applied existentialist ideas more consistently than any other theologian. The excerpt analyses the problem raised by the mythological language of the New Testament, offers a theory of myth as the expression of an existential self-understanding, and points the way to its existential interpretation or demythologizing. Finally, Paul Tillich (1886–1965) shows how reflection on the meaning of biblical faith leads inescapably into the problems of an existential ontology.

2

THE WILL TO BELIEVE

William James

The pragmatism of William James cuts behind the disputes between realists and idealists, holding that such theories are too abstract and intellectualist. James was not indeed averse to speculation (he had sympathy with the kind of metaphysic worked out by Bergson) but he claimed that such speculations must be closely related to practical experience and have a "cash value" in our actual business of living in the world. Religious belief is speculative and cannot be proved, but it is not merely an intellectual belief and has practical consequences. We may therefore be justified in committing ourselves to a religious faith even if the evidence for it is inconclusive, provided that this faith brings forth worthwhile fruits in individual and social life. His famous essay on "The Will to Believe" gives persuasive expression to his view.

IN THE RECENTLY published Life by Leslie Stephen of his brother, Fitz-James, there is an account of a school to which the latter went when he was a boy. The teacher, a certain Mr. Guest, used to converse with his pupils in this wise: "Gurney, what is the difference between justification and sanctification?—Stephen, prove the omnipotence of God!" etc. In the midst of our Harvard freethinking and indifference we are prone to imagine that here at your good old orthodox College conversation continues to be somewhat upon

From *Selected Papers on Philosophy* (London: J. M. Dent, 1917), pp. 99–124.

this order; and to show you that we at Harvard have not lost all interest in these vital subjects, I have brought with me tonight something like a sermon on justification by faith to read to you—I mean an essay in justification *of* faith, a defence of our right to adopt a believing attitude in religious matters, in spite of the fact that our merely logical intellect may not have been coerced. "The Will to Believe," accordingly, is the title of my paper.

I have long defended to my own students the lawfulness of voluntarily adopted faith; but as soon as they have got well imbued with the logical spirit, they have as a rule refused to admit my contention to be lawful philosophically, even though in point of fact they were personally all the time chock-full of some faith or other themselves. I am all the while, however, so profoundly convinced that my own position is correct, that your invitation has seemed to me a good occasion to make my statements more clear. Perhaps your minds will be more open than those with which I have hitherto had to deal. I will be as little technical as I can, though I must begin by setting up some technical distinctions that will help us in the end.

Let us give the name of *hypothesis* to anything that may be proposed to our belief; and just as the electricians speak of live and dead wires, let us speak of any hypothesis as either *live* or *dead*. A live hypothesis is one which appeals as a real possibility to him to whom it is proposed. If I ask you to believe in the Mahdi, the notion makes no electric connection with your nature—it refuses to scintillate with any credibility at all. As an hypothesis it is completely dead. To an Arab, however (even if he be not one of the Mahdi's followers), the hypothesis is among the mind's possibilities: it is alive. This shows that deadness and liveness in an hypothesis are not intrinsic properties but relations to the individual thinker. They are measured by his willingness to act. The maximum of liveness in an hypothesis means willingness to act irrevocably. Practically that means belief; but there is some believing tendency wherever there is willingness to act at all.

Next, let us call the decision between two hypotheses an *option*.

Options may be of several kinds. They may be—(1) *living* or *dead;* (2) *forced* or *avoidable;* (3) *momentous* or *trivial;* and for our purposes we may call an option a *genuine* option when it is of the forced, living, and momentous kind.

A living option is one in which both hypotheses are live ones. If I say to you: "Be a theosophist or be a Mohammedan," it is probably a dead option, because for you neither hypothesis is likely to be alive. But if I say: "Be an agnostic or be a Christian," it is otherwise: trained as you are, each hypothesis makes some appeal, however small, to your belief.

Next, if I say to you: "Choose between going out with your umbrella or without it," I do not offer you a genuine option, for it is not forced. You can easily avoid it by not going out at all. Similarly, if I say, "Either love me or hate me," "Either call my theory true or call it false," your option is avoidable. You may remain indifferent to me, neither loving nor hating, and you may decline to offer any judgment as to my theory. But if I say, "Either accept this truth or go without it," I put on you a forced option, for there is no standing place outside of the alternative. Every dilemma based on a complete logical disjunction, with no possibility of not choosing, is an option of this forced kind.

Finally, if I were Dr. Nansen and proposed to you to join my North Pole expedition, your option would be momentous: for this would probably be your only similar opportunity, and your choice now would either exclude you from the North Pole sort of immortality altogether or put at least the chance of it into your hands. He who refuses to embrace a unique opportunity loses the prize as surely as if he tried and failed. *Per contra,* the option is trivial when the opportunity is not unique, when the stake is insignificant, or when the decision is reversible if it later prove unwise. Such trivial options abound in the scientific life. A chemist finds an hypothesis live enough to spend a year in its verification: he believes in it to that extent. But if his experiments prove inconclusive either way, he is quit for his loss of time, no vital harm being done.

It will facilitate our discussion if we keep all these distinctions well in mind.

The next matter to consider is the actual psychology of human opinion. When we look at certain facts, it seems as if our passional and volitional nature lay at the root of all our convictions. When we look at others, it seems as if they could do nothing when the intellect had once said its say. Let us take the latter facts up first.

Does it not seem preposterous on the very face of it to talk of our opinions being modifiable at will? Can our will either help or hinder our intellect in its perceptions of truth? Can we, by just willing it, believe that Abraham Lincoln's existence is a myth, and that the portraits of him in *McClure's Magazine* are all of some one else? Can we, by any effort of our will, or by any strength of wish that it were true, believe ourselves well and about when we are roaring with rheumatism in bed, or feel certain that the sum of the two one-dollar bills in our pocket must be a hundred dollars? We can *say* any of these things, but we are absolutely impotent to believe them; and of just such things is the whole fabric of the truths that we do believe in made up—matters of fact, immediate or remote, as Hume said, and relations between ideas, which are either there or not there for us if we see them so, and which if not there cannot be put there by any action of our own.

In Pascal's *Thoughts* there is a celebrated passage known in literature as Pascal's wager. In it he tries to force us into Christianity by reasoning as if our concern with truth resembled our concern with the stakes in a game of chance. Translated freely his words are these: You must either believe or not believe that God is—which will you do? Your human reason cannot say. A game is going on between you and the nature of things which at the day of judgment will bring out either heads or tails. Weigh what your gains and your losses would be if you should stake all you have on heads, or God's existence: if you win in such case, you gain eternal beatitude; if you lose, you lose nothing at all. If there were an infinity of chances, and only one for God in this wager, still you ought to stake your all on God; for though you surely risk a finite loss by this procedure, any finite loss is reasonable, even a certain one is reasonable, if there is but the possibility of infinite gain. Go, then, and take holy water, and have masses said; belief will come and stupefy your scruples—*Cela vous fera croire et vous abêtira.* Why should you not? At bottom, what have you to lose?

You probably feel that when religious faith expresses itself thus, in the language of the gaming-table, it is put to its last trumps. Surely Pascal's own personal belief in masses and holy water had far other springs; and this celebrated page of his is but an argument for others, a last desperate snatch at a weapon against the hardness of the unbelieving heart. We feel that a faith in masses and holy water adopted willfully after such a mechanical calculation would lack the inner soul of faith's reality; and if we were ourselves in the place of the Deity, we should probably take particular pleasure in cutting off believers of this pattern from their infinite reward. It is evident that unless there be some pre-existing tendency to believe in masses and holy water, the option offered to the will by Pascal is not a living option. Certainly no Turk ever took to masses and holy water on its account; and even to us Protestants these means of salvation seem such foregone impossibilities that Pascal's logic, invoked for them specifically, leaves us unmoved. As well might the Mahdi write to us, saying, "I am the Expected One whom God has created in his effulgence. You shall be infinitely happy if you confess me; otherwise you shall be cut off from the light of the sun. Weigh, then, your infinite gain if I am genuine against your finite sacrifice if I am not!" His logic would be that of Pascal; but he would vainly use it on us, for the hypothesis he offers us is dead. No tendency to act on it exists in us to any degree.

The talk of believing by our volition seems, then, from one point of view, simply silly. From another point of view it is worse than silly, it is vile. When one turns to the magnificent edifice of the physical sciences, and sees how it was reared; what thousands of disinterested moral lives of men lie buried in its mere foundations; what patience and postponement, what choking down of preference, what submission to the icy laws of outer fact are wrought into its very stones and mortar; how absolutely impersonal it stands in its vast augustness—then how besotted and contemptible seems every little sentimentalist who comes blowing his voluntary smoke-wreaths, and pretending to decide things from out of his private dream! Can we wonder if those bred in the rugged and manly school of science should feel like spewing such subjectivism out of their mouths? The whole system of loyalties which grow up in the schools of science goes dead against its toleration; so that it is only natural that those who have caught the scientific fever should pass over to the opposite extreme, and write sometimes as if the incorruptibly truthful intellect ought positively to prefer bitterness and unacceptableness to the heart in its cup.

> It fortifies my soul to know
> That, though I perish, Truth is so—

sings Clough, while Huxley exclaims: "My only consolation lies in the reflection that, however bad our posterity may become, so far as they hold by the plain rule of not pretending to believe what they have no reason to believe, because it may be to their advantage so to pretend [the word "pretend" is surely here redundant], they will not have reached the lowest depth of immorality." And that delicious *enfant terrible* Clifford writes: "Belief is desecrated when given to unproved and unquestioned statements for the solace and private pleasure of the believer. . . . Whoso would deserve well of his fellows in this matter will guard the purity of his belief with a very fanaticism of jealous care, lest at any time it should rest on an unworthy object, and catch a stain which can never be wiped away. . . . If [a] belief has been accepted on insufficient evidence [even though the belief be true, as Clifford on the same page explains] the pleasure is a stolen one. . . . It is sinful because it is stolen in defiance of our duty to mankind. That duty is to guard ourselves from such beliefs as from a pestilence which may shortly master our own body and then spread to the rest of the town. . . . It is wrong always, everywhere, and for every one, to believe anything upon insufficient evidence."

All this strikes one as healthy, even when expressed, as by Clifford, with somewhat too much of robustious pathos in the voice. Free-will and simple wishing do seem, in the matter of our credences, to be only fifth wheels to the coach. Yet if only one should thereupon assume that intellectual insight is what remains after wish and will and sentimental preference have taken wing, or that pure reason is what then settles our opinions, he would fly quite as directly in the teeth of the facts.

It is only our already dead hypotheses that our willing nature is unable to bring to life again. But what has made them dead for us is for the most part a previous action of our willing nature of an antagonistic kind. When I say "willing nature," I do not mean only such deliberate volitions as may have set up habits of belief that we cannot now escape from—I mean all such factors of belief as fear and hope, prejudice and passion, imitation and partisanship, the circumpressure of our caste and set. As a matter of fact we find ourselves believing, we hardly know how or why. Mr. Balfour gives the name of "authority" to all those influences, born of the intellectual climate, that make hypotheses possible or impossible for us, alive or dead. Here in this room, we all of us believe in molecules and the conservation of energy, in democracy and necessary progress, in Protestant Christianity and the duty of fighting for "the doctrine of the immortal Monroe," all for no reasons worthy of the name. We see into these matters with no more inner clearness, and probably with much less, than any disbeliever in them might possess. His unconventionality would probably have some grounds to show for its conclusions; but for us, not insight, but the *prestige* of the opinions, is what makes the spark shoot from them and light up our sleeping magazines of faith. Our reason is quite satisfied, in nine hundred and ninety-nine cases out of every thousand of us, if it can find a few arguments that will do to recite in case our credulity is criticized by some one else. Our faith is faith in some one else's faith, and in the greatest matters this is most the case. Our belief in truth itself, for instance, that there is a truth, and that our minds and it are made for each other—what is it but a passionate affirmation of desire, in which our social system backs us up? We want to have a truth; we want to believe that our experiments and studies and discussions must put us in a continually better and better position towards it; and on this line we agree to fight out our thinking lives. But if a pyrrhonistic sceptic asks us *how we know* all this, can our logic find a reply? No! certainly it cannot. It is just one volition against another—we willing to go in for life upon a trust or assumption which he, for his part, does not care to make.

As a rule we disbelieve all facts and theories for which we have no use. Clifford's cosmic emotions find no use for Christian feelings. Huxley belabors the bishops because there is no use for sacerdotalism in his scheme of life. Newman, on the contrary, goes over to Romanism and finds all sorts of reasons good for staying there, because a priestly system is for him an organic need and delight. Why do so few "scientists" even look at the evidence for telepathy, so called? Because they think, as a leading biologist, now dead, once said to me, that even if such a thing were true, scientists ought to band together to keep it suppressed and concealed. It would undo the uniformity of Nature and all sorts of other things without which scientists cannot carry on their pursuits. But if this very man had been shown something which as a scientist he might *do* with telepathy, he might not only have examined the evidence, but even have found it good enough. This very law which the logicians would impose upon us—if I may give the name of logicians to those who would rule out our willing nature here—is based on nothing but their own natural wish to exclude all elements for which they, in their professional quality of logicians, can find no use.

Evidently, then, our non-intellectual nature does influence our convictions. There are passional tendencies and volitions which run before and others which come after belief, and it is only the latter that are too late for the fair; and they are not too late when the previous passional work has been already in their own direction. Pascal's argument, instead of being powerless, then seems a regular clincher, and is the last stroke needed to make our faith in masses and holy water complete. The state of things is evidently far from simple; and pure insight and logic, whatever they might do ideally, are not the only things that really do produce our creeds.

Our next duty, having recognized this mixed-up state of affairs, is to ask whether it be simply reprehensible and pathological, or whether, on the contrary, we must treat it as a normal element in making up our minds. The thesis I defend is, briefly stated, this: *Our passional nature not only lawfully may, but must, decide an option between propositions, whenever it is a genuine option that cannot by its nature be decided on intellectual grounds; for to say, under such circumstances, "Do not decide, but leave the question open," is itself a passional decision—just like deciding yes or no —and is attended with the same risk of losing the truth.* The thesis thus abstractly expressed will, I trust, soon become quite clear. But I must first indulge in a bit more of preliminary work.

It will be observed that for the purposes of this discussion we are on "dogmatic" ground—ground, I mean, which leaves systematic philosophical scepticism altogether out of account. The postulate that there is truth, and that it is the destiny of our minds to attain it, we are deliberately resolving to make, though the sceptic will not make it. We part company with him, therefore, absolutely, at this point. But the faith that truth exists, and that our minds can find it, may be held in two ways. We may talk of the *empiricist* way and of the *absolutist* way of believing in truth. The absolutists in this matter say that we not only can attain to knowing truth, but we can *know when* we have attained to knowing it; while the empiricists think that although we may attain it, we cannot in- fallibly know when. To *know* is one thing, and to know for certain *that* we know is another. One may hold to the first being possible without the second; hence the empiricists and the absolutists, al- though neither of them is a sceptic in the usual philosophic sense of the term, show very different degrees of dogmatism in their lives.

If we look at the history of opinions, we see that the empiricist tendency has largely prevailed in science, while in philosophy the absolutist tendency has had everything its own way. The character- istic sort of happiness, indeed, which philosophies yield has mainly consisted in the conviction felt by each successive school or system that by it bottom-certitude had been attained. "Other philosophies are collections of opinions, mostly false; *my* philosophy gives stand-ing-ground forever"—who does not recognize in this the key-note of every system worthy of the name? A system, to be a system at all, must come as a *closed* system, reversible in this or that de-tail, perchance, but in its essential features never!

Scholastic orthodoxy, to which one must always go when one wishes to find perfectly clear statement, has beautifully elabo-rated this absolutist conviction in a doctrine which it calls that of "objective evidence." If, for example, I am unable to doubt that I now exist before you, that two is less than three, or that if all men are mortal then I am mortal too, it is because these things illumine my intellect irresistibly. The final ground of this objective evidence possessed by certain propositions is the *adaequatio intellectus nostri cum re*. The certitude it brings involves an *aptitudinem ad extorquendum certum assensum* on the part of the truth envisaged, and on the side of the subject a *quietem in cognitione,* when once the object is mentally received, that leaves no possibility of doubt behind; and in the whole transaction nothing operates but the *entitas ipsa* of the object and the *entitas ipsa* of the mind. We slouchy modern thinkers dislike to talk in Latin—indeed, we dislike to talk in set terms at all; but at bottom our own state of mind is very much like this whenever we uncritically abandon ourselves: You believe in objective evidence and I do. Of some things we feel that we are certain: we know, and we know that we do know. There is something that gives a click inside of us, a bell that strikes twelve, when the hands of our mental clock have swept the dial and meet over the meridian hour. The greatest empiricists among us are only empiricists on reflection: when left to their instincts, they dogmatize like infallible popes. When the Cliffords tell us how sinful it is to be Christians on such "insuffi-cient evidence," insufficiency is really the last thing they have in mind. For them the evidence is absolutely sufficient, only it makes the other way. They believe so completely in an anti-christian order of the universe that there is no living option: Christianity is a dead hypothesis from the start.

But now, since we are all such absolutists by instinct, what in our quality of students of philosophy ought we to do about the fact? Shall we espouse and endorse it? Or shall we treat it as a weakness of our nature from which we must free ourselves, if we can?

I sincerely believe that the latter course is the only one we can follow as reflective men. Objective evidence and certitude are doubtless very fine ideals to play with, but where on this moonlit and dream-visited planet are they found? I am, therefore, myself a complete empiricist so far as my theory of human knowledge goes. I live, to be sure, by the practical faith that we must go on experiencing and thinking over our experience, for only thus can our opinions grow more true; but to hold any one of them—I absolutely do not care which—as if it never could be reinterpretable or corrigible, I believe to be a tremendously mistaken attitude, and I think that the whole history of philosophy will bear me out. There is but one indefectibly certain truth, and that is the truth that pyrrhonistic scepticism itself leaves standing—the truth that the present phenomenon of consciousness exists. That, however, is the bare starting-point of knowledge, the mere admission of a stuff to be philosophized about. The various philosophies are but so many attempts at expressing what this stuff really is. And if we repair to our libraries what disagreement do we discover! Where is a certainly true answer found? Apart from abstract propositions of comparison (such as two and two are the same as four), propositions which tell us nothing by themselves about concrete reality, we find no proposition ever regarded by any one as evidently certain that has not either been called a falsehood, or at least had its truth sincerely questioned by some one else. The transcending of the axioms of geometry, not in play but in earnest, by certain of our contemporaries (as Zöllner and Charles H. Hinton), and the rejection of the whole Aristotelian logic by the Hegelians are striking instances in point.

No concrete test of what is really true has ever been agreed upon. Some make the criterion external to the moment of perception, putting it either in revelation, the *consensus gentium,* the instincts of the heart, or the systematized experience of the race. Others make the perceptive moment its own test—Descartes, for instance, with his clear and distinct ideas guaranteed by the veracity of God; Reid with his "common-sense"; and Kant with his forms of synthetic judgment *a priori.* The inconceivability of the opposite; the capacity to be verified by sense; the possession of complete organic unity or self-relation, realized when a thing is its own other—are standards which, in turn, have been used. The much-lauded objective evidence is never triumphantly there; it is a mere aspiration or *Grenzbegriff,* marking the infinitely remote ideal of our thinking life. To claim that certain truths now possess it, is simply to say that when you think them true and they *are* true, then their evidence is objective, otherwise it is not. But practically one's conviction that the evidence one goes by is of the real objective brand, is only one more subjective opinion added to the lot. For what a contradictory array of opinions have objective evidence and absolute certitude been claimed! The world is rational through and through—its existence is an ultimate brute fact; there is a personal God—a personal God is inconceivable; there is an extra-mental physical world immediately known—the mind can only know its own ideas; a moral imperative exists— obligation is only the resultant of desires; a permanent spiritual principle is in every one—there are only shifting states of mind; there is an endless chain of causes—there is an absolute first cause; an eternal necessity—a freedom; a purpose—no purpose; a primal One—a primal Many; a universal continuity—an essential discontinuity in things; an infinity—no infinity. There is this—there is that; there is indeed nothing which some one has not thought absolutely true, while his neighbor deemed it absolutely false; and not an absolutist among them ever to have considered that the trouble may all the time be essential, and that the intellect, even with truth directly in its grasp, may have no infallible signal for knowing whether it be truth or no. When, indeed, one remembers that the most striking practical application to life of the doctrine of objective certitude has been the conscientious labors

c. the Holy Office of the Inquisition, one feels less tempted than ever to lend the doctrine a respectful ear.

But please observe, now, that when as empiricists we give up the doctrine of objective certitude, we do not thereby give up the quest or hope of truth itself. We still pin our faith on its existence, and still believe that we gain an ever better position towards it by systematically continuing to roll up experiences and think. Our great difference from the scholastic lies in the way we face. The strength of his system lies in the principles, the origin, the *terminus a quo* of his thought; for us the strength is in the outcome, the upshot, the *terminus ad quem*. Not where it comes from but what it leads to is to decide. It matters not to an empiricist from what quarter an hypothesis may come to him: he may have acquired it by fair means or by foul; passion may have whispered or accident suggested it; but if the total drift of thinking continues to confirm it, that is what he means by its being true.

One more point, small but important, and our preliminaries are done. There are two ways of looking at our duty in the matter of opinion—ways entirely different, and yet ways about whose difference the theory of knowledge seems hitherto to have shown very little concern. *We must know the truth;* and *we must avoid error*—these are our first and great commandments as would-be knowers; but they are not two ways of stating an identical commandment, they are two separable laws. Although it may indeed happen that when we believe the truth *A,* we escape as an incidental consequence from believing the falsehood *B,* it hardly ever happens that by merely disbelieving *B* we necessarily believe *A*. We may in escaping *B* fall into believing other falsehoods, *C* or *D,* just as bad as *B;* or we may escape *B* by not believing anything at all, not even *A*.

Believe truth! Shun error!—these, we see, are two materially different laws; and by choosing between them we may end by coloring differently our whole intellectual life. We may regard the chase for truth as paramount, and the avoidance of error as secondary; or we may, on the other hand, treat the avoidance of error as more imperative, and let truth take its chance. Clifford, in the instructive passage which I have quoted, exhorts us to the latter course. Believe nothing, he tells us, keep your mind in suspense forever, rather than by closing it on insufficient evidence incur the awful risk of believing lies. You, on the other hand, may think that the risk of being in error is a very small matter when compared with the blessings of real knowledge, and be ready to be duped many times in your investigation rather than postpone indefinitely the chance of guessing true. I myself find it impossible to go with Clifford. We must remember that these feelings of our duty about either truth or error are in any case only expressions of our passional life. Biologically considered, our minds are as ready to grind out falsehood as veracity, and he who says, "Better go without belief forever than believe a lie!" merely shows his own preponderant private horror of becoming a dupe. He may be critical of many of his desires and fears, but this fear he slavishly obeys. He cannot imagine any one questioning its binding force. For my own part, I have also a horror of being duped; but I can believe that worse things than being duped may happen to a man in this world: so Clifford's exhortation has to my ears a thoroughly fantastic sound. It is like a general informing his soldiers that it is better to keep out of battle forever than to risk a single wound. Not so are victories either over enemies or over nature gained. Our errors are surely not such awfully solemn things. In a world where we are so certain to incur them in spite of all our caution, a certain lightness of heart seems healthier than this excessive nervousness on their behalf. At any rate, it seems the fittest thing for the empiricist philosopher.

And now, after all this introduction, let us go straight at our question. I have said, and now repeat it, that not only as a matter of fact do we find our passional nature influencing us in our opinions, but that there are some options between opinions in which this influence must be regarded both as an inevitable and as a lawful determinant of our choice.

I fear here that some of you my hearers will begin to scent danger, and lend an inhospitable ear. Two first steps of passion you have indeed had to admit as necessary—we must think so as to avoid dupery, and we must think so as to gain truth; but the surest path to those ideal consummations, you will probably consider, is from now onwards to take no further passional step.

Well, of course, I agree as far as the facts will allow. Wherever the option between losing truth and gaining it is not momentous, we can throw the chance of *gaining truth* away, and at any rate save ourselves from any chance of *believing falsehood,* by not making up our minds at all till objective evidence has come. In scientific questions, this is almost always the case; and even in human affairs in general, the need of acting is seldom so urgent that a false belief to act on is better than no belief at all. Law courts, indeed, have to decide on the best evidence attainable for the moment, because a judge's duty is to make law as well as to ascertain it, and (as a learned judge once said to me) few cases are worth spending much time over: the great thing is to have them decided on *any* acceptable principle, and got out of the way. But in our dealings with objective nature we obviously are recorders, not makers, of the truth; and decisions for the mere sake of deciding promptly and getting on to the next business would be wholly out of place. Throughout the breadth of physical nature facts are what they are quite independently of us, and seldom is there any such hurry about them that the risks of being duped by believing a premature theory need be faced. The questions here are always trivial options, the hypotheses are hardly living (at any rate not living for us spectators), the choice between believing truth or falsehood is seldom forced. The attitude of sceptical balance is therefore the absolutely wise one if we would escape mistakes. What difference, indeed, does it make to most of us whether we have or have not a theory of the Röntgen rays, whether we believe or not in mind-stuff, or have a conviction about the causality of conscious states? It makes no difference. Such options are not forced on us. On every account it is better not to make them, but still keep weighing reasons *pro et contra* with an indifferent hand.

I speak, of course, here of the purely judging mind. For purposes of discovery such indifference is to be less highly recommended, and science would be far less advanced than she is if the passionate desires of individuals to get their own faiths confirmed had been kept out of the game. See, for example, the sagacity which Spencer and Weismann now display. On the other hand, if you want an absolute duffer in an investigation, you must, after all, take the man who has no interest whatever in its results: he is the warranted incapable, the positive fool. The most useful investigator, because the most sensitive observer, is always he whose eager interest in one side of the question is balanced by an equally keen nervousness lest he become deceived. Science has organized this nervousness into a regular *technique,* her so-called method of verification; and she has fallen so deeply in love with the method that one may even say she has ceased to care for truth by itself at all. It is only truth as technically verified that interests her. The truth of truths might come in merely affirmative form, and she would decline to touch it. Such truth as that, she might repeat with Clifford, would be stolen in defiance of her duty to mankind. Human passions, however, are stronger than technical rules. *"Le coeur a ses raisons,"* as Pascal says, *"que la raison ne connaît pas";* and however indifferent to all but the bare rules of the game the umpire, the abstract intellect, may be, the concrete players who furnish him the materials to judge of are usually, each one of them, in love with some pet "live hypothesis" of his own. Let us agree, however, that wherever there is no forced option, the dispassionately judicial intellect with no pet hypothesis, saving us, as it does, from dupery at any rate, ought to be our ideal.

The question next arises: Are there not somewhere forced options in our speculative questions, and can we (as men who may be interested at least as much in positively gaining truth as in merely escaping dupery) always wait with impunity till the coercive evidence shall have arrived? It seems *a priori* improbable that the truth should be so nicely adjusted to our needs and powers as that. In the great boarding-house of nature, the cakes and the butter and the syrup seldom come out so even and leave the plates so clean. Indeed, we should view them with scientific suspicion if they did.

Moral questions immediately present themselves as questions whose solution cannot wait for sensible proof. A moral question is a question not of what sensibly exists, but of what is good, or would be good if it did exist. Science can tell us what exists; but to compare the *worths,* both of what exists and of what does not exist, we must consult not science, but what Pascal calls our heart. Science herself consults her heart when she lays it down that the infinite ascertainment of fact and correction of false belief are the supreme goods for man. Challenge the statement, and science can only repeat it oracularly, or else prove it by showing that such ascertainment and correction bring man all sorts of other goods which man's heart in turn declares. The question of having moral beliefs at all or not having them is decided by our will. Are our moral preferences true or false, or are they only odd biological phenomena, making things good or bad for *us,* but in themselves indifferent? How can your pure intellect decide? If your heart does not *want* a world of moral reality, your head will assuredly never make you believe in one. Mephistophelian scepticism, indeed, will satisfy the head's play-instincts much better than any rigorous idealism can. Some men (even at the student age) are so naturally cool-hearted that the moralistic hypothesis never has for them any pungent life, and in their supercilious presence the hot young moralist always feels strangely ill at ease. The appearance of knowingness is on their side, of *naïveté* and gullibility on his. Yet, in the inarticulate heart of him, he clings to it that he is not a dupe, and that there is a realm in which (as Emerson says) all their wit and intellectual superiority is no better than the cunning of a fox. Moral scepticism can no more be refuted or proved by logic than intellectual scepticism can. When we stick to it that there *is* truth (be it of either kind), we do so with our whole nature, and resolve to stand or fall by the results. The sceptic with his whole nature adopts the doubting attitude; but which of us is the wiser, Omniscience only knows.

Turn now from these wide questions of good to a certain class of questions of fact, questions concerning personal relations, states of mind between one man and another. *Do you like me or not?*— for example. Whether you do or not depends, in countless instances, on whether I meet you half-way, am willing to assume that you must like me, and show you trust and expectation. The previous faith on my part in your liking's existence is in such cases what makes your liking come. But if I stand aloof, and refuse to budge an inch until I have objective evidence, until you shall have done something apt, as the absolutists say, *ad extorquendum assensum meum,* ten to one your liking never comes. How many women's hearts are vanquished by the mere sanguine insistence of some man that they *must* love him! he will not consent to the hypothesis that they cannot. The desire for a certain kind of truth here brings about that special truth's existence; and so it is in innumerable cases of other sorts. Who gains promotions, boons, appointments but the man in whose life they are seen to play the part of live hypotheses, who discounts them, sacrifices other things for their sake before they have come, and takes risks for them in advance? His faith acts on the powers above him as a claim, and creates its own verification.

A social organism of any sort whatever, large or small, is what it is because each member proceeds to his own duty with a trust that the other members will simultaneously do theirs. Wherever a desired result is achieved by the cooperation of many independent persons, its existence as a fact is a pure consequence of the precursive faith in one another of those immediately concerned. A government, an army, a commercial system, a ship, a college, an athletic team, all exist on this condition, without which not only is nothing achieved, but nothing is even attempted. A whole train of passengers (individually brave enough) will be looted by a few highwaymen, simply because the latter can count on one another, while each passenger fears that if he makes a movement of resistance he will be shot before any one else backs him up. If we believed that the whole carful would rise at once with us, we should each severally rise, and train-robbing would never even be attempted. There are, then, cases where a fact cannot come at all unless a preliminary faith exists in its coming. *And where faith in a fact can help create the fact,* that would be an insane logic which should say that faith running ahead of scientific evidence is the "lowest kind of immorality" into which a thinking being can fall. Yet such is the logic by which our scientific absolutists pretend to regulate our lives!

In truths dependent on our personal action, then, faith based on desire is certainly a lawful and possibly an indispensable thing.

But now, it will be said, these are all childish human cases, and have nothing to do with great cosmical matters, like the question of religious faith. Let us then pass on to that. Religions differ so much in their accidents that in discussing the religious question we must make it very generic and broad. What then do we now mean by the religious hypothesis? Science says things are; morality says some things are better than other things; and religion says essentially two things.

First, she says that the best things are the more eternal things, the overlapping things, the things in the universe that throw the last stone, so to speak, and say the final word. "Perfection is eternal," —this phrase of Charles Secrétan seems a good way of putting this first affirmation of religion, an affirmation which obviously cannot yet be verified scientifically at all.

The second affirmation of religion is that we are better off even now if we believe her first affirmation to be true.

Now, let us consider what the logical elements of this situation are *in case the religious hypothesis in both its branches be really true.* (Of course, we must admit that possibility at the outset. If we are to discuss the question at all, it must involve a living option. If for any of you religion be a hypothesis that cannot by any living possibility be true, then you need go no farther. I speak to the "saving remnant" alone.) So proceeding, we see, first, that religion offers itself as a *momentous* option. We are supposed to gain, even now, by our belief, and to lose by our non-belief, a certain vital good. Secondly, religion is a *forced* option, so far as that good goes. We cannot escape the issue by remaining sceptical and waiting for more light, because, although we do avoid error in that way *if religion be untrue,* we lose the good, *if it be true,* just as certainly as if we positively chose to disbelieve. It is as if a man should hesitate indefinitely to ask a certain woman to marry him because he was not perfectly sure that she would prove an angel after he brought her home. Would he not cut himself off from that particular angel-possibility as decisively as if he went and married some one else? Scepticism, then, is not avoidance of option; it is option of a certain particular kind of risk. *Better risk loss of truth than chance of error*—that is your faith-vetoer's exact position. He is actively playing his stake as much as the believer is; he is backing the field against the religious hypothesis, just as the believer is backing the religious hypothesis against the field. To preach scepticism to us as a duty until "sufficient evidence" for religion be found, is tantamount therefore to telling us, when in presence of the religious hypothesis, that to yield to our fear of its being error is wiser and better than to yield to our hope that it may be true. It is not intellect against all passions, then; it is only intellect with one passion laying down its law. And by what, forsooth, is the supreme wisdom of this passion warranted? Dupery for dupery, what proof is there that dupery through hope is so much worse than dupery through fear? I, for one, can see no proof; and I simply refuse obedience to the scientist's command to imitate his kind of option, in a case where my own stake is important enough to give me the right to choose my own form of risk. If religion be true and the evidence for it be still insufficient, I do not wish, by putting your extinguisher upon my nature (which feels to me as if it had after all some business in this matter), to forfeit my sole chance in life of getting upon the winning side— that chance depending, of course, on my willingness to run the risk of acting as if my passional need of taking the world religiously might be prophetic and right.

All this is on the supposition that it really may be prophetic and right, and that, even to us who are discussing the matter, religion is a live hypothesis which may be true. Now, to most of us religion comes in a still further way that makes a veto on our active faith even more illogical. The more perfect and more eternal aspect of the universe is represented in our religions as having personal form. The universe is no longer a mere *It* to us, but a *Thou,* if we are religious; and any relation that may be possible from person to person might be possible here. For instance, although in one sense we are passive portions of the universe, in another we show a curious autonomy, as if we were small active centers on our own account. We feel, too, as if the appeal of religion to us were made to our own active good-will, as if evidence might be forever withheld from us unless we met the hypothesis half-way. To take a trivial illustration: just as a man who in a company of gentlemen made no advances, asked a warrant for every concession, and believed no one's word without proof, would cut himself off by such churlishness from all the social rewards that a more trusting spirit would earn—so here, one who should shut himself up in snarling logicality and try to make the gods extort his recognition willy-nilly, or not get it at all, might cut himself off forever from his only opportunity of making the gods' acquaintance. This feeling, forced on us we know not whence, that by obstinately believing that there are gods (although not to do so would be so easy both for our logic and our life) we are doing the universe the deepest service we can, seems part of the living essence of the religious hypothesis. If the hypothesis *were* true in all its parts, including this one, then pure intellectualism, with its veto on our making willing advances, would be an absurdity; and some participation of our sympathetic nature would be logically required. I, therefore, for one, cannot see my way to accepting the agnostic rules for truth-seeking, or willfully agree to keep my willing nature out of the game. I cannot do so for this plain reason, that *a rule of thinking which would absolutely prevent me from acknowledging certain kinds of truth if those kinds of truth were really there, would be an irrational rule.* That for me is the long and short of the formal logic of the situation, no matter what the kinds of truth might materially be.

I confess I do not see how this logic can be escaped. But sad experience makes me fear that some of you may still shrink from radically saying with me, *in abstracto,* that we have the right to believe at our own risk any hypothesis that is live enough to tempt our will. I suspect, however, that if this is so, it is because you have got away from the abstract logical point of view altogether, and are thinking (perhaps without realizing it) of some particular religious hypothesis which for you is dead. The freedom to "believe what we will" you apply to the case of some patent superstition; and the faith you think of is the faith defined by the schoolboy when he said, "Faith is when you believe something that you know ain't true." I can only repeat that this is misapprehension. *In concreto,* the freedom to believe can only cover living options which the intellect of the individual cannot by itself resolve; and living options never seem absurdities to him who has them to consider. When I look at the religious question as it really puts itself to concrete men, and when I think of all the possibilities which both practically and theoretically it involves, then this command that we shall put a stopper on our heart, instincts, and courage, and *wait*—acting of course meanwhile more or less as if religion were *not* true—till doomsday, or till such time as our intellect and senses working together may have raked in evidence enough—this command, I say, seems to me the queerest idol ever manufactured in the philosophic cave. Were we scholastic absolutists, there might be more excuse. If we had an infallible intellect with its objective certitudes, we might feel ourselves disloyal to such a perfect organ of knowledge in not trusting to it exclusively, in not waiting for its releasing word. But if we are empiricists, if we believe that no bell in us tolls to let us know for certain when truth is in our grasp, then it seems a piece of idle fantasticality to preach so solemnly our duty of waiting for the bell. Indeed we *may* wait if we will—I hope you do not think that I am denying that—but if we do so, we do so at our peril as much as if we believed. In either case we *act,* taking our life in our hands. No one of us ought to issue vetoes to the other, nor should we bandy words of abuse. We ought, on the contrary, delicately and profoundly to respect one another's mental freedom: then only shall we bring about the intellectual republic; then only shall we have that spirit of inner tolerance without which all our outer tolerance is soulless, and which is empiricism's glory; then only shall we live and let live, in speculative as well as in practical things.

I began by a reference to Fitz-James Stephen; let me end by a quotation from him. "What do you think of yourself? What do you think of the world? . . . These are questions with which all must deal as it seems good to them. They are riddles of the Sphinx, and in some way or other we must deal with them. . . . In all important transactions of life we have to take a leap in the dark. . . . If we decide to leave the riddles unanswered, that is a choice; if we waver in our answer, that, too, is a choice: but whatever choice we make, we make it at our peril. If a man chooses to turn his back altogether on God and the future, no one can prevent him; no one can show beyond reasonable doubt that he is mistaken. If a man thinks otherwise and acts as he thinks, I do not see that any one can prove that *he* is mistaken. Each must act as he thinks best; and if he is wrong, so much the worse for him. We stand on a mountain pass in the midst of whirling snow and blinding mist, through which we get glimpses now and then of paths which may be deceptive. If we stand still we shall be frozen to death. If we take the wrong road we shall be dashed to pieces. We do not certainly know whether there is any right one. What must we do? 'Be strong and of a good courage.' Act for the best, hope for the best, and take what comes. . . . If death ends all, we cannot meet death better."[1]

---

[1] *Liberty, Equality, Fraternity* (2d ed.; London, 1874), p. 353.

3

THE KINGDOM OF GOD

Walter Rauschenbusch

Walter Rauschenbusch ranks as one of the leading representatives of the "Social Gospel," an attempt to break away from the individualistic pietism of American Protestantism and to interpret the Christian faith in ethico-social terms. Rauschenbusch drew his inspiration both from the Ritschlians and from American pragmatism. He was wise enough to see that there can be no intelligent or sustained Christian action without a supporting theology, but it seemed to him that traditional theology had been too abstract and intellectualist, and that it needed to be restructured with the idea of the Kingdom of God at its center.

IF THEOLOGY is to offer an adequate doctrinal basis for the social gospel, it must not only make room for the doctrine of the Kingdom of God, but give it a central place and revise all other doctrines so that they will articulate organically with it.

This doctrine is itself the social gospel. Without it, the idea of redeeming the social order will be but an annex to the orthodox conception of the scheme of salvation. It will live like a Negro servant family in a detached cabin back of the white man's house in the South. If this doctrine gets the place which has always been its legitimate right, the practical proclamation and application of social morality will have a firm footing.

To those whose minds live in the social gospel, the Kingdom

Reprinted with permission from *A Theology for the Social Gospel* (New York: The Macmillan Co., 1918), pp. 131–45. Copyright 1917 by The Macmillan Co., renewed 1945 by Pauline E. Rauschenbusch.

of God is a dear truth, the marrow of the gospel, just as the incarnation was to Athanasius, justification by faith alone to Luther, and the sovereignty of God to Jonathan Edwards. It was just as dear to Jesus. He too lived in it, and from it looked out on the world and the work he had to do.

Jesus always spoke of the Kingdom of God. Only two of his reported sayings contain the word "Church," and both passages are of questionable authenticity. It is safe to say that he never thought of founding the kind of institution which afterward claimed to be acting for him.

Yet immediately after his death, groups of disciples joined and consolidated by inward necessity. Each local group knew that it was part of a divinely founded fellowship mysteriously spreading through humanity, and awaiting the return of the Lord and the establishing of his Kingdom. This universal Church was loved with the same religious faith and reverence with which Jesus had loved the Kingdom of God. It was the partial and earthly realization of the divine Society, and at the Parousia the Church and the Kingdom would merge.

But the Kingdom was merely a hope, the Church a present reality. The chief interest and affection flowed toward the Church. Soon, through a combination of causes, the name and idea of "the Kingdom" began to be displaced by the name and idea of "the Church" in the preaching, literature, and theological thought of the Church. Augustine completed this process in his *De Civitate Dei*. The Kingdom of God which has, throughout human history, opposed the Kingdom of Sin, is today embodied in the Church. The millennium began when the Church was founded. This practically substituted the actual, not the ideal Church for the Kingdom of God. The beloved ideal of Jesus became a vague phrase which kept intruding from the New Testament. Like Cinderella in the kitchen, it saw the other great dogmas furbished up for the ball, but no prince of theology restored it to its rightful place. The Reformation, too, brought no renaissance of the doctrine of the Kingdom; it had only eschatological value, or was defined in blurred phrases borrowed from the Church. The present revival of the Kingdom idea is due to the combined influence of the historical study of the Bible and of the social gospel.

When the doctrine of the Kingdom of God shriveled to an undeveloped and pathetic remnant in Christian thought, this loss was bound to have far-reaching consequences. We are told that the loss of a single tooth from the arch of the mouth in childhood may spoil the symmetrical development of the skull and produce malformations affecting the mind and character. The atrophy of that idea which had occupied the chief place in the mind of Jesus, necessarily affected the conception of Christianity, the life of the Church, the progress of humanity, and the structure of theology. I shall briefly enumerate some of the consequences affecting theology. This list, however, is by no means complete.

Theology lost its contact with the synoptic thought of Jesus. Its problems were not at all the same which had occupied his mind. It lost his point of view and became to some extent incapable of understanding him. His ideas had to be rediscovered in our time. Traditional theology and the mind of Jesus Christ became incommensurable quantities. It claimed to regard his revelation and the substance of his thought as divine, and yet did not learn to think like him. The loss of the Kingdom idea is one key to this situation.

The distinctive ethical principles of Jesus were the direct outgrowth of his conception of the Kingdom of God. When the latter disappeared from theology, the former disappeared from ethics. Only persons having the substance of the Kingdom ideal in their minds, seem to be able to get relish out of the ethics of Jesus. Only those church bodies which have been in opposition to organized society and have looked for a better city with its foundations in heaven, have taken the Sermon on the Mount seriously.

The Church is primarily a fellowship for worship; the Kingdom is a fellowship of righteousness. When the latter was neglected in theology, the ethical force of Christianity was weakened; when the former was emphasized in theology, the importance of worship was exaggerated. The prophets and Jesus had cried down sacrifices and ceremonial performances, and cried up righteousness, mercy, solidarity. Theology now reversed this, and by its theoretical discussions did its best to stimulate sacramental actions and priestly importance. Thus the religious energy and enthusiasm which might have saved mankind from its great sins, were used up in hearing and endowing masses, or in maintaining competitive church organizations, while mankind is still stuck in the mud. There are nations in which the ethical condition of the masses is the reverse of the frequency of the masses in the churches.

When the Kingdom ceased to be the dominating religious reality, the Church moved up into the position of the supreme good. To promote the power of the Church and its control over all rival political forces was equivalent to promoting the supreme ends of Christianity. This increased the arrogance of churchmen and took the moral check off their policies. For the Kingdom of God can never be promoted by lies, craft, crime or war, but the wealth and power of the Church have often been promoted by these means. The medieval ideal of the supremacy of the Church over the State was the logical consequence of making the Church the highest good with no superior ethical standard by which to test it. The medieval doctrines concerning the Church and the Papacy were the direct theological outcome of the struggles for Church supremacy, and were meant to be weapons in that struggle.

The Kingdom ideal is the test and corrective of the influence of the Church. When the Kingdom ideal disappeared, the conscience of the Church was muffled. It became possible for the missionary expansion of Christianity to halt for centuries without creating any sense of shortcoming. It became possible for the most unjust social conditions to fasten themselves on Christian nations without awakening any consciousness that the purpose of Christ was being defied and beaten back. The practical undertakings of the Church remained within narrow lines, and the theological thought of the Church was necessarily confined in a similar way. The claims of the Church were allowed to stand in theology with no conditions and obligations to test and balance them. If the Kingdom had stood as the purpose for which the Church exists, the Church could not have fallen into such corruption and sloth. Theology bears part of the guilt for the pride, the greed, and the ambition of the Church.

The Kingdom ideal contains the revolutionary force of Christianity. When this ideal faded out of the systematic thought of the Church, it became a conservative social influence and increased the weight of the other stationary forces in society. If the Kingdom of God had remained part of the theological and Christian consciousness, the Church could not, down to our times, have been salaried by autocratic class governments to keep the democratic and economic impulses of the people under check.

Reversely, the movements for democracy and social justice were left without a religious backing for lack of the Kingdom idea. The Kingdom of God as the fellowship of righteousness, would be advanced by the abolition of industrial slavery and the disappearance of the slums of civilization; the Church would only indirectly gain through such social changes. Even today many Christians cannot see any religious importance in social justice and fraternity because it does not increase the number of conversions nor fill the churches. Thus the practical conception of salvation, which is the effective theology of the common man and minister, has been cut back and crippled for lack of the Kingdom ideal.

Secular life is belittled as compared with church life. Services rendered to the Church get a higher religious rating than services rendered to the community. Thus the religious value is taken out of the activities of the common man and the prophetic services to society. Wherever the Kingdom of God is a living reality in Christian thought, any advance of social righteousness is seen as a part of redemption and arouses inward joy and the triumphant sense of salvation. When the Church absorbs interest, a subtle asceticism creeps back into our theology and the world looks different.

When the doctrine of the Kingdom of God is lacking in theology, the salvation of the individual is seen in its relation to the Church and to the future life, but not in its relation to the task of saving the social order. Theology has left this important point in a condition so hazy and muddled that it has taken us almost a generation to see that the salvation of the individual and the redemption of the social order are closely related, and how.

Finally, theology has been deprived of the inspiration of great ideas contained in the idea of the Kingdom and in labor for it. The Kingdom of God breeds prophets; the Church breeds priests and theologians. The Church runs to tradition and dogma; the Kingdom of God rejoices in forecasts and boundless horizons. The men who have contributed the most fruitful impulses to Christian thought have been men of prophetic vision, and their theology has proved most effective for future times where it has been most concerned with past history, with present social problems, and with the future of human society. The Kingdom of God is to theology what outdoor color and light are to art. It is impossible to estimate what inspirational impulses have been lost to theology and to the Church, because it did not develop the doctrine of the Kingdom of God and see the world and its redemption from that point of view.

These are some of the historical effects which the loss of the doctrine of the Kingdom of God has inflicted on systematic theology. The chief contribution which the social gospel has made and will make to theology is to give new vitality and importance to that doctrine. In doing so it will be a reformatory force of the highest importance in the field of doctrinal theology, for any systematic conception of Christianity must be not only defective but incorrect if the idea of the Kingdom of God does not govern it.

The restoration of the doctrine of the Kingdom has already made progress. Some of the ablest and most voluminous works of the old theology in their thousands of pages gave the Kingdom of God but a scanty mention, usually in connection with eschatology, and saw no connection between it and the Calvinistic doctrines of personal redemption. The newer manuals not only make constant reference to it in connection with various doctrines, but they arrange their entire subject matter so that the Kingdom of God becomes the governing idea.

In the following brief propositions I should like to offer a few suggestions, on behalf of the social gospel, for the theological formulation of the doctrine of the Kingdom. Something like this is needed to give us "a theology for the social gospel."

The Kingdom of God is divine in its origin, progress and consummation. It was initiated by Jesus Christ, in whom the prophetic spirit came to its consummation, it is sustained by the Holy Spirit, and it will be brought to its fulfillment by the power of God in his own time. The passive and active resistance of the Kingdom of Evil at every stage of its advance is so great, and the human resources of the Kingdom of God so slender, that no explanation can satisfy a religious mind which does not see the power of God in its movements. The Kingdom of God, therefore, is miraculous all the way, and is the continuous revelation of the power, the righteousness, and the love of God. The establishment of a community of righteousness in mankind is just as much a saving act of God as the salvation of an individual from his natural selfishness and moral inability. The Kingdom of God, therefore, is not merely ethical, but has a rightful place in theology. This doctrine is absolutely necessary to establish that organic union between religion and morality, between theology and ethics, which is one of the characteristics of the Christian religion. When our moral actions are consciously related to the Kingdom of God they gain religious quality. Without this doctrine we shall have expositions of schemes of redemption and we shall have systems of ethics, but we shall not have a true exposition of Christianity. The first step to the reform of the Churches is the restoration of the doctrine of the Kingdom of God.

The Kingdom of God contains the teleology of the Christian religion. It translates theology from the static to the dynamic. It sees, not doctrines or rites to be conserved and perpetuated, but resistance to be overcome and great ends to be achieved. Since the Kingdom of God is the supreme purpose of God, we shall understand the Kingdom so far as we understand God, and shall understand God so far as we understand his Kingdom. As long as organized sin is in the world, the Kingdom of God is characterized by conflict with evil. But if there were no evil, or after evil has been overcome, the Kingdom of God will still be the end to which God is lifting the race. It is realized not only by redemption, but also by the education of mankind and the revelation of his life within it.

Since God is in it, the Kingdom of God is always both present and future. Like God it is in all tenses, eternal in the midst of time. It is the energy of God realizing itself in human life. Its future lies among the mysteries of God. It invites and justifies prophecy, but all prophecy is fallible; it is valuable in so far as it grows out of action for the Kingdom and impels action. No theories about the future of the Kingdom of God are likely to be valuable or true which paralyze or postpone redemptive action on our part. To those who postpone, it is a theory and not a reality. It is for us to see the Kingdom of God as always coming, always pressing in on the present, always big with possibility, and always inviting immediate action. We walk by faith. Every human life is so placed that it can share with God in the creation of the Kingdom, or can resist and retard its progress. The Kingdom is for each of us the supreme task and the supreme gift of God. By accepting it as a task, we experience it as a gift. By laboring for it we enter into the joy and peace of the Kingdom as our divine fatherland and habitation.

Even before Christ, men of God saw the Kingdom of God as the great end to which all divine leadings were pointing. Every idealistic interpretation of the world, religious or philosophical, needs some such conception. Within the Christian religion the idea of the Kingdom gets its distinctive interpretation from Christ. (a) Jesus emancipated the idea of the Kingdom from previous nationalistic limitations and from the debasement of lower religious tendencies, and made it world-wide and spiritual. (b) He made the purpose of salvation essential in it. (c) He imposed his own mind, his personality, his love and holy will on the idea of the Kingdom. (d) He not only foretold it but initiated it by his life and work. As humanity more and more develops a racial consciousness in modern life, idealistic interpretations of the destiny of humanity will become more influential and important. Unless theology has a solidaristic vision higher and fuller than any other, it cannot maintain the spiritual leadership of mankind, but will be outdistanced. Its business is to infuse the distinctive qualities of Jesus Christ into its teachings about the Kingdom, and this will be a fresh competitive test of his continued headship of humanity.

The Kingdom of God is humanity organized according to the will of God. Interpreting it through the consciousness of Jesus we may affirm these convictions about the ethical relations within the Kingdom: (a) Since Christ revealed the divine worth of life and personality, and since his salvation seeks the restoration and fulfillment of even the least, it follows that the Kingdom of God, at every stage of human development, tends toward a social order which will best guarantee to all personalities their freest and highest development. This involves the redemption of social life from the cramping influence of religious bigotry, from the repression of self-assertion in the relation of upper and lower classes, and from all forms of slavery in which human beings are treated as mere means to serve the ends of others. (b) Since love is the supreme law of Christ, the Kingdom of God implies a progressive reign of love in human affairs. We can see its advance wherever the free will of love supersedes the use of force and legal coercion as a regulative of the social order. This involves the redemption of society from political autocracies and economic oligarchies; the substitution of redemptive for vindictive penology; the abolition of constraint through hunger as part of the industrial system; and the abolition of war as the supreme expression of hate and the completest cessation of freedom. (c) The highest expression of love is the free surrender of what is truly our own, life, property, and rights. A much lower but perhaps more decisive expression of love is the surrender of any opportunity to exploit men. No social group or organization can claim to be clearly within the Kingdom of God which drains others for its own ease, and resists the effort to abate this fundamental evil. This involves the redemption of society from private property in the natural resources of the earth, and from any condition in industry which makes monopoly profits possible. (d) The reign of love tends toward the progressive unity of mankind, but with the maintenance of individual liberty and the opportunity of nations to work out their own national peculiarities and ideals.

Since the Kingdom is the supreme end of God, it must be the purpose for which the Church exists. The measure in which it fulfills this purpose is also the measure of its spiritual authority and honor. The institutions of the Church, its activities, its worship, and its theology must in the long run be tested by its effectiveness in creating the Kingdom of God. For the Church to see itself apart from the Kingdom, and to find its aims in itself, is the same sin of selfish detachment as when an individual selfishly separates himself from the common good. The Church has the power to save in so far as the Kingdom of God is present in it. If the Church is not living for the Kingdom, its institutions are part of the "world." In that case it is not the power of redemption but its object. It may even become an anti-Christian power. If any form of church organization which formerly aided the Kingdom now impedes it, the reason for its existence is gone.

Since the Kingdom is the supreme end, all problems of personal salvation must be reconsidered from the point of view of the Kingdom. It is not sufficient to set the two aims of Christianity side by side. There must be a synthesis, and theology must explain how the two react on each other. The entire redemptive work of Christ must also be reconsidered under this orientation. Early Greek theology saw salvation chiefly as the redemption from ignorance by the revelation of God and from earthliness by the impartation of immortality. It interpreted the work of Christ accordingly, and laid stress on his incarnation and resurrection. Western theology saw salvation mainly as forgiveness of guilt and freedom from punishment. It interpreted the work of Christ accordingly, and laid stress on the death and atonement. If the Kingdom of God was the guiding idea and chief end of Jesus—as we now know it was—we may be sure that every step in His life, including His death, was related to that aim and its realization, and when the idea of the Kingdom of God takes its due place in theology, the work of Christ will have to be interpreted afresh.

The Kingdom of God is not confined within the limits of the

Church and its activities. It embraces the whole of human life. It is the Christian transfiguration of the social order. The Church is one social institution alongside of the family, the industrial organization of society, and the State. The Kingdom of God is in all these, and realizes itself through them all. During the Middle Ages all society was ruled and guided by the Church. Few of us would want modern life to return to such a condition. Functions which the Church used to perform, have now far outgrown its capacities. The Church is indispensable to the religious education of humanity and to the conservation of religion, but the greatest future awaits religion in the public life of humanity.

4

THE ETERNAL THOU

Martin Buber

Different from pragmatism but equally in protest against abstract and speculative approaches to philosophy are the various philosophies of personal being that have arisen during this century. Very influential among them is the work of Martin Buber, who stressed the uniqueness and irreducibility of interpersonal relations in his little classic, I and Thou. *In the following extract, he claims that finite personal relations form a kind of perspective that converges on the "eternal Thou" of God.*

THE EXTENDED LINES of relations meet in the eternal *Thou.*

Every particular *Thou* is a glimpse through to the eternal *Thou;* by means of every particular *Thou* the primary word addresses the eternal *Thou.* Through this mediation of the *Thou* of all beings fulfillment, and non-fulfillment, of relations comes to them: the inborn *Thou* is realized in each relation and consummated in none. It is consummated only in the direct relation with the *Thou* that by its nature cannot become *It.*

Men have addressed their eternal *Thou* with many names. In singing of Him who was thus named they always had the *Thou* in mind: the first myths were hymns of praise. Then the names took refuge in the language of *It;* men were more and more strongly

Reprinted with permission from *I and Thou,* translated by R. Gregor Smith (New York: Charles Scribner's Sons, 1937), pp. 75–81.

moved to think of and to address their eternal *Thou* as an *It*. But all God's names are hallowed, for in them He is not merely spoken about, but also spoken to.

Many men wish to reject the word God as a legitimate usage, because it is so misused. It is indeed the most heavily laden of all the words used by men. For that very reason it is the most imperishable and most indispensable. What does all mistaken talk about God's being and works (though there has been, and can be, no other talk about these) matter in comparison with the one truth that all men who have addressed God had God Himself in mind? For he who speaks the word God and really has *Thou* in mind (whatever the illusion by which he is held), addresses the true *Thou* of his life, which cannot be limited by another *Thou,* and to which he stands in a relation that gathers up and includes all others.

But when he, too, who abhors the name, and believes himself to be godless, gives his whole being to addressing the *Thou* of his life, as a *Thou* that cannot be limited by another, he addresses God.

If we go on our way and meet a man who has advanced towards us and has also gone on *his* way, we know only our part of the way, not his—his we experience only in the meeting.

Of the complete relational event we know, with the knowledge of life lived, our going out to the relation, our part of the way. The other part only comes upon us, we do not know it; it comes upon us in the meeting. But we strain ourselves on it if we speak of it as though it were some thing beyond the meeting.

We have to be concerned, to be troubled, not about the other side but about our own side, not about grace but about will. Grace concerns us in so far as we go out to it and persist in its presence; but it is not our object.

The *Thou* confronts me. But I step into direct relation with it. Hence the relation means being chosen and choosing, suffering and action in one; just as any action of the whole being which means the suspension of all partial actions, and consequently of all sensations of actions grounded only in their particular limitation, is bound to resemble suffering.

This is the activity of the man who has become a whole being, an activity that has been termed doing nothing: nothing separate or partial stirs in the man any more, thus he makes no intervention in the world; it is the whole man, enclosed and at rest in his wholeness, that is effective—he has become an effective whole. To have won stability in this state is to be able to go out to the supreme meeting.

To this end the world of sense does not need to be laid aside as though it were illusory. There is no illusory world, there is only the world—which appears to us as twofold in accordance with our twofold attitude. Only the barrier of separation has to be destroyed. Further, no "going beyond sense-experience" is necessary; for every experience, even the most spiritual, could yield us only an *It*. Nor is any recourse necessary to a world of ideas and values; for they cannot become presentness for us. None of these things is necessary. Can it be said what really is necessary?—Not in the sense of a precept. For everything that has ever been devised and contrived in the time of the human spirit as precept, alleged preparation, practice, or meditation, has nothing to do with the primal, simple fact of the meeting. Whatever the advantages in knowledge or the wielding of power for which we have to thank this or that practice, none of this affects the meeting of which we are speaking; it all has its place in the world of *It* and does not lead one step, does not take *the* step, out of it. Going out to the relation cannot be taught in the sense of precepts being given. It can only be indicated by the drawing of a circle which excludes everything that is not this going out. Then the one thing that matters is visible, full acceptance of the present.

To be sure, this acceptance presupposes that the further a man has wandered in separated being the more difficult is the venture and the more elemental the turning. This does not mean a giving up of, say, the *I*, as mystical writings usually suppose: the *I* is as indispensable to this, the supreme, as to every relation, since relation is only possible between *I* and *Thou*. It is not the *I*, then, that is given up, but that false self-asserting instinct that makes a man flee to the possessing of things before the unreliable, perilous world of relation which has neither density nor duration and cannot be surveyed.

Every real relation with a being or life in the world is exclusive. Its *Thou* is freed, steps forth, is single, and confronts you. It fills the heavens. This does not mean that nothing else exists; but all else lives in *its* light. As long as the presence of the relation continues, this its cosmic range is inviolable. But as soon as a *Thou* becomes *It*, the cosmic range of the relation appears as an offence to the world, its exclusiveness as an exclusion of the universe.

In the relation with God unconditional exclusiveness and unconditional inclusiveness are one. He who enters on the absolute relation is concerned with nothing isolated any more, neither things nor beings, neither earth nor heaven; but everything is gathered up in the relation. For to step into pure relation is not to disregard everything but to see everything in the *Thou*, not to renounce the world but to establish it on its true basis. To look away from the world, or to stare at it, does not help a man to reach God; but he who sees the world in Him stands in His presence. "Here world, there God" is the language of *It*; "God in the world" is another language of *It*; but to eliminate or leave behind nothing at all, to include the whole world in the *Thou*, to give the world its due and its truth, to include nothing beside God but everything in Him—this is full and complete relation.

Men do not find God if they stay in the world. They do not find Him if they leave the world. He who goes out with his whole being to meet his *Thou* and carries to it all being that is in the world, finds Him who cannot be sought.

Of course God is the "wholly Other"; but He is also the wholly Same, the wholly Present. Of course He is the *Mysterium Tremendum* that appears and overthrows; but He is also the mystery of the self-evident, nearer to me than my *I*.

If you explore the life of things and of conditioned being you come to the unfathomable, if you deny the life of things and of conditioned being you stand before nothingness, if you hallow this life you meet the living God.

Man's sense of *Thou,* which experiences in the relations with every particular *Thou* the disappointment of the change to *It,* strives out but not away from them all to its eternal *Thou;* but not as something is sought: actually there is no such thing as seeking God, for there is nothing in which He could not be found. How foolish and hopeless would be the man who turned aside from the course of his life in order to seek God; even though he won all the wisdom of solitude and all the power of concentrated being he would miss God. Rather is it as when a man goes his way and simply wishes that it might be the way: in the strength of his wish his striving is expressed. Every relational event is a stage that affords him a glimpse into the consummating event. So in each event he does not partake, but also (for he is waiting) does partake, of the one event. Waiting, not seeking, he goes his way; hence he is composed before all things, and makes contact with them which helps them. But when he has *found,* his heart is not turned from them, though everything now meets him in the one event. He blesses every cell that sheltered him, and every cell into which he will yet turn. For this finding is not the end, but only the eternal middle, of the way.

It is a finding without seeking, a discovering of the primal, of origin. His sense of *Thou,* which cannot be satiated till he finds the endless *Thou,* had the *Thou* present to it from the beginning; the presence had only to become wholly real to him in the reality of the hallowed life of the world.

God cannot be inferred in anything—in nature, say, as its author, or in history as its master, or in the subject as the self that is thought in it. Something else is not "given" and God then elicited from it; but God is the Being that is directly, most nearly, and lastingly, over against us, that may properly only be addressed, not expressed.

5

MYSTERIUM TREMENDUM

Rudolf Otto

The new philosophies of personal being have found an indispensable tool in the phenomenological method. This approach suspends questions of origin, causation, validity and the like, and seeks simply to provide a careful analytic description of the phenomenon, that is to say, of what shows itself. The method of phenomenology has been widely used in the field of philosophy of religion. One of the earliest and still one of the most valuable and profound attempts to delineate the phenomenology of religious experience is Rudolf Otto's study of the holy.

WE SAID above that the nature of the numinous can only be suggested by means of the special way in which it is reflected in the mind in terms of feeling. "Its nature is such that it grips or stirs the human mind with this and that determinate affective state." We have now to attempt to give a further indication of these determinate states. We must once again endeavor, by adducing feelings akin to them for the purpose of analogy or contrast, and by the use of metaphor and symbolic expressions, to make the states of mind we are investigating ring out, as it were, of themselves.

Let us consider the deepest and most fundamental element in all strong and sincerely felt religious emotion. Faith unto Salvation, Trust, Love—all these are there. But over and above these is an

Reprinted with permission from *The Idea of the Holy,* translated by John W. Harvey (London: Oxford University Press, 1923), pp. 12–24.

element which may also on occasion, quite apart from them, profoundly affect us and occupy the mind with a wellnigh bewildering strength. Let us follow it up with every effort of sympathy and imaginative intuition wherever it is to be found, in the lives of those around us, in sudden, strong ebullitions of personal piety and the frames of mind such ebullitions evince, in the fixed and ordered solemnities of rites and liturgies, and again in the atmosphere that clings to old religious monuments and buildings, to temples and to churches. If we do so we shall find we are dealing with something for which there is only one appropriate expression, *mysterium tremendum*. The feeling of it may at times come sweeping like a gentle tide, pervading the mind with a tranquil mood of deepest worship. It may pass over into a more set and lasting attitude of the soul, continuing, as it were, thrillingly vibrant and resonant, until at last it dies away and the soul resumes its "profane," non-religious mood of everyday experience. It may burst in sudden eruption up from the depths of the soul with spasms and convulsions, or lead to the strangest excitements, to intoxicated frenzy, to transport, and to ecstasy. It has its wild and demonic forms and can sink to an almost grisly horror and shuddering. It has its crude, barbaric antecedents and early manifestations, and again it may be developed into something beautiful and pure and glorious. It may become the hushed, trembling, and speechless humility of the creature in the presence of—whom or what? In the presence of that which is a *Mystery* inexpressible and above all creatures.

It is again evident at once that here too our attempted formulation by means of a concept is once more a merely negative one. Conceptually *mysterium* denotes merely that which is hidden and esoteric, that which is beyond conception or understanding, extraordinary and unfamiliar. The term does not define the object more positively in its qualitative character. But though what is enunciated in the word is negative, what is meant is something absolutely and intensely positive. This pure positive we can experience in feelings, feelings which our discussion can help to make clear to us, in so far as it arouses them actually in our hearts.

1. THE ELEMENT OF AWEFULNESS

To get light upon the positive *quale* of the object of these feelings, we must analyze more closely our phrase *mysterium tremendum,* and we will begin first with the adjective.

"Tremor" is in itself merely the perfectly familiar and "natural" emotion of *fear.* But here the term is taken, aptly enough but still only by analogy, to denote a quite specific kind of emotional response, wholly distinct from that of being afraid, though it so far resembles it that the analogy of fear may be used to throw light upon its nature. There are in some languages special expressions which denote, either exclusively or in the first instance, that "fear" that is more than fear proper. The Hebrew *hiqdîsh* (hallow) is an example. To "keep a thing holy in the heart" means to mark it off by a feeling of peculiar dread, not to be mistaken for any ordinary dread, that is, to appraise it by the category of the numinous. But the Old Testament throughout is rich in parallel expressions for this feeling. Specially noticeable is the *emāt* of Yahweh ("fear of God"), which Yahweh can pour forth, dispatching almost like a demon, and which seizes upon a man with paralyzing effect. It is closely related to the δεῖμα πανικόν of the Greeks. Compare Exodus xxiii. 27: "I will send my fear before thee and will destroy all the people to whom thou shalt come . . ."; also Job ix. 34; xiii. 21 ("Let not his fear terrify me"; "Let not thy dread make me afraid"). Here we have a terror fraught with an inward shuddering such as not even the most menacing and overpowering created thing can instil. It has something spectral in it.

In the Greek language we have a corresponding term in σεβαστός. The early Christians could clearly feel that the title σεβαστός (*augustus*) was one that could not fittingly be given to any creature, not even to the emperor. They felt that to call a man σεβαστός was to give a human being a name proper only to the numen, to rank him by the category proper only to the numen, and that it therefore amounted to a kind of idolatry. Of modern languages English has the words "awe," "aweful," which in their deeper and most special sense approximate closely to our meaning. The phrase, "he stood aghast," is also suggestive in this connection. On the other hand, German has no native-grown expression of its own for the higher and riper form of the emotion we are considering, unless it be in a word like *erschauern,* which does suggest it fairly well. It is far otherwise with its cruder and more debased phases, where such terms as *"grausen"* and *"Schauer,"* and the more popular and telling *gruseln* ("grue"), *gräsen,* and *grässlich* ("grisly"), very clearly designate the numinous element. In my examination of Wundt's Animism I suggested the term *Scheu* (dread); but the special numinous quality (making it *"awe"* rather than *"dread"* in the ordinary sense) would then of course have to be denoted by inverted commas. "Religious dread" (or "awe") would perhaps be a better designation. Its antecedent stage is "demonic dread" (cf. the horror of Pan) with its queer perversion, a sort of abortive offshoot, the "dread of ghosts." It first begins to stir in the feeling of "something uncanny," "eerie," or "weird." It is this feeling which, emerging in the mind of primeval man, forms the starting-point for the entire religious development in history. Demons and gods alike spring from this root, and all the products of mythological apperception or fantasy are nothing but different modes in which it has been objectified. And all ostensible explanations of the origin of religion in terms of animism or magic or folk psychology are doomed from the outset to wander astray and miss the real goal of their inquiry, unless they recognize this fact of our nature— primary, unique, underivable from anything else—to be the basic factor and the basic impulse underlying the entire process of religious evolution.

Not only is the saying of Luther, that the natural man cannot fear God perfectly, correct from the standpoint of psychology, but we ought to go further and add that the natural man is quite unable even to shudder (*grauen*) or feel horror in the real sense of the word. For shuddering is something more than "natural," ordinary fear. It implies that the mysterious is already beginning to loom before the mind, to touch the feelings. It implies the first application of a category of valuation which has no place in the everyday natural world of ordinary experience, and is only possible to a being in whom has been awakened a mental predisposition, unique in kind and different in a definite way from any "natural" faculty. And this newly-revealed capacity, even in the crude and violent manifestations which are all it at first evinces, bears witness to a completely new function of experience and standard of valuation, only belonging to the spirit of man.

Before going on to consider the elements which unfold as the *tremendum* develops, let us give a little further consideration to the first crude, primitive forms in which this numinous dread or *awe* shows itself. It is the mark which really characterizes the so-called Religion of Primitive Man, and there it appears as demonic dread. This crudely naïve and primordial emotional disturbance, and the fantastic images to which it gives rise, are later overborne and ousted by more highly-developed forms of the numinous emotion, with all its mysteriously impelling power. But even when this has long attained its higher and purer mode of expression it is possible for the primitive types of excitation that were formerly a part of it to break out in the soul in all their original naïveté and so to be experienced afresh. That this is so is shown by the potent attraction again and again exercised by the element of horror and shudder in ghost stories, even among persons of high all-round education. It is a remarkable fact that the physical reaction to which this unique dread of the uncanny gives rise is also unique, and is not found in the case of any natural fear or terror. We say: "my blood ran icy cold," and "my flesh crept." The "cold blood" feeling may be a symptom of ordinary, natural fear, but there is something non-natural or supernatural about the symptom of "creeping flesh." And any one who is capable of more precise introspection must recognize that the distinction between such a dread and natural fear is not simply one of degree and intensity. The awe or dread *may* indeed be so overwhelmingly great that it seems to penetrate to the very marrow, making the man's hair bristle and his limbs quake. But it may also steal upon him almost unobserved as the gentlest of agitations, a mere fleeting shadow passing across his mood. It has therefore nothing to do with intensity, and no natural fear passes over into it merely by being intensified. I may be beyond all measure afraid and terrified without there being even a trace of the feeling of uncanniness in my emotion.

We should see the facts more clearly if psychology in general would make a more decisive endeavor to examine and classify the feelings and emotions according to their qualitative differences. But the far too rough division of elementary feelings in general into pleasures and pains is still an obstacle to this. In point of fact pleasures no more than other feelings are differentiated merely by degrees of intensity; they show very definite and specific differences. It makes a specific difference to the condition of mind whether the soul is merely in a state of pleasure, or joy, or aesthetic rapture, or moral exaltation, or finally in the religious bliss that may come in worship. Such states certainly show resemblances one to another, and on that account can legitimately be brought under a common class-concept (pleasure), which serves to cut them off from other psychical functions, generically different. But this class-concept, so far from turning the various subordinate species into merely different degrees of the same thing, can do nothing at all to throw light upon the essence of each several state of mind which it includes.

Though the numinous emotion in its completest development shows a world of difference from the mere demonic dread, yet not even at the highest level does it belie its pedigree or kindred. Even when the worship of demons has long since reached the higher level of worship of gods, these gods still retain as numina something of the ghost in the impress they make on the feelings of the worshipper, viz. the peculiar quality of the uncanny and awful, which survives with the quality of exaltedness and sublimity or is symbolized by means of it. And this element, softened though it is, does not disappear even on the highest level of all, where the worship of God is at its purest. Its disappearance would be indeed an essential loss. The shudder reappears in a form ennobled beyond measure where the soul, held speechless, trembles inwardly to the furthest fibre of its being. It invades the mind mightily in Christian worship with the words: "Holy, holy, holy"; it breaks forth from the hymn of Tersteegen:

> God Himself is present:
> Heart, be stilled before Him:
> Prostrate inwardly adore Him.

The shudder has here lost its crazy and bewildering note, but not the ineffable something that holds the mind. It has become a mystical awe, and sets free as its accompaniment, reflected in self-consciousness, that "creature-feeling" that has already been described as the feeling of personal nothingness and abasement before the awe-inspiring object directly experienced.

The referring of this feeling of numinous tremor to its object in the numen brings into relief a property of the latter which plays an important part in our Holy Scriptures, and which has been the occasion of many difficulties, both to commentators and to theologians, from its puzzling and baffling nature. This is the ὀργή (orgé), the Wrath of Yahweh, which recurs in the New Testament as ὀργὴ θεοῦ, and which is clearly analogous to the idea occurring in many religions of a mysterious *ira deorum*. To pass through the Indian Pantheon of Gods is to find deities who seem to be made up altogether out of such an ὀργή; and even the higher Indian gods of grace and pardon have frequently, beside their merciful, their wrath form. But as regards the Wrath of Yahweh, the strange features about it have for long been a matter for constant remark. In the first place, it is patent from many passages of the Old Testament that this "Wrath" has no concern whatever with moral qualities. There is something very baffling in the way in which it is kindled and manifested. It is, as has been well said, like a hidden force of nature, like stored-up electricity, discharging itself upon any one who comes too near. It is incalculable and arbitrary. Any one who is accustomed to think of deity only by its rational attributes must see in this "Wrath" mere caprice and willful passion.

But such a view would have been emphatically rejected by the religious men of the Old Covenant, for to them the Wrath of God, so far from being a diminution of His Godhead, appears as a natural expression of it, an element of holiness itself, and a quite indispensable one. And in this they are entirely right. This ὀργή is nothing but the *tremendum* itself, apprehended and expressed by the aid of a naïve analogy from the domain of natural experience, in this case from the ordinary passional life of men. But naïve as it may be, the analogy is most disconcertingly apt and striking; so much so that it will always retain its value, and for us no less than for the men of old be an inevitable way of expressing one element in the religious emotion. It cannot be doubted that, despite the protest of Schleiermacher and Ritschl, Christianity also has something to teach of the Wrath of God.

It will be again at once apparent that in the use of this word we are not concerned with a genuine intellectual concept, but only with a sort of illustrative substitute for a concept. "Wrath" here is the ideogram of a unique emotional moment in religious experience, a moment whose singularly *daunting* and awe-inspiring character must be gravely disturbing to those persons who will recognize nothing in the divine nature but goodness, gentleness, love, and a sort of confidential intimacy, in a word, only those aspects of God which turn towards the world of men.

This ὀργή is thus quite wrongly spoken of as "natural" wrath: rather it is an entirely non- or super-natural, i.e. numinous, quality. The rationalization process takes place when it begins to be filled in with elements derived from the moral reason:—righteousness in requital, and punishment for moral transgression. But it should be noted that the idea of the Wrath of God in the Bible is always a synthesis, in which the original is combined with the later meaning that has come to fill it in. Something supra-rational throbs and gleams, palpable and visible, in the Wrath of God, prompting to a sense of terror that no natural anger can arouse.

Beside the Wrath or Anger of Yahweh stands the related expression "Jealousy of Yahweh." The state of mind denoted by the phrase "being jealous *for* Yahweh" is also a numinous state of mind, in which features of the *tremendum* pass over into the man who has experience of it.

2. THE ELEMENT OF OVERPOWERINGNESS (MAJESTAS)

We have been attempting to unfold the implications of that aspect of the *mysterium tremendum* indicated by the adjective, and the result so far may be summarized in two words, constituting, as before, what may be called an ideogram, rather than a concept proper, viz. "absolute unapproachability."

It will be felt at once that there is yet a further element which must be added, that, namely, of might, power, absolute overpoweringness. We will take to represent this the term *majestas,* majesty—the more readily because any one with a feeling for language must detect a last faint trace of the numinous still clinging to the word. The *tremendum* may then be rendered more adequately *tremenda majestas,* or awful majesty. This second element of majesty may continue to be vividly preserved, where the first, that of unapproachability, recedes and dies away, as may be seen, for example, in Mysticism. It is especially in relation to this element of majesty or absolute overpoweringness that the creature-consciousness, of which we have already spoken, comes upon the scene, as a sort of shadow or subjective reflection of it. Thus, in contrast to the overpowering of which we are conscious as an object over against the self, there is the feeling of one's own abasement, of being but "dust and ashes" and nothingness. And this forms the numinous raw material for the feeling of religious humility.

Here we must revert once again to Schleiermacher's expression for what we call "creature-feeling," viz. the "feeling of dependence." We found fault with this phrase before on the ground that Schleiermacher thereby takes as basis and point of departure what is merely a secondary effect; that he sets out to teach a consciousness of the religious *object* only by way of an inference from the shadow it casts upon *self*-consciousness. We have now a further criticism to bring against it, and it is this. By "feeling of dependence" Schleiermacher means consciousness of *being conditioned* (as effect by cause), and so he develops the implications of this logically enough in his sections upon Creation and Preservation. On the side of the deity the correlate to dependence would thus be causality, i.e. God's character as all-causing and all-conditioning. But a sense of this does not enter at all into that immediate and first-hand religious emotion which we have in the moment of worship, and which we can recover in a measure for analysis; it belongs on the contrary decidedly to the *rational* side of the idea of God; its implications admit of precise conceptual determination; and it springs from quite a distinct source. The difference between the feeling of dependence of Schleiermacher and that which finds typical utterance in the words of Abraham already cited might be expressed as that between the consciousness of *createdness* (*Geschaffenheit*) and the consciousness of *creaturehood* (*Geschöpflichkeit*). In the one case you have the creature as the work of the divine creative act; in the other, impotence and general nothingness as against overpowering might, dust and ashes as against majesty. In the one case you have the fact of having been created; in the other, the status of the creature. And as soon as speculative thought has come to concern itself with this latter type of consciousness—as soon as it has come to analyze this majesty—we are introduced to a set of ideas quite different from those of creation or preservation. We come upon the ideas, first, of the annihilation of self, and then, as its complement, of the transcendent as the sole and entire reality. These are the characteristic notes of Mysticism in all its forms, however otherwise various in content. For one of the chiefest and most general features of Mysticism is just this *self-depreciation* (so plainly parallel to the case of Abraham), the estimation of the self, of the personal "I," as something not perfectly or essentially real, or even as mere nullity, a self-depreciation which comes to demand its own fulfillment in practice in rejecting the delusion of selfhood, and so makes for the annihilation of the self. And on the other hand Mysticism leads to a valuation of the trancendent object of its reference as that which through plenitude of being stands supreme and absolute, so that the finite self contrasted with it becomes conscious even in its nullity that "I am nought, Thou art all." There is no thought in this of any causal relation between God, the creator, and the self, the creature. The point from which speculation starts is not a consciousness of absolute dependence—of myself as result and effect of a divine cause—for that would in point of fact lead to insistence upon the reality of the self; it starts from a consciousness of the absolute superiority or supremacy of a power other than myself, and it is only as it falls back upon ontological terms to achieve its end—terms generally borrowed from natural science—that that element of the *tremendum,* originally apprehended as plenitude of power, becomes transmuted into plenitude of being.

This leads again to the mention of Mysticism. No mere inquiry into the genesis of a thing can throw any light upon its essential nature, and it is hence immaterial to us how Mysticism historically arose. But essentially Mysticism is the stressing to a very high degree, indeed the overstressing, of the non-rational or suprarational elements in religion; and it is only intelligible when so understood. The various phases and factors of the non-rational may receive varying emphasis, and the type of Mysticism will differ according as some or others fall into the background. What we have been analyzing, however, is a feature that recurs in all forms of Mysticism everywhere, and it is nothing but the creature-consciousness stressed to the utmost and to excess, the expression meaning, if we may repeat the contrast already made, not feeling of our createdness but feeling of our creaturehood, that is, the consciousness of the littleness of every creature in face of that which is above all creatures.

A characteristic common to all types of Mysticism is the *Identification,* in different degrees of completeness, of the personal self with the transcendent Reality. This identification has a source of its own, with which we are not here concerned, and springs from moments of religious experience which would require separate treatment. Identification alone, however, is not enough for Mysticism; it must be Identification with the Something that is at once absolutely supreme in power and reality and wholly non-rational. And it is among the mystics that we most encounter this element of religious consciousness. Récéjac has noticed this in his *Essai sur les fondements de la connaissance mystique* (Paris, 1897). He writes (p. 90):

"Le mysticisme commence par la crainte, par le sentiment d'une *domination* universelle, *invincible,* et devient plus tard un désir d'union avec ce qui domine ainsi."

And some very clear examples of this taken from the religious experience of the present day are to be found in W. James (*The Varieties of Religious Experience,* Lecture III):

"The perfect stillness of the night was thrilled by a more solemn silence. The darkness held a presence that was all the more felt because it was not seen. I could not any more have doubted that He was there than that I was. Indeed, I felt myself to be, if possible, the less real of the two."

This example is particularly instructive as to the relation of Mysticism to the feelings of Identification, for the experience here recounted was on the point of passing into it.

3. THE ELEMENT OF ENERGY OR URGENCY

There is, finally, a third element comprised in those of *tremendum* and *majestas,* awefulness and majesty, and this I venture to call the *urgency* or *energy* of the numinous object. It is particularly vividly perceptible in the ὀργή or Wrath; and it everywhere clothes itself in symbolical expressions—vitality, passion, emotional temper, will, force, movement, excitement, activity, impetus. These features are typical and recur again and again from the demonic level up to the idea of the "living" God. We have here the factor that has everywhere more than any other prompted the fiercest opposition to the philosophic God of mere rational speculation, who can be put into a definition. And for their part the philosophers have condemned these expressions of the energy of the numen, whenever they are brought on to the scene, as sheer anthropomorphism. In so far as their opponents have for the most part themselves failed to recognize that the terms they have borrowed from the sphere of human conative and affective life have merely value as analogies, the philosophers are right to condemn them. But they are wrong, in so far as, this error notwithstanding, these terms stood for a genuine aspect of the divine nature—its non-rational aspect—a due consciousness of which served to protect religion itself from being rationalized away.

For wherever men have been contending for the living God and for voluntarism, there, we may be sure, have been non-rationalists fighting rationalists and rationalism. It was so with Luther in his controversy with Erasmus; and Luther's *omnipotentia Dei* in his *De Servo Arbitrio* is nothing but the union of majesty—in the sense of absolute supremacy—with this energy, in the sense of a force that knows not stint nor stay, which is urgent, active, compelling, and alive. In Mysticism, too, this element of energy is a very living and vigorous factor, at any rate in the voluntaristic Mysticism, the Mysticism of love, where it is very forcibly seen in that "consuming fire" of love whose burning strength the mystic can hardly bear, but begs that the heat that has scorched him may be mitigated, lest he be himself destroyed by it. And in this urgency and pressure the mystic's love claims a perceptible kinship with the ὀργή itself, the scorching and consuming wrath of God; it is the same energy, only differently directed. "Love," says one of the mystics, is nothing else than quenched Wrath."

6

EXISTENTIAL METAPHYSICS

Nikolai Berdyaev

Existentialism is the type of philosophy that sets out to describe the structures of our own human existence, beginning from our concrete participation in existence itself. The basic concerns of existentialism are admirably set forth by Berdyaev in the extract which follows. He also distinguishes existentialism from pragmatism and other philosophies, and argues that even if Kant demonstrated the impossibility of a rational metaphysic, the existential approach opens the way into a new style of ontology. Man, after all, cannot be understood in isolation. The more he understands himself, the more he is driven to reflection on the wider context in which his existence is set and with which he is in continuous interaction.

THE DISCOVERY of reason by Greek philosophy was an important event in the history of knowledge. Man brought into the light forces which had hitherto been in a dreamlike state within him. He took possession of his reason and reason became independent. The emotional life of man had depended upon his impressions of the world of sense and his thought was entirely under the sway of mythological feelings about the world and of tradition. Reason, however, is both itself free and it is a liberating agent; it both enriches man and impoverishes him.

The philosopher believed that reason lifted him up to the world

Reprinted with permission from *The Beginning and the End,* translated by R. M. French (New York: Harper & Row, 1957), pp. 37–51.

of ideas, to the noumenal world. This opinion Kant subjected to criticism. But almost throughout the history of philosophy the apprehending mind remained faithful to the conviction that cognition is a purely intellectual act, that there exists a universal reason and that reason is always one and the same and remains true to its nature. But in reality cognition is emotional and passionate in character. It is a spiritual struggle for meaning, and it is such not merely in this or that line of thought or school, but in every true philosopher even although he may not recognize the fact himself. Cognition is not a dispassionate understudy of reality. The significance of a philosophy is decided by the passionate intensity of the philosopher as a man, as one who is present behind his effort to know. It is decided by the intensity of the will to truth and meaning; it is the whole man who takes knowledge of a thing. Dilthey, who was one of the forerunners of existential philosophy, says with truth that thinking is a function of life. The whole man, not reason, constructs metaphysics; it is not the autonomy of the intellect which needs to be asserted, but the autonomy of spirit, the autonomy of the knowing person as a complete being.

The process of thinking cannot be separated from the person who thinks and the person who thinks cannot be separated from the corporate experience of his brothers in spirit. The knowing person may, as an effect of his cognition, attain to an objective coolness of expression, but this is a secondary process of objectification. What is primary is the man's intuition as one who exists in the fullness of existence. Man apprehends emotionally to a greater extent than intellectually, and the view that emotional cognition is "subjective" in the bad sense of the word while intellectual cognition is "objective" in the good sense is entirely wrong, and in any case it is expressed in terms which are inaccurate. To quicken the subject matter of knowledge into life is in any case a process which is emotional rather than intellectual in character. The intuitivism of Bergson and Scheler as well as of Schelling, to say nothing of Nietzsche, is non-intellectualist.

Purely intellectual discursive knowledge constructs an objectified world out of touch with reality. What is decisively important in knowledge is not the logical process of thought, which ranks as an instrument, and which takes control only in the center of the path, but the emotional and volitional tension is attributable to the spirit as a whole. Knowledge is a creative activity, not a passive reflection of things, and every act of creation includes knowledge. Intuition is not only the perception of something; it is also a creative penetration into meaning; and more than that, the very existence of meaning presupposes a creative condition of spirit.

Phenomenological philosophy requires passivity on the part of the subject. Existential philosophy, on the other hand, requires activity and passion in the subject. The world of ideas, the noumenal world, assumes this activity and passion of the spirit; it is not a congealed world which is devoid of the movement of life. An act of cognition is an act of transcendence; it is a way out from the closed circle and a way which opens out upwards. It is possible to conceive of the transcendent only because of the existence of such a transcending act. But the transcending act is an intense effort of the whole being. It is its uplifting power and its state of exaltation.

The pursuit of a metaphysics which is completely scientific in form, of metaphysics as a strict and objective science is the pursuit of a will o' the wisp. Metaphysics can only be the apprehension of spirit, in spirit, and through spirit. Metaphysics is in the subject, which creates spiritual values and makes a transcending act, not into the object but into its own self-revealing depth. Metaphysics is empirical in the sense that it is based upon spiritual experience. It is a symbolism of that experience. Philosophical knowledge is knowledge attained by means of images to a greater extent than knowledge reached through concepts. The concept is important only as playing a secondary part. In Hegel the concept does not possess its traditional logical significance; it acquires not only a metaphysical but even an almost mystical meaning.

The principal and decisive thing about the philosopher has not by any means been the assertions which he has contributed for objective use. The apprehending mind has never discovered truth by the assistance of the logical apparatus by which he endeavors to convince others. Philosophical knowledge is the knowledge of truth, of what is true and right, not of being, for the apprehension of truth is an uplifting movement of the spirit towards truth; it is a spiritual ascent, an entering into truth. There is, however, a social aspect of knowledge and too little attention has been paid to it. Knowledge is a form of communication and intercourse among human beings. At the same time knowledge is above all a gesture on the part of him who seeks it, which places him face to face not with some other, or others in general, but face to face with truth. It is to stand facing the primary reality which philosophers have been fond of calling "being." Human knowledge, and philosophical knowledge in particular, depends upon the spiritual condition of men, upon the scope of their minds, and the forms of communion and community which exist among men have an enormous part to play in this.

Philosophical knowledge is personal in character and the more personal it is the more important it is. But the personal character of knowledge does not mean the isolation of personality. Personality gets to know things in communion and community with the world and with men; it enters into union with world experience and world thought. Knowledge is at the same time personal and social. The degrees of spiritual community which hold among men are here of very great importance. All this leads to the fundamental truth, that knowledge is anthropological, but this will not by any means denote relativism.

There is one very important truth which must be recognized in the theory of knowledge, and that is that the person who knows is himself existent, that he himself is "being," and that the recognition of the meaning of the world is possible only in the subject, not in the object, that is to say in human existence. It is indeed in this that the truth of existential philosophy is to be found. If it is not to be naïvely and unconsciously anthropocentric, philosophy must be consciously and critically anthropocentric. Philosophy is anthropocentric but the philosopher ought to be theocentric.

Comprehension of the mystery of the world in human existence is a possibility only because man is a microcosm and a microtheos.

There is no cosmos in the object world of phenomena. There is no God in the objective world order, but there is a cosmos in man. God is in man, and through man there is a way out into another world. That protagonist of the humanist theory of knowledge, F. S. Schiller, says with truth that a depersonalization and dehumanization of knowledge has taken place and that the personalizing and humanizing of it is imperative. Man is the measure of things, but there is a higher measure than man. St. Augustine was perhaps the first to turn to the existential philosophy of the subject. He set forth the principle of interior experience and of the credibility of the mind to itself. He recognized doubt as a source of credibility and as a proof of one's own existence. To him the soul was the whole personality.

The theory of orderly and regular development in knowledge does not settle accounts with the invasion of individuality. It may be taken as beyond doubt that the act of appraisal which has such an immense part to play in cognition, is performed above all by feeling not by the intellect. Nietzsche, who did his philosophizing with a sledge hammer, said that the philosopher ought to be one who gives instructions and imposes commands. This means that in philosophical knowledge a rearrangement of values and the creation of values take place. Philosophy seeks to break out from the slavery of this world into another world, towards a perfect free life, and deliverance from the suffering and ugliness of the world as we have it. To strive after objective knowledge is an illusion and in any case it is a mistake in terminology. Dispassionate knowledge there cannot be and never has been among real philosophers; it can only exist in dissertations which are devoid of any creative gift. Even in Spinoza himself knowledge was nothing if not passionate. Intellectual passion may be a source of perceptual transcendence. Plato, the greatest of all philosophers, was an erotic philosopher. There was an erotic pull in the rationalist Spinoza, and in the panlogist Hegel, to say nothing of such philosophers as Kierkegaard and Nietzsche.

The philosopher has fallen in love with wisdom. In real true-born philosophy there is the eros of truth; there is the erotic attraction of the infinite and the absolute. Philosophical creativity is intoxicated with thought. Philosophical cognition can only be based upon experience, upon spiritual experience, and within that it is the spirit as one whole which accomplishes the act of cognition. There is bitterness in knowledge. But knowledge is by nature a liberating agent. Philosophical knowledge is called upon to set man free from the power of the objectified world and from his intolerable servitude to it. Not the will to power but the will to meaning and to freedom is the driving force of philosophical knowledge. As a system of concepts metaphysics is an impossibility, it is possible only as the symbolism of spiritual experience.

The conflict between subject and object, between freedom and necessity, between meaning and the lack of it is, in the language of metaphysics, a symbolic conflict which in this provides symbols of another. Behind the finite the infinite is concealed, and it gives signs of its presence. The depth of my ego is steeped in infinity and eternity and it is only a superficial layer of my ego which is illuminated by the mind, rationalized, and recognized on the basis of the antithesis between subject and object. But out of the depth signs are given, whole worlds are there, and there is all our world and its destiny. Hartman is right when he says that the problem of cognition is a metaphysical problem, and Heidegger is right when he says that we understand the *Existenziale* as an interpretation of our own selves. But what is truth? That is the eternal question. The answer that the Gospels give to this question has its importance even in philosophy.

The aim of philosophical knowledge certainly does not consist in the knowledge of being, in a reflection of reality in the mind of the person who knows. Its aim is the knowledge of truth, the discovery of meaning, its purpose is to give an intelligible sense to reality. Philosophical knowledge, therefore, is not passive reflection, it is an active break-through, it is victory in the conflict with the meaninglessness of world reality. What I want to know is not reality but the truth about it, and I can recognize this truth only because there is in me myself, in the knowing subject, a source of truth, and union with truth is a possibility. The fact that there is in front of me a writing-table and I am writing with a pen on paper is not truth. It is something received by the senses and a statement of fact. The problem of truth is already posed in my writing. There is no truth of any sort in the object; truth is only in the subject.

Truth is related not to the phenomenal world but to the noumenal, to the world of ideas. Truth is a relation, but this relation is by no means the one between subject and object; it is not the repercussion of the object in the subject. Truth is not to be understood in the spirit of epistemological realism or at any rate if it is to be taken as realism, then it is realism of an entirely different kind. Truth has two meanings. There is truth in the sense of knowledge of reality and there is truth which is reality itself. Truth is not only an idea, and a value, it is also an entity, something which exists. "I am the Truth." Truth is not that which exists; it is the meaning of that which exists, the Logos of it; but this meaning is that which, or he who, exists.

According to Heidegger truth exists only to the extent that *Dasein* exists. Truth does not exist outside and above us; it is a possibility because we are within it. Heidegger is of the opinion that absolute truth is a remnant of Christian theology, but in point of fact it is precisely Christianity which must deny truth outside that which exists and outside him who exists. Truth is a creative act of spirit in which meaning is brought to birth. Truth stands higher than the reality which exercises compulsion upon us, higher than the "real" world. But still higher than truth is God, or to put it more truly—God is Truth.

A thorough-going materialism has to reject the idea of truth as pragmatism has to reject it. Marx, still preserving some connection with German idealism, has a divided mind in this matter; Lenin is naïve; but their descendants refuse truth and so do Nietzsche's. Nietzsche was alone in boldly acknowledging the truth of illusions, the offspring of the will to power, but he still recognizes an aristocratic quality which those who have popularized him deny. There is in truth an aristocracy of ideas and meaning. But the idea and the meaning are not to be torn away from the existent and existence. Truth is the meaning of the existent, and meaning is the truth of the existent. This found its expression in the doctrine of the Logos which is not bound to be tied to the limits of Platonism and to a static ontology. Truth is meaning born in God before all ages, in God the existent One. And this birth is repeated in all who exist, and because of it personality emerges into view.

Personality is not the offspring of a generic process; it is the child of meaning, of truth. There is a concrete universalism in truth which not only is not opposed to personality but presupposes its existence. Truth is not a reflection of the world as it is and as it appears, it is a conflict with the darkness and evil of the world. The apprehension of truth is a self-kindling of the light (the Logos) in existence (in being) and this process takes place in the depth of being; it is not in opposition to being. I use the word "being" in the conventional sense before investigating the essence of the problem of "being."

Truth is certainly not knowledge of the object. Truth is a victory over objectification, in other words over the illusory and transparent nature of object being. Truth certainly reflects nothing, just as the reality of spirit reflects nothing. Truth is spiritual, it is in the spirit, it is the victory of spirit over the non-spiritual objectivity of the world, the world of things. Spirit is not an epiphenomenon of anything, everything is an epiphenomenon of spirit. Truth is the awakening of the spirit in man; it is communion with spirit.

It may be supposed that all that I have just said refers to Truth but not to truths, not to those partial and relative truths which science discovers in the natural phenomenal world. What is there of the noumenal in such truths as "twice two are four" and "all bodies expand when heated"? Is meaning revealed in such truths? There is Truth with a capital letter and there is truth with a small letter. This needs elucidation. All the little and partial truths receive their light from the whole major Truth. All rays of light come from the sun. Philosophers have in their different ways expressed this in the doctrine of the Logos, of universal reason, of the general validity of transcendental thought.

But transcendental thought is mobile and its structure depends upon the character and quality of the cognitive mind and upon the subject matter to which cognition is directed. The Logos is a sun which shines down upon a fallen objectified world, and the logical apparatus of cognition is worked out to correspond with the state of that world of objects. This is epistemological adjustment to the world for the sake of victory over the world. If science is under the sway of determinism, if it is looking for causal links and does not discover primary creative movements in the life of the world, the blame for this does not lie with science but with the state of the world. But the light which science sheds upon the world arises, albeit not in a direct line, from the primary source of the Sun of Truth. The lie begins with the affirmation of scientism, that is to say, with a false philosophy.

But can the acknowledgment of the one whole entire Truth of the universal Logos be combined with the existential type of philosophy? If philosophy has to be personal, if it is based upon personal experience, if the subject puts his own experience with all its contradictions into the act of knowing, does not universal Truth disintegrate into partial truths and do we not fall into the power of relativism? The usual and generally accepted views on this point must be dismissed. They are due to the limitations of rationalism. The old antithesis between the individually personal and the individually common is false and has to be superseded. Truth lies outside that antithesis; the individually personal is the most existential of all things and perhaps the most universal too; it is the most spiritual, and it is that which is most closely linked with meaning. The ego is steeped in its own depth and there it comes into touch with the noumenal spiritual world. This has been better understood by mystics than by philosophers.

But the universality and entirety of self-revealing Truth is certainly not the same thing as general validity. General validity exists precisely for the objectified world, for the world of phenomena. It indicates forms of communication within this disconnected world. It is an adjustment to a fallen state. What is of general validity is due to discontinuity, it is communication within discontinuity.

The whole logical apparatus of proof exists for the sake of those who are disconnected from me, and do not see the Truth which is perceptible to me; it exists for those with whom I am not united in the Truth. There is an analogy between general validity in the field of logic and general validity in the field of jurisprudence. Truths which are of general validity and are proved are, therefore, just those that are least universal; they are under the power of objectification. Universal Truth, on the other hand, lies outside the process of objectification. It is in the highest degree existential, and it is derived from spirit, not from the world. In spirit, that is in spirit which has not been objectified, the universal and the individually personal are united. Truth is not revealed through objectification nor through subordination to the world; it is revealed through the transcending act, through a way-out which lies beyond the confines of the antithesis between the subject and object. Truth is not objective, it is subjective, but subjective in the sense of spiritual depth, removed from that superficial subjectivity which stands in opposition to objectivity.

Where, however, is the criterion of truth to be sought? Too often this criterion is looked for in something which lies on a lower level than truth, it is sought in an objectified world with its general validity. People look for the criterion of the spirit in the material world, and thus they fall into a vicious circle. Discursive thought can provide no criteria at all for final truth; its place is wholly in the middle part of the road; it is unaware of that which belongs to the beginning as well as of that which belongs to the end. All proof rests upon the undemonstrable, upon what can be postulated, perceived and created. There is a chance but there is no guarantee. The very search for guarantees is a false line to take: it means the subordination of the higher to the lower. The freedom of the spirit knows nothing of guarantees.

The one and only standard of truth is Truth itself, it is the radiant light of its sunshine. All other criteria exist only for the objective world of the commonplace and for the sake of social intercourse. I never demonstrate truth for my own sake. I have to demonstrate it only for the sake of others. In regard to knowledge

I live in two worlds, on the one hand in a world which is primary, existential, and in which communion with Truth is possible, and on the other hand in a secondary world, an objectified world, in which Truth is communicated to others and is demonstrated, a world in which Truth is crumbled into a multitude of truths as a consequence of adjustment to the fallen state of the world. Florensky says that the credibility of truth is given potentially, not actually. This means that the Truth is within me, in the depth of me, in the depth of the knowing subject, since I have my roots in the noumenal spiritual world. But it is within me in a drowsy state and awaking of it demands a creative act on my part. The awakening of the spirit within me is an awakening to truth. The criterion of truth is in the spirit, in spirituality, in the subject which has come to recognize itself through the spirit. It is not in the object. Truth is not received from without, it is received from within. The knowledge of truth makes me free. But the actual knowledge of truth cannot but be free itself. Every external criterion of truth which is derived from the lower world is opposed to freedom of the spirit in the apprehension of truth, and it does not liberate. Truth is not due to the object, not even to "objective being." It is due to the spirit. Spirit is in the subject, not in the object, in the noumenon, not in the phenomenon. And science which knows the world of phenomena, the object world, the world of necessities, moves out of the spirit and down from it, descending by degrees of objectification, by stages of dissociation and general validity.

Pragmatism was an attempt to provide a new answer to the question of the criterion of truth, by starting from the true proposition that knowledge is a function of life. Pragmatism is right in regard to the technical results of science, but truth is nevertheless in direct opposition to pragmatism. A vitally flourishing state of affairs, success, profit, interest, all these things are marks rather of falsity than of truth. Truth is certainly not a useful and serviceable thing in this world; it renders no services, it may even be destructive and ruinous to the ordering of the things of this world; it demands sacrifices and has even led to martyrdom. Truth does not so much liberate and save within this world as liberate and save from this world. The thorough-going acceptance of the truth of the Gospel right through to the end, an agreement to bring it to effective realization, would lead to the destruction of States, civilizations, and societies which are organized according to the law of this world. It would lead to the perishing of this world which is in every respect opposed to the Truth of the Gospel.

And so people and nations have amended the Gospel. They have filled it up with "truths" that belong to this world, "truths" which were really pragmatic because they were a lie and an adjustment to a lie. The recognition and confession of Truth have no connection with use and profit; their connections are with hazard and danger. But pragmatism in all its forms has no knowledge of Truth, which stands above the world and judges it. It is only the tragic pragmatism of Nietzsche which is free from this adjusting optimism, if indeed it is in place to speak of his pragmatism. The pathos of Nietzsche is due to his *amor fati* and with him victory is associated with ruin. Bergson's philosophy of life and his biological metaphysics are likewise optimistic.

Existential philosophy must be distinguished both from the philosophy of life and from pragmatic philosophy. It is associated with the experience of tragic conflict. There is in it no cult of life as the highest criterion; it is not biological in character. Life has judgment passed upon it by Truth-and-Right. What is important is not the quantitative maximum of life, not its flourishing condition in the world, nor its power, but the quality of it, its intensity, its moving and pathetic character, which carries over and beyond the frontiers of life.

The recognition of Truth does not by any means indicate a primitively joyful blooming of life and an increase of its strength. It may mean the exposure of the fallen state of the world, the testing experience of the pain which accompanies all life, the conflict between personal destiny and the destiny of the world, between existential experience and enslaving objectification, the struggle of freedom with the necessity which it encounters. Truth is saving, but it saves for another world, for the eternal world which begins in temporal life, but begins with suffering, with grief and frequently with what seems like hopelessness. The acceptance of Truth right through to the end, to the last of its vital deductions, is to give assent to the perishing of this world and to its coming to an end.

I am not speaking of truths which denote adjustment to the world of phenomena, to the inevitable process of objectification, but I am speaking about Truth, as the primary source of light, as what is true and right in its entirety. Knowledge within the objectified world does admittedly reveal truths. There is a reflected light in it which helps us to take our bearings in the darkness of this world, but it does not reveal primary and original Truth, which is the beginning and the end. It is science, not philosophy, which is the discoverer of principles and laws which give men their bearings within reality. But supreme Truth is eschatological and by this very fact exposes the conventional lie of pragmatism, the falsehood of an optimistic cult of life.

Truth is not of the world but of the spirit. It is known only in the transcendence of the object-world. Truth is the end of this object-world, and it demands assent to this end of it. Such is the Truth of Christianity when freed from social adjustments and distortions. But such also is in essence the Truth which was to some extent revealed to the messianic prophetic thought of ancient Israel, to the religious philosophy of India, to Persian dualist eschatology and to many thinkers, such as Plato, Plotinus, Eckhardt, Boehme, Pascal, Kant, Schopenhauer, Kierkegaard, Dostoyevsky and Tolstoy.

All philosophy, theory of knowledge, ethics, philosophy of history should be constructed with an eschatological outlook, but, as we shall see, by no means eschatological in the sense in which the word is usually understood. Knowledge seeks the Truth and truths; it ardently seeks to be purified from all that darkens and distorts the process of Knowing, to achieve the self-purification of the subject. But he who knows may know the falsehood of the world, its defilement and pollution. Knowledge may be the discovery of the truth about a lie. In that case truth is a judgment upon the falsity of the world, it is light which exposes the darkness. And the proclamation of the Truth is the end of the world of falsehood. In every true act of knowing the end of the world comes, the end of en-slaving objectivity.

There have always been different types of philosophers. They have been distinguished from one another by a varying structure of the mind behind which lay different directions in which the spirit moved. In Greece there were Parmenides and Heraclitus, Democritus and Plato; they endeavored to establish types of philosophical world outlook. The distinction among the types depended upon what principle was taken as the basis of classification. One and the same philosopher may fall into one class in one connection and in another connection into another class. Dilthey proposes to recognize three types of philosophical world-outlook: naturalism, objective idealism and idealism of freedom. In this conventional classification I should decidedly be placed in the class of idealism of freedom. On the same grounds this might be called realism of freedom so long as reality is not understood in a naturalistic way. I would suggest the following series of antitheses:

1. Philosophy of the subject and philosophy of the object.

2. Philosophy of the spirit and naturalistic philosophy.

3. Philosophy of freedom and determinist philosophy.

4. Philosophy which is dualistically pluralist and monistic philosophy.

5. Philosophy which is creatively dynamic and statically ontological philosophy.

6. Personalist philosophy or the philosophy of personality and the philosophy of universal common sense.

7. Eschatological philosophy, the philosophy of discontinuity and evolutionary philosophy; the philosophy of continuity.

Within this list of antitheses I define my own philosophy as being of the subject, of spirit, of freedom; as being dualistically pluralist, creatively dynamic, personalist and eschatological. Up to the present time philosophy has to a very small extent been eschatological. Eschatology has been related to the sphere of religion only. But eschatology can have and ought to have its epistemological and transcendental metaphysical expression, and I shall aim at such an expression. It is imperative to build up a philosophy of the End. This has little in common with the various interpretations of the Book of the Revelation and it does not imply an expectation of the end in some definite year. Eschatological philosophy springs from a philosophical problem raised already by Plato.

Philosophical monism was an attempt to solve the eschatological problem within the confines of this world, to assert a unity without taking the end into its purview. In my opinion the central thought of eschatological philosophy is connected with the interpretation of the Fall as objectification, and of the end as the final and decisive victory over objectification. The choice of the type of philosophy is settled by the spirit of the philosopher as a whole, by decision and emotion rather than by the intellect. But the human intellect itself is also inseparable from the existence of the whole man, from choice of his will and from his emotional experience.

7

GENERAL AND SPECIAL
REVELATION

Emil Brunner

*The rise of the new philosophies of existentialism and of personal
being coincided with the revolution in theology associated with the
names of Barth, Brunner, and others. The influence of Søren Kierkegaard (1813–55), sometimes called the "father of existentialism,"
was important in the early stages of this theological revolution. The
following excerpt from Brunner shows the stress that the new theologians were laying on the particularity and concreteness of the
Christian revelation as a unique personal and historical event, and
how they regarded this as the differentiating mark of the Christian
revelation as distinct from the timeless and general revelations claimed
by mystical and idealist religions. Although Brunner was more gen-
erous than Barth toward the non-Christian religions, he found the
special claim of Christianity to lie precisely in the unique, historical,
personal, once-for-all character of its revelation, and in this respect
he stands at the opposite extreme from the idealist philosophers and
theologians of the early part of the century.*

THROUGH GOD alone can God be known. This is not a specifically
Christian principle; on the contrary, it is the principle which is
common to all religion and indeed, to the philosophy of religion

Reprinted with permission from *The Mediator,* translated by Olive Wyon
(Philadelphia: The Westminster Press, copyright 1947, W. L. Jenkins),
pp. 21–32.

as a whole. There is no religion which does not believe itself to be based upon divine revelation in one way or another. There is no religion worth the name which does not claim to be "revealed religion." Further, there is no speculative philosophy of religion which does not endeavor to base its statements about God and divine Truth upon a self-disclosure of the divine ground in the spirit of Man. The issue is clear: either religion is based upon Divine revelation, or it is simply the product of the phantasy of the mind which desires it. The statement: "Through God alone can God be known" might be made equally well by a Christian, a Neo-Platonist religious philosopher, a Parsee, or a Hindu. For many of our contemporaries this is sufficient reason to declare that the general principle of relativity applies also to the sphere of religion. I do not intend to enter into any discussion of this problem of apologetics; the question with which we are here concerned is a preliminary question, and indeed it is one which, if it were answered in a satisfactory way, might even make all apologetic superfluous. The preliminary question is this: wherever the appeal is made to revelation, is the word "revelation" used in the same sense?

This question at once makes us aware of a striking difference. All living popular religions appeal to revelations; they feel it essential to be able to produce a large number of revelations, theophanies and divine oracles, miraculous incidents of all kinds, in which the divine and personal character of the supersensible world manifests itself in this temporal world. The whole cultus with its conceptions and its ritual action, in fact, its life as a religion is based upon manifestations of this kind. The religious man believes that the reality of the object of his faith is guaranteed by the concrete character of such revelations. Through them he "knows" that his god, or his gods, are beings which have a personal relation with him and with his world.

The philosophy of religion, religious speculation, and the mysticism which is connected with this school of thought, have a different conception of the nature of revelation. In their origin, indeed, they might actually be regarded as a conscious corrective to the "primitive," "falsely realistic," "revealed" character of the popular religions. To this type of thought "revelation" does not possess this solid character of historic fact which, in the majority of cases, is nothing more than an illusion based on an overstimulated imagination, due to lack of rational knowledge of the world and primitive psychology. In the "higher" relation to God of speculation and mysticism, in the "religion of educated people," revelation means rather the emergence of the eternal basis of all phenomena into consciousness, the perception of something which was always true, the growing consciousness of a Divine Presence, which might have been perceived before, since it was there all the time. Hence in this connection both revelation and religion are spoken of in the singular. Revelation as the objective element, and religion as the subjective element, are fundamentally everywhere one and the same; this is the "essence of religion," and its basis, even when it cannot be recognized as such by man owing to the hampering limitations of his sense-environment. Fundamentally, indeed, there is only one religion, and the differences between the various religions are due simply to the precise individual form of that which is ever the same, a non-essential modification of the "essence" of religion itself. Revelation of every kind means that the eternal Divine Presence behind all phenomena shines through the phenomena; religion means—however dimly and imperfectly—the realization of this divine reality. Religion, however, is not fully developed until it is freed from the trammels of these accidental elements, that is, from all that is historical and contingent. Thus the idea of revelation as "primitive" man conceives it, in the sense of a characteristic divine and objective event, a fact which has actually taken place in the world of time and space, has here become transformed into knowledge, vision, the sense of a Divine Being which, although in itself it is active and creative, is yet at the same time in absolute repose; the manifestation of this Being is not based upon any actual historical self-manifestation in particular, but simply upon the fact that certain hindrances within the individual have disappeared; hence this "revelation" is based upon a subjective process—like throwing back the shutters and opening the windows that the light of morning may stream into the darkened room—upon the unfolding of the soul to the Divine Light, upon the attainment of the right degree of "recollection," or "introversion," or "solitude," or "sinking into the Divine Ground" or some other expression which is characteristic of religion of this type.

Thus, while it belongs to the very essence of the living popular religions that they should be based upon "special revelations," it is of the very essence of religious speculation, religious idealism, and mysticism, to be independent of all special "external" revelations and, indeed, to regard them as merely subjectively determined forms of something different, namely, of the one fundamental revelation which is always and everywhere the same, a process freed from all the "accidents" of an historical process in time and space. The distinction is clear: on the one side are many revelations in the sense of actual incidents; on the other, a revelation which does not take place at all but simply "is"; on the one hand the idea of revelation is connected with definite events, on the other it means the consciousness of freedom from all that is actual in the sense of bondage to the world of time and space, from all external, "sense-bound" events; on the one hand revelation is "special"; on the other it is "general."

The Christian religion belongs neither to the first nor to the second group. It is opposed to both and yet connected with both. In common with the popular religions it points to an actual divine reality, which has been made known in a definite particular way through an act of revelation. It is based wholly upon something which has actually happened, within this world of time and space, and indeed, to put it still more plainly, it is based upon something which has taken place once for all. By its very nature it is absolutely opposed to that saying of Fichte's (which is an amazingly plain statement of the speculative and mystical idea of a divine "ground"): "It is the metaphysical element alone, and not the historical, which saves us." In the Christian religion "salvation" is always indissolubly connected with an historical fact: with the fact of the Incarnation of the Divine Word, with the fact of Atonement by Jesus Christ. Although the time and space element, that is, the element of historical contingency, does not, in itself, constitute a revelation, yet the revelation upon which the Christian faith is based is founded upon this fact alone, and apart from it Christianity itself could not exist.

On the other hand, the Christian religion is equally opposed to all forms of popular religion, since it is not based upon a series of events, but upon one single event; moreover, it is fully conscious that this one fact of revelation, this event which took place once for all, is unique. Ἐφ' ἅπαξ, once for all, this is the category to which the Christian revelation belongs. The Scriptures bear witness to this unique character of the Christian revelation—a revelation which can never be repeated. There is nothing accidental about the unique and unrepeatable character of revelation in the Christian religion; it is an integral element, or rather, it is not one element alone, but constitutes its very essence. The whole meaning of this revelation would be destroyed if it could be severed from this unique event which took place once for all. This means, however, that this idea of revelation, since it is of its very nature that it should be unique, is, essentially, entirely different from the conception of revelation in other forms of religion. The fact that this revelation has taken place once for all does not constitute an arithmetical difference, but a positive difference, a difference in quality. In its essence a revelation which, by its very nature, can only take place once, differs absolutely from a revelation which, also by its very nature, can necessarily be repeated an indefinite number of times.

In order to see this more clearly let us return to the conception of "special revelations."

The fact that special revelations—as, for example, theophanies and incarnations—are said to have happened several times really means that nothing happened at all. The element which was repeated in each of these events was not final. A final event *can* only happen once. A final decision is made once, or it is not made at all. The serious nature of the decision can be gauged by the fact that inevitably the decisive event takes place once for all, and once only. A factor which recurs constantly belongs to the cyclic rhythm of Nature. Hence the mythological element—that is, the revelation which is frequently repeated—belongs to the realm of Nature. The essential rhythm of Nature is reflected in the recurrent type of revelation; the revelation-myth belongs to the sphere of natural religion. The myths of the Saviour-God who dies and then returns to life are typical of this kind of religion.

The distinction between the historical and the natural element lies in the fact that the historical event can only happen once; it cannot be repeated. But in history, as we know it, this absolute historical element does not exist; all that it possesses is the tendency towards that which cannot be repeated (*Einmaligkeit*). Just as Nature is not wholly without the tendency towards that which cannot be repeated, so also History contains some elements which recur. The distinction between History and Nature consists in the tendency to non-repetition. The distinction is, however, not absolute; therefore History has an aspect of natural law, and Nature has an historical aspect. If some historical event could be proved to have taken place once for all, it would be an absolutely decisive event. Such an event, however, cannot be discovered within history; for if such an event could be discovered, it would be the end of all history, the "fullness of time." It is precisely an event of this kind which the Christian religion regards as revelation. Revelation means the unique historical event which, *by its very nature,* must either take place once or not at all. And it is *only* revelation in this Christian sense which contains this element of absolute and never-recurring actuality. Here the word "uniqueness" (*Einmaligkeit*) has its full and absolute meaning; the relative element which is implied when we speak of something which only happened once has been eliminated. Hence by revelation we mean that historical event which is at the same time the end of history, that is, an event which, if it really did take place, by its very force shattered the framework of history; in other words, that in fulfilling the purpose of history it ends it. Here, however, we can only speak of a special revelation in the strict sense of the word. For where the opposite takes place, that is to say, where revelations are frequent, there can be no valid revelation in the ultimate sense of the word. In each of these revelations what was said to have happened did not take place; for if it had actually taken place it could not have happened repeatedly. This point of view is supported by the fact that these "revelations" on which certain religions are based are not actual events. They are not *Individual* but *General*. They are myths which, in the strict sense of the word, can lay no serious claim to historicity. The mythical element eliminates historical reality from the actual event, and also prevents us from regarding the "revelation" as a serious decisive element; in both instances for the same reason.

Hence, in the last resort, the so-called "special" revelations of the various religions come to the same thing as the speculative assertions of the philosophy of religion and mysticism: namely, that revelation is merely an individual concrete instance of a general truth, or, in other words, the accidental incarnation of that Essence which reigns supreme beyond the confines of time and space, in the realm of eternal Being. The important distinction, therefore, is not that which exists between the Christian revelation and these mythological religions, with their recurring revelations, but the distinction between the Christian belief in the revelation which has taken place once for all, and this general kind of religion, with its conception of a general diffused type of revelation, and its non-historical outlook, since, in point of fact, the primitive type of religion tends either to be absorbed into this diffused type of religion, or into the Christian religion itself. More and more the distinction centers round one point, and the issue is clear: either the mystical, idealistic, ethical, general kind of religion (in all its various forms), which lays no claim to "revelation" in the concrete sense of the word, but which rejects such a conception of religion as "crude," "unspiritual," "sense-bound," "external," or the Christian belief in the unique revelation of Jesus Christ. Stated in this way, however, we can see that it is not correct to say that one claim to revelation is opposed to the other. A claim to revelation in the Christian, concrete, and at the same time absolutely serious sense is made only by the Christian religion. This may be regarded as settled without in the least anticipating any further conclusions. There is, however, a very sharp contrast between these two conceptions: the religion of general revelation, and the Christian belief in the unique and final revelation in the fact of Jesus Christ, a contrast which cannot be removed by any attempts at compromise. Attempts at reconciliation have been made, it is true; we shall be dealing with them in the next chapter; our first endeavor, however, must be to look steadily at the distinction itself, and then to keep it, as clearly as possible, before our minds.

When the mystic, the idealist, or the Neo-Platonist speaks of revelation he means that contact between the Divine and the soul of man, that union between the infinite and the finite, between the Creator and the creature in the highest act of knowledge, in contemplation, intuition, in mystical experience, which by its very nature can take place anywhere and at any time; a "revelation" which, so far as it does take place, is independent of all the "accidents of history." But the "Aristotelian" also who finds proofs of the existence of God in Nature, the adherent of a religion based on ethics and on reason, who bases his faith upon the moral order of the world or upon the moral law—all these also, in spite of other forms of difference, unite with the mystic and the idealist in affirming Fichte's statement that "Man is saved by the metaphysical element alone, and not by the historical." All have this in common: they present a united front against the conception of a revelation which claims to be final and unique, and thus, since they also base their faith upon "revelation," they are one in the assertion that revelation is timeless and universal. It is of course true that the form of illumination or experience which they regard as a revelation of the Divine is not immediate, but that it is mediated to them through Nature and through history; nevertheless, so far as the content of the revelation is concerned, it is wholly detached from the time process; it is an act of direct contact with the Divine, with the eternal "ground of the soul." For a revelation of this kind all "mediation through history" is regarded merely as an accidental element, as the "vehicle" of the revelation, as a stimulus, or a symbol. It is like the scaffolding which can be removed as soon as the building itself has been completed. It is like the teacher whom everyone needs, but whose usefulness is over as soon as the required knowledge has been gained. Hence it may even be re-garded as necessary from the psychological point of view—since apart from it an experience of this kind cannot be attained; but by its very nature this knowledge, and the revelation upon which it is based, can easily be detached from the historical element. For it is "the metaphysical element alone and not the historical which saves." To this category belong the contemplation of the Neo-Platonist, the knowledge of the "Ideas" of the idealist, the thought of the metaphysician who has arrived at the conclusion of his proofs for the existence of God, the moral postulate of the Kantian who grasps the Absolute in the moral imperative, as well as the faith of the simple adherent of the philosophy of the Enlighten-ment who bases his religion on "God in Nature and in the Moral Law"; moreover, to it also belong the vision and experience of the mystic who "released from images of every kind" sinks down into the depths of being, or the vision of the religious artist to whom the Infinite and the Eternal is revealed through his artistic inspiration, as, for instance, in the famous saying of Beethoven, "Music is a higher revelation than all wisdom and all philosophy." This is why I summarize all these varieties of religion under the concept of "universal religion": because the revelation upon which it is based is regarded as something universal in character, inde-pendent of the particular event, or a fact which has taken place once for all.

Christianity, and Christianity alone, is the absolute opposite of this form of religion. For the very existence of the Christian re-ligion depends on vital connection with an "accidental" fact of history, with a real event in time and space, which, so it affirms, is the unique, final revelation, for time and for eternity, and for the whole world. In principle, therefore, its relation with God is not immediate but is mediated. Between the soul and God, between humanity and God, between the world and God, there stands a third element, or rather a third Person, who, although He unites man with God, yet equally maintains the absolute distinction be-tween them; through Him alone that reconciliation takes place through which God reveals Himself: the Mediator. In the one form of religion it is claimed as fundamental that God reveals Himself directly to the human soul, in the other as fundamental that God reveals Himself through the Mediator. This is the fundamental distinction.

But this distinction is not simple. It is of course true that the "religion of universal revelation" excludes this faith. This, however, is not done explicitly and deliberately; rather in its own characteristic way, by its inclusiveness; that is, it regards the connection between the Christian faith and the Mediator—its insistence on the historical event which took place once for all in time—as a feature which, by its very nature, is merely a non-essential variety of the universal essence of religion or of revelation. In the Christian religion, so it is said, the universal religion, the "essence of religion" is specialized in such a way that in it the historical phenomenon of Jesus plays a certain part. But how ever well disposed this religion without a Mediator may be towards this faith with a Mediator, and however ready it may be to join forces with it, the fact still remains that the Christian religion feels that it is bound to protest against this misinterpretation. For here it can see nothing but two opposing points of view. For it is evident that there can be no connection between these two assertions: everything depends upon the fact—and "at bottom" everything does *not* depend upon the fact—that religion has a Mediator or it has not. For each side—if they listen to each other properly—only one of these statements can be true.

This does not mean, however, that the Christian faith altogether denies this idea of "universal revelation." Over and over again a great deal of misunderstanding has arisen, even in the most recent theological discussion, through mistaking the first distinction for this second one. Certainly the Christian faith stakes everything on the fact of the distinction between it, as the faith in that fact of revelation, in the Mediator, and the religion of idealism and of mysticism which, in principle, does not see any necessity for a Mediator at all. But this does not mean that it is unable to discern traces of truth in all forms of religion and traces of God in all existence and in all thought. In point of fact the Christian religion does admit this.

It is impossible to believe in a Christian way in the unique revelation, in the Mediator, without believing also in a universal revelation of God in creation, in history, and especially in the human conscience. But, on the other hand, a believer in the universal revelation who is a Christian and believes in the Mediator, can no longer be an idealist or a mystic. This twofold point of view is based on the fact that the Christian believer regards "general" revelation as an indirect (*gebrochen*) form of revelation. In so far as the idealist and the mystic are aware of its existence they have the truth. But in so far as they do not recognize that it is merely an indirect (*gebrochen*) revelation and think that in it they have an authentic knowledge of God they are not in the truth. The recognition of the indirect (*gebrochen*) general revelation is the presupposition of the Christian religion of revelation, with its unique character.

8

THE MESSAGE OF JESUS AND THE PROBLEM OF MYTHOLOGY

Rudolf Bultmann

How can the writings of the New Testament, composed back in the first century of our era, still communicate with men who live in the very different thought-world of today? The New Testament writers conceived their world mythically, whereas we have all been influenced by the scientific view of the world. Rudolf Bultmann has seen in existentialism a possibility of reinterpreting the New Testament teaching in a manner that can once again show its relevance for life. The process of "demythologizing" involves the translation of the New Testament message out of the language of myth into the language of human existence. Bultmann's method of interpretation is one of the major events in religious hermeneutics in a long time, and some of the basic principles are expounded by him in the following excerpt.

THE HEART of the preaching of Jesus Christ is the Kingdom of God. During the nineteenth century exegesis and theology understood the Kingdom of God as a spiritual community consisting of men joined together by obedience to the will of God which ruled in their wills. By such obedience they sought to enlarge the sphere of His rule in the world. They were building, it was said, the Kingdom of God as a realm which is spiritual but within the world,

Reprinted by permission from *Jesus Christ and Mythology* (New York: Charles Scribner's Sons, 1958), pp. 11–21.

active and effective in this world, unfolding in the history of this world.

The year 1892 saw the publication of *The Preaching of Jesus about the Kingdom of God* by Johannes Weiss. This epoch-making book refuted the interpretation which was hitherto generally accepted. Weiss showed that the Kingdom of God is not immanent in the world and does not grow as part of the world's history, but is rather eschatological; i.e., the Kingdom of God transcends the historical order. It will come into being not through the moral endeavor of man, but solely through the supernatural action of God. God will suddenly put an end to the world and to history, and He will bring in a new world, the world of eternal blessedness.

This conception of the Kingdom of God was not an invention of Jesus. It was a conception familiar in certain circles of Jews who were waiting for the end of this world. This picture of the eschatological drama was drawn in Jewish apocalyptic literature, of which the book of Daniel is the earliest still extant. The preaching of Jesus is distinguished from the typical apocalyptic pictures of the eschatological drama and of the blessedness of the coming new age in so far as Jesus refrained from drawing detailed pictures. He confined himself to the statement that the Kingdom of God will come and that men must be prepared to face the coming judgment. Otherwise he shared the eschatological expectations of his contemporaries. That is why he taught his disciples to pray,

> Hallowed be thy name,
> Thy Kingdom come,
> Thy will be done on earth as it is in heaven.

Jesus expected that this would take place soon, in the immediate future, and he said that the dawning of that age could already be perceived in the signs and wonders which he performed, especially in his casting out of demons. Jesus envisaged the inauguration of the Kingdom of God as a tremendous cosmic drama. The Son of Man will come with the clouds of heaven, the dead will be raised and the day of judgment will arrive; for the righteous the time of bliss will begin, whereas the damned will be delivered to the torments of hell.

When I began to study theology, theologians as well as laymen were excited and frightened by the theories of Johannes Weiss. I remember that Julius Kaftan, my teacher in dogmatics in Berlin, said: "If Johannes Weiss is right and the conception of the Kingdom of God is an eschatological one, then it is impossible to make use of this conception in dogmatics." But in the following years the theologians, J. Kaftan among them, became convinced that Weiss was correct. Perhaps I may here refer to Albert Schweitzer who carried the theory of Weiss to extremes. He maintains that not only the preaching and the self-consciousness of Jesus but also his day-to-day conduct of life were dominated by an eschatological expectation which amounted to an all-pervading eschatological dogma.

Today nobody doubts that Jesus' conception of the Kingdom of God is an eschatological one—at least in European theology and, as far as I can see, also among American New Testament scholars. Indeed, it has become more and more clear that the eschatological expectation and hope is the core of the New Testament preaching throughout.

The earliest Christian community understood the Kingdom of God in the same sense as Jesus. It, too, expected the Kingdom of God to come in the immediate future. So Paul, too, thought that he would still be alive when the end of this world was to come and the dead were to be raised. This general conviction is confirmed by the voices of impatience, of anxiety and of doubt which are already audible in the synoptic gospels and which echo a little later and louder, for example, in the Second Epistle of Peter. Christianity has always retained the hope that the Kingdom of God will come in the immediate future, although it has waited in vain. We may cite Mark 9:1, which is not a genuine saying of Jesus but was ascribed to him by the earliest community: "Truly, I say to you, there are some standing here who will not taste death before they see the kingdom of God come with power." Is not the meaning of this verse clear? Though many of the contemporaries of

Jesus are already dead, the hope must nevertheless be retained that the Kingdom of God will still come in this generation.

This hope of Jesus and of the early Christian community was not fulfilled. The same world still exists and history continues. The course of history has refuted mythology. For the conception "Kingdom of God" is mythological, as is the conception of the eschatological drama. Just as mythological are the presuppositions of the expectation of the Kingdom of God, namely, the theory that the world, although created by God, is ruled by the devil, Satan, and that his army, the demons, is the cause of all evil, sin and disease. The whole conception of the world which is presupposed in the preaching of Jesus as in the New Testament generally is mythological; i.e., the conception of the world as being structured in three stories, heaven, earth and hell; the conception of the intervention of supernatural powers in the course of events; and the conception of miracles, especially the conception of the intervention of supernatural powers in the inner life of the soul, the conception that men can be tempted and corrupted by the devil and possessed by evil spirits. This conception of the world we call mythological because it is different from the conception of the world which has been formed and developed by science since its inception in ancient Greece and which has been accepted by all modern men. In this modern conception of the world the cause-and-effect nexus is fundamental. Although modern physical theories take account of chance in the chain of cause and effect in subatomic phenomena, our daily living, purposes and actions are not affected. In any case, modern science does not believe that the course of nature can be interrupted or, so to speak, perforated, by supernatural powers.

The same is true of the modern study of history, which does not take into account any intervention of God or of the devil or of demons in the course of history. Instead, the course of history is considered to be an unbroken whole, complete in itself, though differing from the course of nature because there are in history spiritual powers which influence the will of persons. Granted that not all historical events are determined by physical necessity and that persons are responsible for their actions, nevertheless nothing happens without rational motivation. Otherwise, responsibility would be dissolved. Of course, there are still many superstitions among modern men, but they are exceptions or even anomalies. Modern men take it for granted that the course of nature and of history, like their own inner life and their practical life, is nowhere interrupted by the intervention of supernatural powers.

Then the question inevitably arises: is it possible that Jesus' preaching of the Kingdom of God still has any importance for modern men and the preaching of the New Testament as a whole is still important for modern men? The preaching of the New Testament proclaims Jesus Christ, not only his preaching of the Kingdom of God but first of all his person, which was mythologized from the very beginnings of earliest Christianity. New Testament scholars are at variance as to whether Jesus himself claimed to be the Messiah, the King of the time of blessedness, whether he believed himself to be the Son of Man who would come on the clouds of heaven. If so, Jesus understood himself in the light of mythology. We need not, at this point, decide one way or the other. At any rate, the early Christian community thus regarded him as a mythological figure. It expected him to return as the Son of Man on the clouds of heaven to bring salvation and damnation as judge of the world. His person is viewed in the light of mythology when he is said to have been begotten of the Holy Spirit and born of a virgin, and this becomes clearer still in Hellenistic Christian communities where he is understood to be the Son of God in a metaphysical sense, a great, pre-existent heavenly being who became man for the sake of our redemption and took on himself suffering, even the suffering of the cross. It is evident that such conceptions are mythological, for they were widespread in the mythologies of Jews and Gentiles and then were transferred to the historical person of Jesus. Particularly the conception of the pre-existent Son of God who descended in human guise into the world to redeem mankind is part of the Gnostic doctrine of redemption, and nobody hesitates to call this doctrine mythological. This raises in an acute form the question: *what is the importance of the preaching of Jesus and of the preaching of the New Testament as a whole for modern man?*

For modern man the mythological conception of the world, the conceptions of eschatology, of redeemer and of redemption, are over and does with. Is it possible to expect that we shall make a sacrifice of understanding, *sacrificium intellectus,* in order to accept what we cannot sincerely consider true—merely because such conceptions are suggested by the Bible? Or ought we to pass over those sayings of the New Testament which contain such mythological conceptions and to select other sayings which are not such stumbling-blocks to modern man? In fact, the preaching of Jesus is not confined to eschatological sayings. He proclaimed also the will of God, which is God's demand, the demand for the good. Jesus demands truthfulness and purity, readiness to sacrifice and to love. He demands that the whole man be obedient to God, and he protests against the delusion that one's duty to God can be fulfilled by obeying certain external commandments. If the ethical demands of Jesus are stumbling-blocks to modern man, then it is to his selfish will, not to his understanding, that they are stumbling-blocks.

What follows from all this? Shall we retain the ethical preaching of Jesus and abandon his eschatological preaching? Shall we reduce his preaching of the Kingdom of God to the so-called social gospel? Or is there a third possibility? We must ask whether the eschatological preaching and the mythological sayings as a whole contain a still deeper meaning which is concealed under the cover of mythology. If that is so, let us abandon the mythological conceptions precisely because we want to retain their deeper meaning. This method of interpretation of the New Testament which tries to recover the deeper meaning behind the mythological conceptions I call *de-mythologizing*—an unsatisfactory word, to be sure. Its aim is not to eliminate the mythological statements but to interpret them. It is a method of hermeneutics. The meaning of this method will be best understood when we make clear the meaning of mythology in general.

It is often said that mythology is a primitive science, the intention of which is to explain phenomena and incidents which are strange, curious, surprising, or frightening, by attributing them to supernatural causes, to gods or to demons. So it is in part, for example, when it attributes phenomena like eclipses of the sun or of the moon to such causes; but there is more than this in mythology. Myths speak about gods and demons as powers on which man knows himself to be dependent, powers whose favor he needs, powers whose wrath he fears. Myths express the knowledge that man is not master of the world and of his life, that the world within which he lives is full of riddles and mysteries and that human life also is full of riddles and mysteries.

Mythology expresses a certain understanding of human existence. It believes that the world and human life have their ground and their limits in a power which is beyond all that we can calculate or control. Mythology speaks about this power inadequately and insufficiently because it speaks about it as if it were a worldly power. It speaks of gods who represent the power beyond the visible, comprehensible world. It speaks of gods as if they were men and of their actions as human actions, although it conceives of the gods as endowed with superhuman power and of their actions as incalculable, as capable of breaking the normal, ordinary order of events. It may be said that myths give to the transcendent reality an immanent, this-worldly objectivity. Myths give worldly objectivity to that which is unworldly. (In German one would say, *"Der Mythos objektiviert das Jenseitige zum Diesseitigen."*)

All this holds true also of the mythological conceptions found in the Bible. According to mythological thinking, God has his domicile in heaven. What is the meaning of this statement? The meaning is quite clear. In a crude manner it expresses the idea that God is beyond the world, that He is transcendent. The thinking which is not yet capable of forming the abstract idea of transcendence expresses its intention in the category of space; the transcendent God is imagined as being at an immense spatial distance, far above the world: for above this world is the world of the stars, of the light which enlightens and makes glad the life of men.

When mythological thinking forms the conception of hell, it expresses the idea of the transcendence of evil as the tremendous power which again and again afflicts mankind. The location of hell and of men whom hell has seized is below the earth in darkness, because darkness is tremendous and terrible to men.

These mythological conceptions of heaven and hell are no longer acceptable for modern men since for scientific thinking to speak of "above" and "below" in the universe has lost all meaning, but the idea of the transcendence of God and of evil is still significant.

Another example is the conception of Satan and the evil spirits into whose power men are delivered. This conception rests upon the experience, quite apart from the inexplicable evils arising outside ourselves to which we are exposed, that our own actions are often so puzzling; men are often carried away by their passions and are no longer master of themselves, with the result that inconceivable wickedness breaks forth from them. Again, the conception of Satan as ruler over the world expresses a deep insight, namely, the insight that evil is not only to be found here and there in the world, but that all particular evils make up one single power which in the last analysis grows from the very actions of men, which form an atmosphere, a spiritual tradition, which overwhelms every man. The consequences and effects of our sins become a power dominating us, and we cannot free ourselves from them. Particularly in our day and generation, although we no longer think mythologically, we often speak of demonic powers which rule history, corrupting political and social life. Such language is metaphorical, a figure of speech, but in it is expressed the knowledge, the insight, that the evil for which every man is responsible individually has nevertheless become a power which mysteriously enslaves every member of the human race.

9

BIBLICAL RELIGION AND THE
SEARCH FOR ULTIMATE REALITY

Paul Tillich

*Contemporary theology has reawakened an appreciation for the mean-
ing of revelation and has shown the relevance of the Bible to our
life and action in the world. But we cannot bypass the questions of
truth and validity. Paul Tillich has been outstanding in relating the
existential and ontological aspects of the Christian faith. The following passage shows how biblical faith and ontological reflection are
bound up together.*

THE TITLE "Biblical Religion and the Search for Ultimate Reality"
itself may have raised a number of skeptical questions. This skepti-
cism may be increased when I say that, in spite of the tremendous
tension between biblical religion and ontology, they have an ultimate unity and a profound interdependence. In reaction to such a
statement some will certainly ask: Is not the very nature of biblical
religion opposed to philosophy? Does not biblical religion destroy
the strongholds of human thought by the power of the divine revelation to which it gives witness? Was not the great theological event
of the last decades Karl Barth's prophetic protest against the synthesis between Christianity and humanism? Did not Barth rein-
terpret for our time the radical dissociation of Christianity and

Reprinted with permission from *Biblical Religion and the Search for Ultimate Reality* (Chicago: University of Chicago Press, 1955), pp. 1–10.

philosophy found in Kierkegaard a century ago? Is not the conviction that the advancement and the application of the gospel are served in the attempt to relate philosophy and biblical religion an unfortunate return to the theological situation at the turn of the century? These are among the questions which will concern us throughout this analysis.

The term "biblical religion" poses some problems. If the Bible is considered to be the document of God's final self-manifestation, in what sense can one speak of biblical religion? Religion is a function of the human mind; according to recent theologians, it is the futile attempt of man to reach God. Religion moves from man toward God, while revelation moves from God to man, and its first work is to confound man's religious aspirations. There are many students of theology, especially in Continental Europe, who contrast divine revelation not only with philosophy but also with religion. For them religion and philosophy stand under the same condemnation, since both are attempts of man to be like God; both are demonic elevations of man above his creatureliness and finitude. And, of the two, religion is the more dangerous, because philosophy, at least in principle, can be restricted to the technical problems of logic and epistemology. If this were true, a confrontation of philosophy and biblical religion would be impossible, because there would not be such a thing as biblical religion. And philosophy would be either harmless logical inquiry or demonic *hubris*. The adjective "biblical" would demand "revelation" and not "religion" as its noun.

We must take this argument seriously. It may be surprising to Americans to know that I have been strongly criticized by German readers of my books because the word "religion" appears frequently in them. Although these critics are in sympathy with my general point of view, they cannot understand that a modern theologian would use the word "religion" in a positive sense. For them, the greater part of what we call "religion" is the devil's work. To speak of "biblical religion" is to deprive the Bible of its revelatory character and to consider it a work of men or, even worse, a demonic creation.

But, in saying this, these people show that they too have a religion. They forget that revelation must be received and that the name for the reception of revelation is "religion." They forget that revelation becomes more revealing the more it speaks to man in his concrete situation, to the special receptivity of his mind, to the special conditions of his society, and to the special historical period. Revelation is never revelation in general, however universal its claim may be. It is always revelation for someone and for a group in a definite environment, under unique circumstances. Therefore, he who receives revelation witnesses to it in terms of his individuality and in terms of the social and spiritual conditions in which the revelation has been manifested to him. In other words, he does it in terms of his religion. This makes the concept "biblical religion" meaningful. Every passage of the Old and New Testaments is both revelation and religion. The Bible is a document both of the divine self-manifestation and of the way in which human beings have received it. And it is not that some words and sentences belong to the former and others to the latter but that in one and the same passage revelation and the reception of revelation are inseparably united. He who gives an account of divine revelation simultaneously gives an account of his own religion. The basic error of fundamentalism is that it overlooks the contribution of the receptive side in the revelatory situation and consequently identifies *one* individual and conditioned form of receiving the divine with the divine itself. But there are other forms. Even in the Bible we find differences between the priestly and the prophetic writings, between early and late traditions in the Four Gospels. We find them, too, in the classics of church history and in the denominational interpretations of the Bible today. These different ways characterize the religious side of the biblical and church tradition; they are receptacles of revelation.

Revelation cannot be separated from them. Those who ignore this situation are forced to deny the differences on the receptive side and to confuse their own form of reception with an assumedly undiluted and untransformed revelation. But there is no pure revelation. Wherever the divine is manifest, it is manifest in "flesh," that is, in a concrete, physical, and historical reality, as in the religious receptivity of the biblical writers. This is what biblical religion means. It is itself a highly dialectical concept.

This character of biblical literature makes possible and necessary the confrontation of biblical religion with philosophy. But a confrontation would be impossible if philosophy were logical analysis and epistemological inquiry only, however important may be the development of these tools for philosophical thought. Yet philosophy, "love of wisdom," means much more than this. It seems to me that the oldest definition given to philosophy is, at the same time, the newest and that which always was and always will be valid: Philosophy is that cognitive endeavor in which the question of being is asked. In accordance with this definition, Aristotle summarized the development of Greek philosophy, anticipating the consequent periods up to the Renaissance and preparing the modern ways of asking the same question. The question of being is not the question of any special being, its existence and nature, but it is the question of what it means to *be*. It is the simplest, most profound, and absolutely inexhaustible question—the question of what it means to say that something *is*. This word "is" hides the riddle of all riddles, the mystery that there is anything at all. Every philosophy, whether it asks the question of being openly or not, moves around this mystery, has a partial answer to it, whether acknowledged or not, but is generally at a loss to answer it fully. Philosophy is always in what the Greeks called *aporia* ("without a way"), that is, in a state of perplexity about the nature of being. For this inquiry I like to use the word "ontology," derived from *logos* ("the word") and *on* ("being"); that is, the word of being, the word which grasps being, makes its nature manifest, drives it out of its hiddenness into the light of knowledge. Ontology is the center of all philosophy. It is, as Aristotle has called it, "first philosophy," or, as it was unfortunately also called, "metaphysics," that which follows the physical books in the collection of Aristotelian writings. This name was and is unfortunate, because it conveys the misconception that ontology deals with transempirical realities, with a world behind the world, existing only in speculative imagination. In all areas of theology—historical, practical, systematic—there are theologians who believe that they can avoid the confrontation of philosophy and biblical religion by identifying philosophy with what they call "metaphysical speculation," which they can then throw onto the garbage heap of past errors, intellectual and moral. I want to challenge as strongly as possible all those who use this language to tell us what they mean by metaphysics and speculation and, after they have done so, to compare their description with what the classical philosophers from Anaximander to Whitehead have done. *Speculari,* the root of the word "speculation," means "looking at something." It has nothing to do with the creation of imaginary worlds, an accusation which the philosophers could make against the theologians with equal justification. It is infuriating to see how biblical theologians, when explaining the concepts of the Old or New Testament writers, use most of the terms created by the toil of philosophers and the ingenuity of the speculative mind and then dismiss, with cheap denunciations, the work from which their language has been immensely enriched. No theologian should be taken seriously as a theologian, even if he is a great Christian and a great scholar, if his work shows that he does not take philosophy seriously.

Therefore, to avoid the "black magic" of words like "metaphysical speculation," let us speak of ontology as the basic work of those who aspire to wisdom (*sophia* in Greek, *sapientia* in Latin), meaning the knowledge of the principles. And, more specifically, let us speak of ontological *analysis* in order to show that one has to look at things as they are given if one wants to discover the principles, the structures, and the nature of being as it is embodied in everything that is.

On the basis of such an ontological analysis, philosophy tries to show the presence of being and its structures in the different realms of being, in nature and in man, in history and in value, in knowledge and in religion. But in each case it is not the subject matter as such with which philosophy deals but the constitutive principles of being, that which is always present if a thing participates in the power to be and to resist nonbeing.

Philosophy in this sense is not a matter of liking or disliking. It is a matter of man as man, for man is that being who asks the question of being. Therefore, every human being philosophizes, just as every human being moralizes and acts politically, artistically, scientifically, religiously. There are immense differences in degree, education, and creativity among different human beings in the exercise of these functions, but there is no difference in the character of the function itself. The child's restless question, "Why is this so; why is that not so?" and Kant's grandiose description, in his critique of the cosmological argument, of the God who asks himself, "Why am I?" are the same in substance although infinitely distinguished in form. Man is by nature a philosopher, because he inescapably asks the question of being. He does it in myth and epic, in drama and poetry, in the structure and the vocabulary of any language.

It is the special task of philosophy to make this question conscious and to elaborate the answers methodologically. The prephilosophical ways of putting and answering the question of being prepare the philosophical way. When philosophy comes into its own, it is not without a long prehistory. Without Homer's poetry, the Dionysian festivals, and the Solonic laws, and, above all, without the genius of the Greek language, no Western philosophy as we have it now would have developed. And everyone who participates in the language and the art and the cult and the social life of a culture is a collaborator in the creation of its philosophy. He is a prephilosophical philosopher, and most people are in this situation even after a methodical philosophy has been born. But one thing has changed since this birth: not only does prephilosophy determine philosophy but also philosophy determines prephilosophy. The language in nonphilosophical literature and common usage, which is a form of prephilosophy too, is determined by previous philosophical usage. Nor do those who are antiphilosophical escape this. Even the despiser of philosophy is not only a collaborator with, but also a pupil of, the subject of his contempt. This interdependence between prephilosophy and philosophy is also true of the biblical and all other religious and theological literature, even if written under a strong, antiphilosophical bias. The fundamentalist minister who said to me, "Why do we need philosophy when we possess all truth through revelation?" did not realize that, in using the words "truth" and "revelation," he was determined by a long history of philosophical thought which gave these words the meaning in which he used them. We cannot avoid philosophy, because the ways we take to avoid it are carved out and paved by philosophy.